M000308210

Contemporary Perspectives on Research on Motivation in Early Childhood Education

A Volume in Contemporary Perspectives on
Research in Early Childhood Education

Series Editor

Olivia N. Saracho
University of Maryland

Contemporary Perspectives in Early Childhood Education

Olivia N. Saracho, Series Editor

(Series list continues on next page)

*Contemporary Perspectives on Social Learning in
Early Childhood Education* (2007)
edited by Olivia N. Saracho and Bernard Spodek

*Contemporary Perspectives on Socialization and Social Development in Early
Childhood Education* (2007)
edited by Olivia N. Saracho and Bernard Spodek

*Contemporary Perspectives on Language Policy and Literacy Instruction in
Early Childhood Education* (2006)
edited by Olivia N. Saracho and Bernard Spodek

*Contemporary Perspectives on Families, Communities and Schools for
Young Children* (2006)
edited by Olivia N. Saracho and Bernard Spodek

International Perspectives on Research in Early Childhood Education (2005)
edited by Bernard Spodek and Olivia N. Saracho

Studying Teachers in Early Childhood Settings (2003)
edited by Bernard Spodek and Olivia N. Saracho

Contemporary Perspectives on Play in Early Childhood Education (2003)
edited by Olivia N. Saracho and Bernard Spodek

Contemporary Perspectives on Literacy in Early Childhood Education (2002)
edited by Olivia N. Saracho and Bernard Spodek

Contemporary Perspectives on Early Childhood Curriculum (2002)
edited by Olivia N. Saracho and Bernard Spodek

Contemporary Perspectives on Research on Motivation in Early Childhood Education

edited by

Olivia N. Saracho
University of Maryland

INFORMATION AGE PUBLISHING, INC.
Charlotte, NC • www.infoagepub.com

Library of Congress Cataloging-in-Publication Data

CIP record for this book is available from the Library of Congress
http://www.loc.gov

ISBNs: 978-1-64113-489-7 (Paperback)

978-1-64113-490-3 (Hardcover)

978-1-64113-491-0 (ebook)

Copyright © 2019 Information Age Publishing Inc.

All rights reserved. No part of this publication may be reproduced, stored
in a retrieval system, or transmitted, in any form or by any means, electronic,
mechanical, photocopying, microfilming, recording or otherwise, without written
permission from the publisher.

Printed in the United States of America

Editorial Advisory Board

Doris Bergen
Miami University. Oxford, OH

Anne Haas Dyson
University of Illinois

Roy Evans
Brunel University, Twickenham, Middlesex, United Kingdom

Joe Frost
University of Texas at Austin, Austin, TX

Eugene García
Arizona State University, Tempe, AZ

Celia Genishi
Teachers College, Columbia University, New York, NY

Amos Hatch
University of Tennessee, Knoxville, TN

Mary Renck Jalongo
Indiana University of Pennsylvania, Indiana, Pennsylvania

Esther Elena López-Mulnix
American University of Iraq, Sulaimani

Michaelene Ostrosky
University of Illinois at Urbana-Champaign, Champaign IL

Douglas Powell
Purdue University

Kelvin Seifert
University of Manitoba, Winnipeg, MB, Canada

Consulting Editors

Sara Abercrombie

Stephen Aguilar

Hyun Seon Ahn

Kay Alderman

David Allen

Andrea Allio

Michael Barger

Anne M. DeFelippo

Maria K. DiBenedetto

Annie Dubeau

Hebbah El-Moslimany

Tierra Freeman

Frances Hancock

Aisling Leavy

Wayne Slater

Allan Wigfield

CONTENTS

PART I

MOTIVATION IN EARLY CHILDHOOD EDUCATION

CHAPTER 1

MOTIVATION THEORY IN THE 21ST CENTURY

Research Implications and Issues

Olivia N. Saracho

Society considers motivation to be important; therefore, educational researchers and scholars have been investigating it. In the 21st century, motivation will continue to contribute to society, but it is important to consider the numerous transformations that will guide new research areas in all of the countries. The motivation goals may differ in each country, but educational psychology can assist in identifying and assessing them. A major problem to solve in the 21st century is how to deal successfully with individual differences in learning rates.

DEFINING MOTIVATION

The overall view of motivation is that it is extremely related to conscious or subconscious motives that describe individuals' selections (Theodotou, 2014). Pintrich (2003) stated that "the term motivation is derived from the Latin verb movere, which means to move. In other words, motivational theories attempt to answer questions about what gets individuals moving

Contemporary Perspectives on Research on
Motivation in Early Childhood Education, pp. 3–19
Copyright © 2019 by Information Age Publishing
All rights of reproduction in any form reserved.

(energization) and toward what activities or tasks" (p. 669). Motivation is a complicated view with challenging strictures (Theodotou, 2014). Leo and Galloway (1996) describe it as an extremely complex construct, which they liken to "a coat of many colours" (p. 36).

Motivational researchers strive to define the way individuals rationalize their behaviors. The definition for motivation is rather vague and many researchers have difficulty agreeing on one. A foremost struggle in the psychology of motivation has been the absence of agreement on its definition. Psychologists disagree on its definition. For example, Bolles (1975) stated:

> There is little agreement among different proposals about what the defining criteria [of motivation] should be.... What one proposes as a definition of motivated behavior seems to depend more on his theoretical commitments than upon anything in the behavior itself. (p. 1)

Several authors have acknowledged the difficulties of defining motivation. For example, Littman (1958) states, "it is evident ... that there is still no substantial agreement about what motivation is. I think there is something wrong when something like this persists for as long a time as it has" (p. 115). Brown (1961) protested that

> the ubiquity of the concept of motivation, in one guise or another, is nevertheless surprising when we consider that its meaning is often scandalously vague.... We thus find ourselves in the position of trying to deal with an allegedly vital factor in the face of violent disagreements as to its origins, its essential nature, and its particular rules as a behavioral determinant. (p. 24)

Several psychologists (e.g., Dewsbury, 1978; Verplanck, 1957) have proposed forsaking the idea of motivation completely. Nonetheless, bearing in mind the popularity and obvious practicality of various motivational thoughts and theories, the psychologists reject such a proposal. They have recommended several alternatives. For example, Bernard, Mills, Swenson, and Walsh (2005) suggested an evolutionary theory of human motivation, in which motivation is termed as focused behavior that is finally targeted in the direction of the basic purpose of comprehensive capability. They also encourage for motivation to be determined in relation to individual differences. Since motivation concentrates on human behavior,

> Most psychologists and educators use motivation as a word to describe those processes that can (a) arouse and instigate behavior; (b) give direction and purpose to behavior; (c) continue to allow behavior to persist; and (d) lead to choosing or preferring a particular behavior. (Wlodkowski, 1984, p. 12)

In an effort to clearly define motivation, Kleinginna and Kleinginna (1981) assembled 102 definitions of motivation from different sources. Table 1.1 presents examples of such definitions.

Table 1.1.
Theorists and Their Definition on Motivations

Theorists	Date	Definitions of Motivation
Abraham Maslow	1955	The original criterion of motivation and the one that is still used by all human beings except behavioral psychologists is the subjective one. I am motivated when I feel desire or want or yearning or wish or lack.
G. Lindzey, C. S. Hall, & R. F. Thompson,	1978	The three major characteristics of motivated behavior are: arousal, direction, and desire.
Raymond J. Wlodkowski	1978	Motivation is the word used to describe those processes that can (a) arouse and instigate behavior; (b) give direction or purpose to behavior; (c) continue to allow behavior to persist; and (d) lead to choosing or preferring a particular behavior.
Horace B. English & Ava C. English (psychological dictionary)	1958	The nonstimulus variables controlling behavior: the general name for the fact that an organism's acts are partly determined in direction and strength by its own nature (or enduring structure) and/or internal state. When the term is thus used, it contrasts with two other determinants of action: *ability*, and the *stimulus* or *situation*. But since the stimulus is conceived as touching off the motivation, it is sometimes half included under that term.
Dalbir Bindra & Jane Stewart	1971	Any goal-directed action is instigated by a central motivational state, which itself is created by an interaction within the brain between the neural consequences of bodily organismic states ("drives") and neural consequences of environmental incentives ("reinforcers").
Jackson Beatty	1975	Motivation is a term used by psychologists to denote internal processes such as hunger that serve to direct the behavior of the organism. Motivational processes are inferred from changes in the direction, intensity, or persistence of behavior.
Hugh Brown	1976	Motivation is the change in the biological state of the organism that relates to behaviors directed at self and species preservation. Secondary emphasis: directional/functional
Pintrich & Schunk	1996	Motivation is the process by which children's goal-directed activity is prompted and maintained.

In addition, Transformation Research Networks and JustListsNetwork Affiliate (n.d) surveyed academic, scholarly, peer-reviewed and refereed journals and books to identify and briefly summarize current scholarly definitions for motivation. Table 1.2 provides some examples of their current definitions.

Table 1.2.

Contemporary Definitions From Academic, Scholarly, Peer-Reviewed Refereed Journals, and Books

Researchers	Date	Definitions of Motivation
Goudas, Biddle, & Fox	2011	Motivation is an ongoing process.
Thijs	2011	Motivation is dependent on the fulfillment of fundamental, innate psychological needs for competence, relatedness, and autonomy.
Davis & Singh	2011	Motivation is system oriented.
De Cooman, De Gieter, Pepermans, & Jegers	2011	Motivation is a broad concept.
Pavey, Greitemeyer, & Sparks	2011	Motivation suggests there are unsatisfied needs.
King, & Teo	2012	Motivation is the 'want-to' component of individuals' actions.
Oudeyer, & Kaplan	2008	Motivation is defined as the doing of an activity.
Mayer	2011	Motivation is generally considered to be an internal state that initiates and maintains goal directed behavior.

The aforementioned definitions have an overall agreement that motivation is an internal state or condition (occasionally called a need, desire, or want) that stimulates or strengthens behavior and offer guidance.

THE SCIENTIFIC STUDY OF MOTIVATION

Researchers from different disciplines (e.g., physiological, psychological, philosophical) have investigated motivation using multiple approaches. For example, in physiology (the scientific study of the normal function in living systems such as biology), researchers may use "electrical and chemical stimulation of the brain, the recording of electrical brain-wave activity with the electroencephalograph, and lesion techniques, where a portion of the brain (usually of a laboratory animal) is destroyed and subsequent changes in motivation are noted" (Petri & Cofer, 2017). Physiological studies mainly conducted with animals, other than humans, have revealed the significance of particular brain structures in the control of fundamental motives such as hunger, thirst, sex, aggression, and fear. In psychology, researchers may study the individuals' behaviors to understand their actions. In sociology, researchers may examine how individuals' interactions influence their behavior. For instance, in the classroom students and teachers behave in expected ways, which may differ when they are outside the classroom. Saracho (2003) examined the students' academic achievement when they matched or mismatched their teachers' way of thinking. She identified both the teachers and students' individual differences and defined consistencies in their cognitive processes. In philosophy, researchers can study the individuals' theoretical position such as supporting Maslow's (1943) concept that motivation can create behaviors that augments motivation in the future. Abraham H. Maslow's theory of self-actualization supports this theoretical position (Petri & Cofer, 2017).

These areas and others are represented in this volume. This volume is devoted to understanding mutual and contemporary themes in the individuals' motivation and its relationship to cognition. The current literature covers several methods to the multifaceted relationships between motivational and cognitive processes. Comprehensive reviews of the literature focus on prominent cognitive perspectives on motivation with young children, which includes ages from birth to 8 years of age. The chapters in this special volume reviews and critically analyze the literature on several aspects of the relationships between motivational and cognitive processes and demonstrate the breadth and theoretical effectiveness of this domain. This brief introduction acknowledges the valuable contributions of these chapters to the study of human motivation. This volume can be a valuable tool to researchers who are conducting studies in the motivation field. It focuses on important contemporary issues on motivation in early childhood education (ages 0 to 8) to provide the information necessary to make judgments about these issues. It also motivates and guides researchers to explore gaps in the motivation literature.

MOTIVATION IN EARLY CHILDHOOD EDUCATION

Motivation is the convincing motive in all experiences and is the basis to learning. All children are born with curiosity and a desire to explore their environment. Developmental theorists (e.g., Hunt, 1965; Piaget, 1952; White, 1959) hypothesized that young children are motivated learners and explore their world, which is their learning source. Young children are immersed in their surroundings, are self-assured that they are capable to learn more, and develop their abilities but difficult experiences restrain them. When young children become adept in their situation, it is considered to be motivation. While experiences generate mastery motivation, their determination to be skillful and engage in continuing learning has a crucial impact on most of them. Studies indicate that some young children respond to exterior motives when they participate in learning. They need to *show* proficiency by achieving better than others or obtaining approval which describes extrinsic motivation (Senko, Durik, & Harackiewicz, 2008). The first section provides back ground information on motivation in early childhood education. In the first chapter titled, "Motivation in the 21st Century: New Issues and Research Implications," Olivia N. Saracho discusses the importance of motivation, the disagreement on its definition, and the role of stimuli. She identifies, describes, and compares different definitions and the doubts about the frequently used definitions.

Motivation theories have contributed to the development of guidelines to improve human performance. The majority of motivation theories presume that individuals initiate and continue behaviors to the degree that they consider that the behaviors will lead to expected goals. Beginning with the work of Lewin (1936) and Tolman (1932), this foundation has directed motivation researchers to examine the psychological worth individuals attribute to goals (e.g., Kasser & Ryan, 1996; Vroom, 1964), individuals' expectations about achieving goals (e.g., Abramson, Seligman, & Teasdale, 1978; Bandura, 1989; Rotter, 1966), and the means that sustain individuals to progress toward chosen goals (e.g., Carver & Scheier, 1998).

Several theories of motivation have been described to provide insights about the reason behavior is prompted, sustained, guided, and on and on (Graham & Weiner, 1996). Cherry (2017) raises the question, "What exactly lies behind the motivations for why we act?" Psychologists have developed several motivation theories (e.g., drive theory, instinct theory, humanistic theory). In fact, numerous distinctive effects have an impact on the individuals' motivations. In the next chapter titled, "Motivation Theories, Theorists, and Theoretical Conceptions," Olivia N. Saracho describes several influences on the study of motivation, such as theories, theorists, theoretical conceptions, and specific principles. She describes how the motivation theories assume that individuals initiate and continue behaviors to the degree that they consider that the behaviors will lead to expected goals. In addition, she shows the relationship between motivation and personality. Personality has had a disproportionate past in motivation research. The majority of researchers would indirectly concur that individual differences exist in motivation and such differentiations can be found in personality predispositions (Judge & Ilies, 2002). In addressing the individual differences in motivation, Austin and Klein (1996) remarked, "Despite studies addressing individual differences within each of the perspectives, a considerable amount of research is needed before precise statements can be made about their role" (p. 239). Gellatly (1996) observed that "attempts to empirically link personality characteristics with motivational variables have produced inconsistent results" (p. 474). Lastly, Kanfer and Heggestad (1997) determined, "Until recently, the status of traits in most work motivation theories has been like that of a distant and not well-liked relative attending a family reunion" (p. 13). A fundamental problem in the investigation of dispositional influences on work behavior stems from the current lack of a unified theoretical perspective for understanding how and which personality constructs influence the motivational system (Kanfer, 1990, p. 155). Nevertheless, motivation research has reached considerable theoretical headway, especially in relation to the theory for which arguably the most progress has been made.

ACADEMIC ACHIEVEMENT

During the last decades, studies on motivation have multiplied. They provide evidence concerning the nature of the children's motivation, the way it develops, affects school performance changes, and is influenced by teacher practices, classroom environments. Generally, motivation theorists want to know the reasons for the individuals' behavior such as the motives for their actions (Weiner, 1992). In relation to school performance, educational researchers examine influences such as the children's selections about academic activities, their determination to continue with the activities, and the amount of effort they use to complete the tasks (Wigfield, Eccles, & Rodriguez, 1998).

Motivation indicates the reasons for the individuals' behaviors. In relation to academic achievement, motivational issues refer to the causes that certain students have to complete their tasks regardless of huge impediments, whereas various students would quit at the smallest difficulties, or the reasons several students form credibly high expectations for themselves that failure is inevitable to take place (Weiner, 1995). Numerous studies show the influence of motivation on academic achievement, but most of them have examined the effect of motivation on the older children's learning behaviors and academic achievement

(Gottfried, Fleming, & Gottfried, 1998; Wentzel & Wigfield, 1998; Steinmayr & Spinath, 2009).

Recently, studies show the impact of preschool children's motivation and its impact on later academic achievement and success. In the chapter titled, "The Development of Motivation in Preschoolers and its Effect on Academic Achievement," Sandy L. R. Dietrich and Robert Pasnak examine and report current literature of findings on preschool children's motivation and their academic achievement. They emphasize the importance of understanding the preschool children's development of motivation before their formal education. Sandy L. R. Dietrich and Robert Pasnak discuss how the different motivation theories have guided the use of various motivation constructs and components. Since preschool children have limited cognitive abilities, these theories, constructs, and elements have challenged the assessment of motivation in young children. Additionally, they implement an ecological model of development to examine the effects of internal and external factors on the development of motivation during the preschool years. Lastly, they conclude with implications for future research and practice that may enhance motivation in preschool children which in turn could better equipped them to attain academic success.

Young children's mathematic abilities are essential in helping them develop their academic achievement throughout their school years (Duncan et al., 2007; Jordan, Kaplan, Ramineini, & Locuniack, 2009; Siegler et al., 2012). It is important to find the means to improve the children's mathematics abilities as early as possible (Aunola, Leskinen, Lerkkanen, & Nurmi, 2004) such as in the home environment. Parents assume an important role in their children's mathematics development (Ramani & Siegler, 2014; Sonnenschein, Metzger, & Thompson, 2016). Researchers on parent involvement in their children's education referred to it as parents' academic socialization, which focuses on their beliefs and practices concerning their children's academic development. The parents' socialization practices affect their children's motivation in developing their academic abilities. Since there is limited research on this area (Jacobs, Davis-Kean, Bleeker, Eccles, & Malanchuk, 2005), in the chapter titled, "Parents' Socialization of Their Young Children's Interest in Math," Susan Sonnenschein and Rebecca Dowling examine and discuss the available research on that topic. They review studies that support that the home learning environment is an important component for children's mathematic development. They focus on the parents' socialization of young children's interest in mathematics. Susan Sonnenschein and Rebecca Dowling take the approach that parents' beliefs and practices facilitate children's interest in mathematics which, in turn, fosters their engagement in mathematics activities, and subsequent mathematics development. As appropriate, they discuss racial/ethnic, socioeconomic status, and child gender differences in the parents' practices. In addition, they discuss any relevant research on reading. In the next chapter titled, "Motivation and Mathematics in Early Childhood," Nicole R. Scalise, Jessica R. Gladstone, and Geetha B. Ramani discuss the variability in young children's mathematics skills. One source of this variability is young children's motivational beliefs about mathematics, including their mathematics ability beliefs, interest in mathematics, and mathematics anxiety. These motivational beliefs predict children's concurrent and future mathematics achievement, and follow developmental patterns that begin in early childhood education. They summarize the research on the social interactions that children share with parents and early childhood educators that may inform the development of their math-related motivational beliefs. In the final section, Nicole R. Scalise, Jessica R. Gladstone, and Geetha B. Ramani describe ways in which future research could extend the rich knowledge about older students' mathematics motivation to younger children, and provide suggestions for parents, teachers, and policy makers who are interested in promoting young children's early motivational beliefs.

MASTERY MOTIVATION

Motivation behaviors are a usual phenomenon or characteristic of young children when they interact with the world. Teachers attempt to reinforce and motivate children's learning with interesting methods, but they recurrently encounter numerous problems in establishing the circumstances that can nurture the children's learning. Alison K. Billman and Bryce L. C. Becker studied this phenomenon to understand how to promote and maintain children's motivation at an early age. In their chapter titled, "Dragonflies, Fireflies, and Dinosaurs: Harnessing Motivation Through Student-Based Inquiry," they define motivation in early childhood classrooms and how to foster motivation through children's interests and student-based inquiry, as framed by the interests of one child, Sam. Informed by both sociocognitive and sociocultural perspectives, Alison K. Billman and Bryce L. C. Becker described motivation as both intrinsically based and extrinsically influenced. In this way, they highlight its connection to several additional factors, such as personal interest, agency, goal-oriented behavior, and self-evaluation. Next, they describe the 6-Cs (Turner & Paris, 1995) of motivational contexts and teachers' roles in harnessing and sustaining student motivation. In particular, project-based learning and student-based inquiry are considered effective approaches for doing so in early childhood settings. The authors turn to science as a discipline that lends itself particularly well to such inquiry, and provide examples of science and literacy integrated curricula that have been shown to support children's motivation to learn. They conclude with their own recommendations for fostering motivation in classrooms, as well as recommendations from Sam himself.

When individuals are involved in an interesting experience, they are greatly motivated. Motivation researchers, scholars, psychologists, and educators are conscious of this reality. They have proposed several ways to improve motivation. Some focus on "intrinsic" motivation (Deci, 1975) or motivational "flow" (Csikszentmihalyi, 1975, 1990), where situations are formed to enhance interest in learning and knowledge are pursued for their personal sake. The preschool years are considered to be crucial with regard to children's intrinsic motivation, which has been shown to be associated with several child-related outcomes. Consequently, identifying conducive and obstructive factors to promote preschool children's intrinsic motivation is of major interest. In the chapter titled, "Fostering children's intrinsic motivation in preschool." Wilfried Smidt and Stefanie Kraft use Helmke's (2007) framework to describe several characteristics that may influence the preschool children's intrinsic motivation. They review and critically discuss findings concerning the direct effects of didactical characteristics (e.g., granting of autonomy, working with peers, task characteristics) on intrinsic motivation. They take into account the factors regarding the preschool (1) teachers' characteristics, (2) children's characteristics, and (3) contextual characteristics. They report that there is some research evidence on the predictive role of children's personal characteristics; however, findings concerning indirect relations between preschool teachers' personal characteristics and contextual preschool class characteristics with children's intrinsic motivation is still scarce, and further research is required to shed more light on possibilities and barriers for the promotion of children's intrinsic motivation in preschool.

Motivating others requires considering their individual needs. Psychology theorists and researchers show that all individuals have a unique way of developing including particular drives and desires as a result of their experiences. Two individuals need their own unique motivation because they differ in their background and experiences. For example, twins who have been raised in the same environment differ in their personality characteristics, which suggest that individual needs must be considered when attempting to motivate someone beginning at an early age (Baumeister & Bushman, 2016).

Children are born with an instinctive yearning to learn about their world. Their motivation depends on their experiences. Their motivation needs to be adapted to their individual differences to promote their development. In the chapter titled, "Developmental Differences in Young Children's Intrinsic, Extrinsic, and Mastery Motivation," Olivia N. Saracho provides information on the theory of young children's motivation, the way it develops in relation to the children's functioning, and how it is formed by their environment. She also discusses the difference between intrinsic and extrinsic motivation as well as mastery motivation. Mastery motivation is a multidimensional, intrinsic psychological influence that motivates individuals to make an effort to overcome their tendency to quit before completing a task (Morgan, Józsa, & Liao, 2017). It is a "psychological force that stimulates an individual to attempt independently, in a focused and persistent manner, to solve a problem or master a skill or task which is at least moderately challenging for him or her" (Morgan, Harmon, & Maslin-Cole, 1990, p. 319). Then Olivia N. Saracho describes the children's developmental patterns and sequence of motivation in relation to their age differences and their age and behavior differences.

SOCIAL MOTIVATION

Social withdrawal is an umbrella term that encompasses different underlying motivations as to why children choose to remove themselves from opportunities for social interaction. It has been argued that *all* children who experience a relative lack of age-normative social interactions are at increased risk for a range of maladaptive outcomes at school. However, more recent research suggests differential outcomes among subtypes of withdrawn children. For example, *shy* children (i.e., who desire but also fear social contact) demonstrate a greater risk for social, emotional, and school difficulties as compared to *unsociable* children (i.e., who are content to play alone). In the current chapter titled, "Teachers' Beliefs About Socially Withdrawn Young Children," Kristen A. Archbell, Amanda Bullock, and Robert J. Coplan review research studies that examine teachers' beliefs, responses, and emotional reactions to socially withdrawn children in the early educational setting. Topics covered include, an overview of social withdrawal and its underlying social motivations, early perspectives on teachers' beliefs toward social withdrawal, and more recent research examining teachers' beliefs about distinct subtypes of social withdrawal (i.e., shyness and unsociability). Further, they consider intervention strategies that teachers can incorporate into the educational environment. They conclude with some caveats and posit directions for future research.

Motivation assumes a fundamental function for early childhood classrooms, students, practitioners, and parents alike. When motivation runs high, teachers and parents can be powerful allies in the implementation of evidence-based practices that support children's growth and development in both school and home settings. The rising prevalence of social and behavioral challenges in early childhood programs have educational researchers and program administrators advocating for evidence-based practices that provide better methods for communicating with teachers and parents in ways that support their motivation and effective implementation of interventions that target these issues. Coaching has emerged as a vehicle for ongoing teacher professional development and parent education and training. Coaching offers a framework for practitioners to provide positive social influence to parents and teachers as they face new changes. Erchul (2011) suggests "the added value of this social influence lens to change teacher's beliefs, attitudes, and behaviors to enhance the implementation of evidence-based practices is considerable," and that "intervention integrity is fundamentally an exercise in social influence and, once viewed in this way, there are multiple viable frameworks to be applied" (pp. 76–77). It has indicated potential outcomes for teachers, parents, and children. Similarly, Erchul's reports about teachers can be considered to be paralleled to parents as well, and that of a modification of a specific theory and motivational interviewing (Miller & Rollnick, 2012), offers such a framework of influence and corresponds with the goal of promoting changes in teacher and parent behavior. Motivational interviewing (MI) has become more prominent in early childhood research, addressing the motivations of teachers and parents to implement evidence-based practices with fidelity. In their chapter titled, "Coaching to Improve Motivation in Early Childhood Practitioners and Parents," Jon Lee, Andy J. Frey, Zachary Warner, and Laura Kelley advocate for the promise of MI as a framework for coaching that both prioritizes adult motivation and provides a blueprint for the structure, processes, and content of effective coaching mechanisms. They (1) describe MI and its application in the context of school-based coaching, (2) analyze the coaching interventions that have cited MI as part of their logic model using Powell and Diamond's (2013) framework, (3) highlight some of the strengths and potential challenges of MI-based coaching approaches, and (4) conclude with a discussion of some possible areas for future research.

Throughout the last half-century, Western scholars have focused on Japanese students' learning processes, including motivation and engagement. Japanese students have continuously shown high academic performance in international tests of mathematics, science, and language arts (Organization for Economic Co-operation and Development [OECD], 2016), Western scholars have identified key elements that explain the Japanese students' academic achievement, their important qualities that build a foundation to motivate young children to learn, and how Japanese early childhood education teachers try to build strong motivational values in young children that can carry on to their later years of life. In the chapter titled, "*Ganbari*: Cultivating Perseverance and Motivation in Early Childhood Education in Japan," Yoko Yamamoto and Eimi Satoh introduce a distinctive Japanese concept to emphasize a cultural virtue and offer a unique perspective to motivate children's learning in Japanese childcare, preschools, and elementary schools. The authors introduce and describe the Japanese concept of *ganbari*, which means the exertion of hard work and effort, is considered to be a virtue and attitude shaping an individual's long-term learning motivation in Japan. They also explore the role of *ganbari* in children's motivation and learning processes and how Japanese teachers and schools try to cultivate *ganbari* in young children by examining and reviewing interdisciplinary studies. Yoko Yamamoto and Eimi Satoh first explain the concept of *ganbari*, including its definitions, meanings, and its relationship to learning through motivation. In addition, they explain the structure of early childhood education in Japan and the role of *ganbari* in children's educational processes. Then, they elaborate on how early childhood education teachers implicitly and explicitly cultivate *ganbari* in young children. Yoko Yamamoto and Eimi Satoh conclude with a discussion focusing on what we can learn from our examination of *ganbari*, as well as the drawbacks and challenges associated with the concept itself.

CONCLUSION

Motivation has been important to society, particularly among educational researchers, scholars, and educators. Recently, many motivation theorists and researchers have been validating its accountability for motivational and psychological patterns on educational behaviors. Pakdel (2013) analyzes the process of social, psychological and educational motivations in relation to the theories about the individual motivations. Individuals are inquisitive, energetic, and self-motivated (Ryan & Deci, 2000). In the last chapter titled, "Motivation Research, Contributions, and Recommendations," Olivia N. Saracho reviews some research developments. She also describes the contributions of motivation. Finally, she provides several recommendations for research and practice, to establish new motivation theories, and on how to broaden, modify, and develop new motivation models that contribute to future society.

REFERENCES

Abramson, L. Y., Seligman, M. E. P., & Teasdale, J. D. (1978). Learned helplessness in humans: Critique and reformulation. *Journal of Abnormal Psychology, 87*, 49–74.

Aunola, K., Leskinen, E., & Nurmi, J.-E. (2006). Developmental dynamics between mathematical performance, task motivation, and teachers' goals during the transition to primary school. *British Journal of Educational Psychology, 76*, 21–40. doi:10.1348/000709905X51608.

Austin, J. T., & Klein, H. J. (1996). Work motivation and goal striving. In K. R. Murphy (Ed.), *Individual differences and behavior in organizations* (pp. 209–257). San Francisco, CA: Jossey-Bass.

Bandura, A. (1989). Human agency in social cognitive theory. *American Psychologist, 44*, 1175–1184.

Baumeister, R. F., & Bushman, B. J. (2016). *Social psychology and human nature.* Belmont, CA: Wadsworth.

Bernard, L. C., Mills, M., Swenson, L., & Walsh, R. P. (2005). An evolutionary theory of human motivation. *Genetic, Social, and General Psychology Monographs, 131*(2), 129–184. doi:10.3200/MONO.131.2.129-184

Bolles, R. C. (1975). *Theory of motivation* (2nd ed.). New York, NY: Harper & Row.

Brown, J. S. (1961). *The motivation of behavior.* New York, NY: McGraw-Hill.

Carver, C. S., & Scheier, M. F. (1998). *On the self-regulation of behavior.* New York, NY: Cambridge University Press.

Cherry, K. (2017). *Motivation: Psychological factors that guide behavior.* Retrieved from https://www.verywell.com/what-is-motivation-2795378

Csikszentmihalyi, M. (1975). *Beyond boredom and anxiety.* San Francisco, CA: Jossey-Bass.

Csikszentmihalyi, M. (1990). *Flow: The psychology of optimal experience.* New York, NY: Harper and Row.

Deci, E. (1975). *Intrinsic motivation.* New York, NY: Plenum Press.

Dewsbury, D. A. (1978). *Comparative animal behavior.* New York, NY: McGraw-Hill.

Duncan, G. J., Dowsett, C. J., Dlaessens, A., Magnuson, K., Huston, A. C., Klebanov, P., ... Japel, C. (2007). School readiness and later achievement. *Developmental Psychology, 43*, 1428–1446. doi:10.1037/0012-1649.43.6.1428

Erchul, W. P. (2011). School consultation and response to intervention: A tale of two literatures. *Journal of Educational and Psychological Consultation, 21*(3), 191–208.

Gellatly, I. R. (1996). Conscientiousness and task performance: Test of cognitive process model. *Journal of Applied Psychology, 81*(5), 474–482.

Gottfried, A. E., Fleming, J. S., & Gottfried, A. W. (1998). Role of cognitively stimulating home environment in children's academic intrinsic motivation: A longitudinal study. *Child Development, 69*(5), 1448–1460. doi:10.1111/j.1467-8624.1998.tb06223.x

Graham, S., & Weiner, B. (1996). Theories and principles of motivation. In D. C. Berliner & R. C. Calfee (Eds.), *Handbook of educational psychology* (pp. 63–84). New York, NY: Macmillan Library Reference.

Helmke, A. (2007). *Unterrichtsqualität erfassen, bewerten, verbessern* [Capturing, evaluating, and improving classroom quality]. Seelze-Velber, Germany: Kallmeyer.

Hunt, J. McV. (1965). Intrinsic motivation and its role in psychological development. In Nebraska symposium on motivation. In D. Levine (Ed.), *Nebraska symposium on motivation* (pp. 189–282). Lincoln, NE: University of Nebraska Press.

Jacobs, J. E., Davis-Kean, P., Bleeker, M., Eccles, J. S., & Malanchuk, O. (2005). 'I can, but I don't want to': The impact of parents, interests, and activities on gender differences in math. In A. M. Gallagher & J. C. Kaufman (Eds.), *Gender differences in mathematics: An integrative psychological approach* (pp. 246–263). New York, NY: Cambridge University Press.

Jordan, N. C., Kaplan, D., Ramineini, C., & Locuniak, M. N. (2009). Early math matters: Kindergarten number competence and later mathematics outcomes. *Developmental Psychology, 45*, 850–867. doi:10.1037/a0014939

Judge, T. A., & Ilies, R. (2002). Relationship of personality to performance motivation: A meta-analytic review. *Journal of Applied Psychology, 87*(4), 797–807.

Kanfer, R. (1990). Motivation theory and industrial and organizational psychology. In M. D. Dunnette & L. M. Hough (Eds.), *Handbook of industrial and organizational psychology* (Vol. 1, pp. 75–170). Palo Alto, CA: Consulting Psychologists Press.

Kanfer, R., & Heggestad, E. D. (1997). Motivation traits and skills: A person-centered approach to work motivation. *Research in Organizational Behavior, 19*, 1–5.

Kasser, T., & Ryan, R. M. (1996). Further examining the American dream: Differential correlates of intrinsic and extrinsic goals. *Personality and Social Psychology Bulletin, 22*(3), 280–287. doi:10.1177/0146167296223006

Kleinginna, P., Jr., & Kleinginna A. (1981). A categorized list of motivation definitions, with suggestions for a consensual definition. *Motivation and Emotion, 5*(3), 263–291. doi:10.1007/BF00993889

Leo, E. L. & Galloway, D. (1996). Evaluating research on motivation: Generating more heat than light? *Evaluation and Research in Education, 10*(1), 35–47.

Lewin, K. (1936). *Principles of topological psychology*. New York, NY: McGraw-Hill.

Littman, R. A. (1958), Motives, history and causes. In M. R. Jones (Ed.) *Nebraska symposium on motivation* (Vol. 6, pp. 114–168). Lincoln, NE: University of Nebraska Press.

Maslow, A. H. (1943). A theory of human motivation. *Psychological Review, 50*(4), 370–396. doi:10.1037/h0054346

Miller, W. R., & Rollnick, S. (2012). *Motivational interviewing: Helping people change*. New York, NY: Guilford Press.

Morgan, G., Harmon, R., & Maslin-Cole, C. (1990). Mastery Motivation: Definition and measurement. *Early Education & Development, 1*(5), 318–339. doi:10.1207/s15566935eed0105_1

Morgan, G. A., Józsa, K., & Liao, H.-F. (2017). Introduction to the special issue on mastery motivation: Measures and results across cultures and ages. *Hungarian Educational Research Journal, 7*(2), 5–14. doi:10.14413/HERJ/7/2/1

Organization for Economic Co-operation and Development. (2016). *Launch of 2015 results of the OECD Programme for International Student Assessment (PISA)*. Retrieved from http://www.oecd.org/pisa/launch-of-pisa-2015-results.htm

Pakdel, B. (2013). The historical context of motivation and analysis theories individual motivation. *International Journal of Humanities and Social Science, 3*(18). Retrieved from http://www.ijhssnet.com/journals/Vol_3_No_18_October_2013/23.pdf

Petri, H. L., & Cofer, C. N. (2017). *Motivation behavior*. Retrieved from https://www.britannica.com/topic/motivation#ref12677

Piaget, J. (1952). *The origins of intelligence in children*. New York, NY: International Universities Press.

Pintrich, P. R. (2003) A motivational science perspective on the role of student motivation in learning and teaching context. *Journal of Educational Psychology*, *95*(4), 667–686. doi:10.1037/0022-0663.95.4.667

Powell, D. R., & Diamond, K. E. (2013). Studying the implementation of coaching-based professional development. In T. Halle, A. Metz, & I. Martinez-Beck (Eds.), *Applying implementation science in early childhood programs and systems* (pp. 97–116). Baltimore, MD: Paul J. Brooks.

Ramani, G. B., & Siegler, R. S. (2014). How informal learning activities can promote children's numerical knowledge. In R. C. Kadosh & A. Dowker (Eds.), *Oxford handbook of mathematical cognition* (pp. 1135–1155). Oxford, England: Oxford University Press.

Rotter, J. (1966). Generalized expectancies for internal versus external control of reinforcement. *Psychological Monographs*, *80*(1, Whole No. 609, 1–28.

Ryan, R. M.; Deci, E. L. (2000). Self-determination theory and the facilitation of intrinsic motivation, social development, and well-being. *American Psychologist*. *55*(1), 68–78. doi:10.1037/0003-066X.55.1.68

Saracho, O. N. (2003). Matching teachers' and students' cognitive styles, *Early Child Development and Care*, *173*(2-3), 161–173.

Senko, C., Durik, A., & Harackiewicz, J. (2008). Historical perspectives and new directions in achievement goal theory. In J. Shah & W. Gardner (Eds.), *Handbook of motivation science* (pp. 100–113). New York, NY: Guilford Press.

Siegler, R. S., Duncan, G. J., Davis-Kean, P. E., Duckworth, K., Claessens, A., Engel, M., & Chen, M. (2012). Early predictors of high school mathematics achievement. *Psychological Science*, *23*, 691–669. doi:10.1177/0956797612440101

Sonnenschein, S., Metzger, S. R., & Thompson, J. A. (2016). Low-income parents' socialization of their preschoolers' early reading and math skills. *Research in Human Development*, *13*, 207–224. doi:10.1080/15427609.2016.1194707

Steinmayr, R., & Spinath, B. (2009). The importance of motivation as a predictor of school achievement. *Learning and Individual Differences*, *19*(1), 80–90.

Theodotou, E. (2014). Early years education: Are young students intrinsically or extrinsically motivated towards school activities? A discussion about the effects of rewards on young children's learning. *Research in Teacher Education*, *4*(1), 17–21.

Tolman, E. C. (1932). *Purposive behavior in animals and men*. New York, NY: Appleton-Century.

Transformation Research Networks and JustListsNetwork Affiliate (n.d.). How scholars define motivation. Retrieved from https://sites.google.com/site/howscholarsdefinemotivation/

Turner, J., & Paris, S. G. (1995). How literacy tasks influence children's motivation for literacy. *The Reading Teacher*, *48*(8), 662–673.

Verplanck, W. S. (1957). A glossary of some terms used in the objective study of behavior. *Psychological Review*, *1957*, *64*(Suppl.), 1–42.

Vroom, V. H. (1964). *Work and motivation*. New York, NY: Wiley.

Weiner, B. (1992). *Human motivation: Metaphors, theories and research*. Thousand Oaks, CA: SAGE.

Weiner, B. (1995). Lessons from the past. *Psychological Inquiry, 6*(4), 319–321.

Wentzel, K. R., & Wigfield, A. (1998). Academic and social motivational influences on students' academic performance. *Educational Psychology Review, 10*(2), 155–175.

White, R. W. (1959). Motivation reconsidered: The concept of competence. *Psychological Review, 66*(5), 297–333. doi:10.1037/h0040934

Wigfield, A., Eccles, J. S., & Rodriguez, D. (1998). The development of children's motivation in school contexts. In A. Iran-Nejad & P. D. Pearson (Eds.), *Review of research in education* (Vol. 23, pp. 73–118). Washington, DC: American Educational Research Association.

Wlodkowski, R. J. (1984). *Motivation and teaching: A practical guide.* Washington, DC: National Education Association.

CHAPTER 2

MOTIVATION THEORIES, THEORISTS, AND THEORETICAL CONCEPTIONS

Olivia N. Saracho

Our ancestors constructed bridges long before engineering programs and knowledge of the laws of physics existed while prehistoric primitive healers diagnosed treatments before medical programs and knowledge of the laws of biology existed. The development of these laws contributed to society. For example, the laws of physics assisted in building the Golden Gate Bridge while the laws of biology aided in the elimination of smallpox. In a parallel way, motivation theories have contributed to the development of guidelines to improve human performance. Several theories of motivation provide insights concerning the cause behavior is prompted, sustained, guided, and on and on (Graham & Weiner, 1996). Cherry (2017b) raises the question, "What exactly lies behind the motivations for why we act?" Psychologists have developed several motivation theories (e.g., drive theory, instinct theory, humanistic theory). In fact, numerous distinctive effects have an impact on the individuals' motivations. This chapter discusses some influences on the study of motivation, such as theories, theorists, theoretical conceptions, and specific principles.

Contemporary Perspectives on Research on
Motivation in Early Childhood Education, pp. 21–44
Copyright © 2019 by Information Age Publishing
All rights of reproduction in any form reserved.

SOURCES OF MOTIVATION: THE SEARCH FOR INSTINCTS

Prior to the scientific study of motivation, the sources of motivation were anonymous. Various psychologists, like William McDougall (1923), attempted to determine the individuals' instincts or natural feelings, that is, the needs that drive behavior. McDougall proposed a list of 18 human instincts that ranged from reproductive method to fearful circumvention, and the instincts were considered to stimulate the organism toward certain end states (Graham & Weiner, 2012).

The instincts frequently were perceived as fine-tuned means instead of simply awarding growth to inflexible forms of behavior. Numerous instinct theorists incorporated different instincts in their lists. Possibly the greatest parsimonious supporter of this situation was Sigmund Freud (1915/1925), who advocated the dominance of sexual and possibly aggressive instincts and their countless indications. Such debatable scheme continued as the scientific study of motivation materialized. Nevertheless, the pursuit for the fundamental expansions in accomplishments and the construction of lists on instincts continued in the study of motivation, even though it surely diminished in prominence. Instead, drive or need replaced the principle of instinct. Needs varied from instincts in that they frequently incorporated deficits such as hunger and the physiological foundations that instincts needed (Graham & Weiner, 2012).

Prescientific societies agree with this principle of motivation. Many additional principles of motivation have been offered. For instance, it has been found that the quest for knowledge will be hindered if other motivations that are essential for survival (such as hunger) are more urgent (Maslow, 1943b) that useful compensations accruing from performance will augment the possibility of succeeding replications of this aspired behavior (Skinner, 1953). Henry Murray (1938) established an extensive taxonomy of human needs (e.g., achievement, aggression, autonomy) that moderately met these standards. Several years later, Maslow (1943b) proposed a hierarchy of needs.

MASLOW'S HIERARCHY OF NEEDS

Maslow's (1943b) hierarchy of needs is a motivational theory that has a five-tier representation of human needs, frequently portrayed as hierarchical levels within a pyramid. This pyramid of needs continues to be amongst the most cited work in motivation. Maslow proposed a hierarchy of needs that were based on his observations of humans' instinctive curiosity. His hierarchy defines phases of the individuals' development. Maslow's hierarchy of needs is usually presented in a hierarchical pyramid with five levels:

physiological, safety, belonging and love, esteem, and self-actualization. The low level of the pyramid is labeled physiological needs, whereas the top level of the pyramid is identified as self-actualization. The lower level has to be fulfilled before a higher level can be able to influence behavior. Additionally, the needs are assumed to vary in importance and developmental order (Graham & Weiner, 2012). According to Maslow, individuals have the following needs:

- At the bottom of the pyramid are the individuals' "Basic needs or Physiological needs" : food, water, sleep, sex, homeostasis, and excretion.
- In the second level are the individuals' "Safety Needs: Security, Order, and Stability," which are essential for their physical survival.
- In the third level are the individuals' psychological needs of "Love and Belonging," which includes family and friends.
- In the fourth level are the individuals' "Esteem Needs," which refers to their feeling of accomplishments as a result of status and success level.
- At the top of the pyramid are the individuals' "Need for Self-actualization," which is when they have achieved their full potential.

These five levels can be divided into deficiency needs and development needs. The first four levels are usually considered deficiency needs (D-needs) while the top level is thought of as growth or being needs (B-needs). Deficiency needs emerge due to the individuals' lack of motivation when they are not satisfied. Furthermore, the motivation to attain these needs become stronger the longer they are not fulfilled. For instance, the longer individuals do not have food, the hungrier they will become (McLeod, 2017). Initially, Maslow (1943b) indicated that individuals need to fulfill lower level deficit needs before proceeding to satisfy higher level developmental needs. Though, he later explained that fulfillment of a need is not an "all-or-none" phenomenon. He acknowledged that his previous statements may have presented "the false impression that a need must be satisfied 100% before the next need emerges" (Maslow, 1987, p. 69). Throughout numerous periods, Maslow persisted in improving his hierarchy of needs theory (Maslow, 1943b; 1987, McLeod, 2017).), which continues to be a very predominant framework in various areas such as psychology, sociology, and early childhood education. For example, Douglas Kenrick, a professor at Arizona State University, believes that the interest of Maslow's hierarchy is observed in the young children's developmental patterns. He states, "I have a child who is six-years-old and I noticed that when he was an infant he couldn't care less about public opinion." Kenrick adds, "

In kindergarten he (his child) started to worry about making friends but he didn't really care about getting respect from those people. And now he's in the first grade and you can see he's beginning to think about his friends' opinions and what status they hold him in. (Kremer & Hammond, 2013)

The overall perception of motivation is intensely associated with conscious or subconscious explanations based on the individuals' selections. Pintrich (2003) attributes that *the term motivation is derived from the Latin verb movere, which means to move. In other words, motivational theories attempt to answer questions about what gets individuals moving (energization) and toward what activities or tasks* (p. 669, emphasis added). Consequently, motivational researchers pursue to establish *how* individuals rationalize their behaviors. Motivation is a complicated idea with simple boundaries. It is a very intricate concept, which Leo and Galloway (1996) describe as "a coat of many colours" (p. 36), because motivational theorists embrace various theoretical frameworks to study the individuals' behavior (Theodotou, 2014).

MOTIVATION AND PERSONALITY

The majority of motivation theories presume that individuals initiate and continue behaviors to the degree that they consider the behaviors will lead to expected goals. Beginning with the work of Lewin (1936) and Tolman (1932), that set the foundation that stimulated motivation researchers to examine the psychological worth individuals attribute to goals (e.g., Kasser & Ryan, 1993; Vroom, 1964), individuals' expectations about achieving goals (e.g., Abramson, Seligman, & Teasdale, 1978; Bandura, 1989; Rotter, 1966), and the means that sustain individuals progressing toward their chosen goals (e.g., Carver & Scheier, 1998).

Motivation is considered a personality characteristic or set of characteristics (Kanfer & Heggestad, 1997). Personality has had a disproportionate past in motivation research. The majority of researchers would indirectly concur that individual differences exist in motivation and such differentiations can be found in personality predispositions (Judge & Ilies, 2002). In addressing the individual differences in motivation, Austin and Klein (1996) remarked, "Despite studies addressing individual differences within each of the perspectives, a considerable amount of research is needed before precise statements can be made about their role" (p. 239). Gellatly (1996) observed that "attempts to empirically link personality characteristics with motivational variables have produced inconsistent results" (p. 474). Lastly, Kanfer and Heggestad (1997) determined, "Until recently, the status of traits in most work motivation theories has been like that of a distant and not well-liked relative attending a family reunion" (p. 13). A fundamental problem in the investigation of dispositional influences on work behavior stems from the current lack of a unified theoretical perspective for understanding how and which personality constructs influence the motivational system (Kanfer, 1990, p. 155). Nevertheless, motivation research has made considerable theoretical progress, especially in relation to theory.

The individuals' characteristics are grounded in well-articulated motivation theories. The personality attributes are extremely wide-ranging in application, intercepting more than motivation (e.g., achievement striving, competence, order, dutifulness), or characteristics that influence motivation in specific situations (Judge & Ilies, 2002). Thus, personality is integrated in motivational theory.

MOTIVATION THEORIES

History is an effective procedure. The scientific study of motivation was initiated approximately in 1930. Originally, there was an overall transition from the construction of all-inclusive, wide-ranging theories to more precise, confined "mini"-theories and the examination of definite characteristics of motivated behavior. Both general and educational psychologists have abandoned the search of general developments of behavior to focus on theories of achievement behavior and principles that might strengthen or obstruct strenuous efforts in achievement.

Theories of motivation are intended to describe the reason for the individuals' behavior. Motivation theory was developed with irrelevant influence at various historical stages. Psychologists proposed that individuals were essentially designed to act in specific ways, based on the behavioral cues they received. Twentieth century researchers-initiated studies on probable reasons for individual differences in motivation. Researchers concentrated on exploring different explanations for motivated behavior such as internal drives, the outcomes of learning, and how individuals respond to their present behavior based on the effects of the individuals' past behavior, and cognitive processes (e.g., their views about future events).

MOTIVATION THEORISTS

Some stimulus responses motivate individuals' actions. Based on an experimentalist point of view motivational principles related to the classroom have an empirical emphasis in finding those theories that emerged from experimental data. Psychologists have proposed different theories to explain motivation. Psychological theories and historical understandings vary based on their followers. The following sections discuss a group of motivation researchers who may differ in their theoretical orientation. Table 2.1 provides a summary of these motivation theorists and their theories.

Table 2.1.
Summary of Motivation Theorists and Their Theories

Theorist	Theory	Description
Robert W. White (1904–2001)	Personality theory. Introduced the concepts of competence and "effectance" in motivation.	Recognized the individuals' emotions, interests, behaviors, relationship with others, etc. Effectively interact with the environment.
Gordon Willard Allport (1897-1967)	Personality theory. Trait theory. Value scales.	Focused on the individuals' social interactions, distinctiveness, and current situations. Focused on the individual's unique traits that are static through time and situations. Psychological inventories that identify the individuals' priorities.
Abraham Harold Maslow (1908–1970)	Maslow's hierarchy of needs.	Physiological needs. Safety Needs. Love and Belonging. Esteem Needs. Self-actualization.
Clark Leonard Hull (1884–1952)	Theories of learning and behaviors. Drive theory or systematic behavior theory. Drive reduction theory or drive-stimulus reduction learning.	Behaviors develop through reinforcement. Physiological needs (e.g., thirst, hunger) drive individuals, producing tension or arousal.

(Table continues on next page)

Table 2.1.
(Continued)

Theorist	Theory	Description
Edward Chace Tolman (1886–1959)	Purposive behaviorism. Instinct theory.	Goal expectations and demands motivate behavior.
		Instinctive nature or individual attributes motivate behavior.
David Clarence McClelland (1917–1998)	Achievement motivation theory. Theory of needs.	Need to achieve. Need for achievement, affiliation, and power.
		Avoidance.
William McDougall (1871–1938)	Human instinctive behavior.	Inherent qualities of mind and character cause behavior.
John Broadus Watson (1878–1958)	Scientific theory of behaviorism.	Predict and control of behavior under certain conditions (conditioned response).
Carl Gustav Jung (1875–1961)	"Individuation" process. Myers-Briggs Type Indicator (MBTI).	Psychological method using opposites (e.g., conscious vs unconscious, introverts vs extroverts, rational vs irrational).
		Self-report questionnaire to identify how individuals view the world and make decisions.
Henry Alexander Murray (1893–1988)	Theory of personality termed "personology." Thematic Apperception Test (TAT).	Identifies the individuals' needs, motives, and unique characteristics.
		A projective test that assesses an individual's personality and self-understanding.

Robert W. White (1904–2001)

Robert W. White, an American psychologist, was initially a historian. He began teaching at Harvard University in 1937 and retired from teaching in 1964. He became head of Harvard's clinical psychology program and chairman of the social relations department. White studied the surviving approaches of normal individuals. In the 1930s, White and other psychologists at Harvard (e.g., Henry A. Murray) advocated personality theory. He used a historian's perspective to study the personality of both normal and abnormal people. In 1948, he published his book titled, *Origins of Abnormal Psychology* (White, 1948), which became the regular textbook on the subject for decades. His curiosity in human behavior modified his research focus toward individual psychology. White was among the first American advocates of personality psychology, which attempted to recognize the individuals' emotions, interests, behaviors, and other attributes, particularly as they influence their relationship with others. He assumed that the individuals' needs motivated them to be competent and effective. In his article titled, "Motivation Reconsidered: The Concept of Competence," White (1959) introduced the concepts of competence and "effectance" in motivation which he described as the "the desire for effective interaction with the environment" (p. 317). He examined important issues to develop methods and abilities to completely function in their environment (Sabir, 2014) and identified the individuals' behavior that guides them to the effective outcomes. This kind of motivation is neither internal nor external rather it is generated when a difficult job is satisfactorily completed.

White concentrated on studying the individuals' lives, described them, and published them in his book titled, *Lives in Progress: A Study of the Natural Growth of Personality* (White, 1952). In this book he provided profiles of regular individuals and described how biology, psychology, and culture developed their personalities.

Gordon Willard Allport (1897–1967)

Gordon Willard Allport was an American psychologist whose major contributions emphasized the study of personality, trait theory, and value scales. He is considered a twentieth century personality theorist (Haggbloom et al., 2002). He introduced the study of personality; therefore, he is frequently described as one of the most prominent names in the psychology of personality. He opposed both the psychoanalytic and behavioral methods to personality. He considered that the psychoanalytic process to personality usually was extremely profound while the behavioral process was superficial. In particular, Allport considered the uniqueness of the individual. To identify the individuals' personality, he focused on the individuals' distinctiveness and their current rather than their past situations. He studied intricate social interactions. He merged individual personality characteristics that were found in most individuals, which contributed to his trait theory. He is one of the original contemporary trait theorists (Nicholson, 2003).

Unlike the humanistic and psychoanalytic theories of personality, the trait theory examined the trait method to focus on individual distinctions in attributes that are static through time and situations. Thus, Allport is also known as a "trait" psychologist. He developed his trait theory in personality. To understand his theory of traits, it is important to know how he approached psychology and in particular traits and personality. To identify the individuals' traits, he surveyed two of the utmost all-inclusive dictionaries of the English language and identified approximately 18,000 words that he believed could describe an individual. From this list, the number of words was reduced to approximately 4,500 personality-describing adjectives. Allport (1937) organized these traits into a hierarchy of three levels:

- *Cardinal traits* control and form the individuals' behavior. These are the dominant passions/obsessions, like the need for money, attention, fame etc.
- *Central traits* are common characteristics (e.g., honesty, loyalty, kindness, agreeableness, friendliness) that differ in levels for each individual.
- *Secondary traits* are characteristics (e.g., dislikes or likes, attitudes, beliefs) that are rarely observed except under certain situations.

Allport (1955) theorized that internal and external forces affect the individuals' behavior and personality. He participated in the development of the values scales, which were originally created by an international group of psychologists. The values scales are psychological inventories that are used to identify the individuals' priorities in their lives. This self-report assessment is used to determine the individuals' intrinsic and extrinsic values (Allport, Vernon, & Lindzey, 1970). Psychologists, political scientists, economists, and other interested individuals use the scales to explain what persons appreciate and assess the final purpose of their values (Johnston, 1995). They simplify the awareness of both work and common values that people sustain. Also they evaluate the meaning of each value in people's lives and the way they struggle toward self-realization through work and supplementary life responsibilities, such as parenting. The earliest values scale assessed the individuals' ability utilization, achievement, advancement, aesthetics, altruism, authority, autonomy, creativity, cultural identity, and economic rewards.

Abraham Harold Maslow (1908–1970)

Abraham Maslow, a prominant American psychologist, was assumed to be one of the forefathers of humanist psychology. While at Brandeis University he met Kurt Goldstein, a German neurologist and psychiatrist. He originated a holistic theory of the organism and the concept of self-actualization, which he wrote in his well-known book, *The Organism* (Goldstein, 1939/1934). During this time, he started his movement for a humanistic psychology, which he felt was more essential than his own theory. His theory of motivation was influenced by Wertheimer (1920, 1945), Goldstein (1934/1939), Freud (1933), and Adler (1938). This union may subjectively be termed a "general-dynamic" theory. His theory in psychology was proposed in his 1943 paper "A Theory of Human Motivation," which was published in *Psychological Review* (Maslow, 1943b). Later he expanded the concept to incorporate his observations of the humans' innate curiosity.

Maslow's (1943b) theory explains the utmost essential premises of the motivation theory, while considering his definition "of humanist psychology, " The major proposition of his theory of motivation is that all human needs are capable of being classified into a hierarchy of needs consisting of the following:

- Human beings should be viewed as an integrated unit.
- Most human beings' needs are felt more unconsciously than conciously.
- Human beings are perpetually wanting animals.
- A complex set of conscious and unconscious needs motivates behavior.
- One single need is usually not enough to explain behavior. (Maslow, 1943a)

Maslow's hierarchy of needs is frequently depicted in the shape of a pyramid with the prevalent, most basic needs at the bottom and the need for self-actualization and self-transcendence at the top. His classification has a a five-level hierarchy. Starting from the most prepotent needs, the hierarchy is the following:

1. Physiological needs, such as—breathing, drinking, eating, staying warm (homeostasis).
2. Safety needs—the personal mental and physical safety.
3. Love/belonging needs—finding a partner, establishing relationships, building a community.
4. Esteem needs—finding a status/reputation in the community.
5. Self-actualization needs—unleashing the internal creative power.

Maslow refers to the first four levels of needs as "deficit needs," because all individuals have these needs. After any of these needs are met, the motivation is discontinued. He considers the fifth level of needs as "the being need." It varies from the lower levels, because full satisfaction is never achieved. Maslow (1954) theorizes that even though individuals are mainly busy trying to meet their pressing "lower" needs, it is the self-actualization need that drives them to the actual innovation and satisfaction. A famous quote from his article states: "what a *man* can be, he *must* be!"(p. 9, emphasis added). According to Rennie (2008), "The satisfaction of higher needs is contingent on the lower needs having been met" (p. 445).

Clark Leonard Hull (1884–1952)

Clark Leonard Hull, an American psychologist, studied learning and motivation. His major focus was on theories of learning and behaviors that contribute to learning. At Yale University, Hull began to create his theory. Several scholars (e.g., Charles Darwin, Ivan Pavlov, John. B. Watson, Edward L. Thorndike) influenced him. Thorndike's (1898, 1911) law of effect, Ivan Pavlov's (1927) concept of conditional reflexes, and Watson's (1913) system of behaviorism influenced Hull's theory of learning (Hilgard & Bower, 1975). He based his theory on the idea of homeostasis, which states that the body energetically works to preserve a definite state of balance or equilibrium. For instance, the individuals' body controls its temperature to be able to guarantee that they are not very hot or cold. Hull (1935) thought that the individuals' behavior control how an organism sustains this balance. Hull concluded that all motivation occurs as a result of these biological needs; therefore, Hull named it drive theory. He established his own learning theory, which is also called drive theory or systematic behavior theory (Hovland, 1952). His systematic behavior theory or drive theory refers to how behaviors are developed when they are reinforced because they meet a need. Such satisfaction of needs produces habits of behaviors. Explicitly, Hull's theory suggests that behaviors that satisfy needs decrease these desires. He labeled this idea drive-reduction or drive-stimulus reduction learning (Hilgard & Bower, 1975).

During the 1940s and 1950s, drive reduction theory of motivation was used to describe behavior, learning, and motivation. Hull (1935) believed that the reduction of drive is the main strength for motivation. The condition of tension or arousal is produced by biological or physiological needs that drive the individual. Drives may consist of thirst, hunger and the need for warmth. A drive produces an unpleasant state; a strain that needs to be reduced (Cherry, 2017a). Hull's work was on experimentation, an organized theory of learning, and the nature of habits that he believed had a relationship between a stimulus and a response (Friedman & Schustack, 2015). Many considered Hull's method to be very difficult and his

drive-reduction theory neglected to completely describe human motivation. However, his theory has had an impact on psychology and theories
of motivation (Hovland, 1952).

Edward Chace Tolman (1886–1959)

Edward Tolman, an American psychologist, established purposive
behaviorism, which focuses on objective learning of behavior although it
also bears in mind the reason or goal of behavior (Schultz & Schultz, 2012).
He labeled his motivational system "purposive behaviorism," claiming that
behavior "reeks of purpose." Tolman's purposive behaviorism focused on
meaningful behavior, such as kicking a ball. He introduced this term in his
book titled, *Purposive Behavior in Animals and Men* (Tolman, 1932). Tolman
(1932) believed that motivated behavior is guided by goal expectations and
demands, the latter comprising internal needs and the properties of the
goal object. He believed that learning grew from knowledge about the environment and the way the organism relates to its environment. Tolman also
advocated latent learning which was initially created by Blodgett (1929). It
is a type of learning that is not instantly conveyed in an apparent reaction;
it transpires without any clear reinforcement of the behavior or relationships that are learned (Wade & Tavris, 1997).

In addition to his influence in learning theory (e.g., purposive behaviorism and latent learning), Tolman (1949) described his position on methods
of learning. He published his research on behaviorism and cognition as well
as theoretical analysis of the relations concerning psychology, sociology,
and anthropology. He described how the three disciplines of physiology,
psychology, and sociology are related to each other; therefore, they need
to be considered in its entirety (Tolman, 1932). In his article, "A Theoretical Analysis of the Relations between Psychology and Sociology," Tolman
(1952) took independent, dependent, and intervening variables under
the framework of psychology and sociology. Then he integrated them to
show their relationship to several research variables. He made a plea for
both disciplines to establish an obvious methodological system to have a
better relationship. He believed that for both sociology and psychology, the
threefold division of *independent variables, intervening variables,* and *dependent variables* offers a vital and practical method of analysis (Tolman, 1952).

A major scientific contribution to motivation was the emergence of
Tolman's instinct theory, because his theory indicated that motivation was
affected by an instinctive nature or individual attribute. The cause may be
within the individual and/or the situation. For instance, achievement attempts
can differ based on the intensity of a personality characteristic such as being

meticulous, staying in control, or having a great desire to achieve (Weiner, 1965). Tolman (1920) created a two-level theory of instinct to psychology. Instinct was divided into two parts: (1) determining or driving adjustments and (2) subordinate acts. Adjustments are motivations that follow subordinate acts, while the subordinate acts achieve that purpose. Adjustments are the reaction to a stimulus and can be positioned in a hierarchy with the lowest adjustment creating subordinate acts. Subordinate acts are randomized independent acts. A stimulus determines an adjustment or a hierarchy or adjustments. The lowest adjustment then prompts subordinate acts that continue until the adjustment is achieved. Tolman provided the following example:

> we may suppose that on a given occasion an individual's leg and foot move-
> ments are directly subordinate to what may be called the walking adjust-
> ment. This walking adjustment, however, we may assume is subordinate to
> an anger adjustment. (The man may be on his way to confront a business
> opponent.) This anger adjustment will then be subordinate to a business
> adjustment and, finally, this business adjustment itself may be assumed
> to be subordinate to what may be called the man's general sociodomestic
> adjustment. In the case of such a hierarchy of adjustments it is obvious that
> the function of all, save the lowest one in the sequence, consists in a release
> of a lower determining adjustment rather than in a release of actual subor-
> dinate acts. (p. 220)

Individuals have a distinctive way of thinking what to do in advance, which Tolman referred to as thoughts-of-acts or thinking-of-acts. This helps indi-viduals to avoid making different failing attempts until they find something that ultimately functions. Thinking-of-acts activates an inhibitory progres-sion of actions that stops the determining adjustment from prompting subordinate acts. After thinking, a prepotent stimulus directs those views into actions. A stimulus can be a prepotent: (a) the initial adjustment is pre-ferred to the act generated by the anticipated stimulus or (b) the stimulus generates a different adjustment that is more promising than the previous one. For instance, individuals are trapped in a burning building. Without thinking, they try to escape. This is the individuals' lowest determining adjustment that leads to several actions. They may run around randomly staggering to find an escape route. Or, they may pause, reflect, and recall that there was an entrance in the corner that leads to a hallway, stairwell, a set of doors, and the street. In this example of thinking-of-acts, the street is the prepotent stimulus because it creates a preferred act to the first stimu-lus. In turn, the stairwell might be a hazardous option since smoke may be found but going to a window to call for help might be a better choice. This is an alternate form of a prepotent stimulus because it creates a different adjustment that is more satisfactory than the previous one. Individuals may consider that it is safer to remain close to a window and call for help, which is a better choice rather than to go further into the burning building, generating a self-preservation adjustment (Tolman, 1920).

David Clarence McClelland (1917–1998)

David Clarence McClelland was well-known for his work on motivation. McClelland is credited with developing the achievement motivation theory (McClelland, 1961) commonly referred to as need achievement. He was ranked as the 15th most cited psychologist of the 20th century (Haggbloom et al., 2002). He generated McCelland's (1961) theory of needs (also known as three needs theory or the learned needs theory), because he believed that the individuals' particular needs are attained throughout time and are formed by one's early life experiences. According to McClelland, most human needs and/or motives can be classified as **achievement, affiliation,** and **power.** He found that these three needs affect the individuals' motivation and effectiveness. Below is a brief description of McClelland's three needs theory of motivational needs.

1. **Affiliation.** The need to have friendly relationships with others and personal interactions.
2. **Power.** The need to be in charge and have authority, which can occur in two systems: personal and institutional.
3. **Achievement.** The need to seek achievement, attainment of realistic but challenging goals, and advancement in an occupation. Individuals are motivated to improve their personal status and prestige.

According to McClelland, individuals usually have all three needs. One need will dominate based on the individuals' character, personality, and experience. Later, McClelland (1988) identified a fourth need.

4. **Avoidance**. The need to motivate individuals to circumvent conditions and others where they will experience disagreeable experiences. These avoidance causes may consist of fear of rejection, failure, success, and anxiety. He emphasized that both voluntary and involuntary intentions have an impact on an individual's motivation.

McClelland established that competence rather than intelligence is fundamental to the goal of teaching knowledge, which differs from intelligence.

William McDougall (1871–1938)

William McDougal, a motivation theorist, wrote textbooks on social and abnormal psychology. He was a forerunner in human instinctual behavior and was against mechanical explanations of human behavior. McDougall (1908) believed that human behavior relied on three abilities (e.g., intellect, emotion, willpower), which are part of instinctive control. McDougall was unable to determine the number of instincts that existed and the circular reasoning about their authenticity. Holt (1931) taunted him by saying, "if he twiddles his thumbs, it is the thumb-twiddling instinct; if he does not twiddle his thumbs, it is the thumb-not-twiddling instinct" (p. 428). McDougall developed a Darwinian theory of human behavior based on the belief that instinct is hereditary. His major contribution is that behavior is predominantly caused by the individuals' inherent qualities of mind and character, which he refers to as dispositional qualities. These dispositional behaviors identify the individuals' character and/or personality. They are established in quantity and divided by individuals but differ in strength. McDougall defined his concept of motivation in his first textbook in social psychology titled, *An Introduction to Social Psychology* (McDougall, 1908). This renowned book influenced the development of social psychology. He promoted what he identified as *hormic* (impulse) *psychology*, declaring the individuals' inherited instincts or predispositions that motivated them. Such instincts prompt intentional behaviors concerning preferred aims. McDougall also suggested that each instinct affects interpretation (focusing on stimuli pertinent to that instinct) and emotion. For instance, the instinct of fright is provoked by items communicating danger and is related with distress.

John Broadus Watson (1878–1958)

John B. Watson was a groundbreaking psychologist who contributed to the development of behaviorism. He promoted scientific theory with behaviorism. He thought that psychology should mainly be based on systematic observable behavior. He stimulated a transformation in psychology through his 1913 article titled, "Psychology as the Behaviorist Views It" (Watson, 1913) where he identified the key elements of his new philosophy of psychology, called "behaviorism." In the first paragraph he summarized his behaviorist position: "Psychology as the behaviorist views it" is a purely objective experimental branch of natural science. Its theoretical goal is the prediction and control of behavior. Introspection forms no essential part of its methods, nor is the scientific value of its data dependent upon the readiness with which they lend themselves to interpretation in terms of consciousness.

> The behaviorist, in his efforts to get a unitary scheme of animal response, recognizes no dividing line between man and brute. The behavior of man, with all of its refinement and complexity, forms only a part of the behaviorist's total scheme of investigation. (Watson, 1913, p. 158)

He used this behaviorist approach to conduct research on animal behavior, child rearing, and advertising. He also conducted his most famous controversial experiment known as "Little Albert" (Watson & Rayner, 1920) where a young child was conditioned to fear a white rat, which was guided by Ivan Pavlov's (1897/1902) studies on classical conditioning. Watson recorded the boy's conditioned as fear to justify his major view that all behavior is learned rather than being inborn instincts. He also proposed that his well-known research on the conditioning process could be generalized to other comparable items. In 2002, Haggbloom and colleagues conducted a survey that was published in the journal titled, *Review of General Psychology*. The results indicated that Watson was the 17th most cited psychologist of the 20th century and identified him to be among the 100 most eminent psychologists of the 20th century.

Carl Gustav Jung (1875–1961)

Carl Gustav Jung, a Swiss psychiatrist and psychoanalyst, launched analytical psychology to address Sigmund Freud's psychoanalysis. He introduced the concepts of extraverted and introverted personality, archetypes, and the collective unconscious. His work influenced the fields of psychiatry, anthropology, archaeology, literature, philosophy, and religious studies. Sigmund Freud, the founder of psychoanalysis, became aware of Jung's distinguished research. They corresponded at length and joined forces to work on human psychology. Since Jung and Freud had a shared interest in the unconscious, Jung supported Freud's work. Therefore, Freud thought that Jung would continue his "new science" of psychoanalysis. However, Jung's research and personal vision did not support Freud's work rather he was influenced by Murray and his study of achievement motivation. The majority of Jung's suppositions of his analytical psychology reveal his theoretical differences with Freud. For instance, although Jung concurred with Freud that the individuals' childhood experiences established their future behavior, he also thought that the individuals' ambitions also contribute to their future. Among Jung's pursuits were to determine the substances of both the so-called personal unconscious and the shared unconscious (Jung, 1934). To understand the personal unconscious, he developed an experimental technique to study the latency and the substance of word associations (Jung, 1903, 1905/1973). Jung proposed that this projective assessment would provide knowledge about the personality "complexes" that contributed to the development of dysfunctional behaviors. He also investigated the individuals' dreams and other symbols to compare if any of these were found across cultures and all the way through history. Additionally, Jung (1923) identified and assessed concerns about the unconscious to examine the individuals' personality and create a typology of individual traits. He designed the "individuation" process, which is the psychological method of incorporating the opposites, involving the conscious with the unconscious but yet preserves their reasonable independence. It is considered to be the fundamental system of human development. Individuation is the central concept of analytical psychology. His structure distinguishes between what he referred to as introverts and extroverts as well as between "rational" and "irrational" kinds of individuals. He proposed and developed the concepts of the extraverted and the introverted personality, archetypes, and the collective unconscious. Jung shared with Murray his trouble with personality features, their taxonomy, the presence of the unconscious, and the undertaking of discriminating these unknown forces. Jung's (1921/1971, 1923) theory also had a major impact on The Myers-Briggs Type Indicator (MBTI), a prevalent psychometric measure, and the conceptions of socionics (theory of managing information and type of personality). It is an introspective self-report questionnaire intended to specify psychological preferences in the way individuals view the world and make decisions that will assist them to be successful in life. Isabel Briggs, developer of the Myers-Briggs Type Indicator® instrument (Myers & Myers, 1980/1995, 2014), had been steadily developing concepts of individual differences in healthy personalities to improve coherence and effectiveness in assorted groups. She implemented the concepts from Jung's (1921/1971) book titled, *Psychological Types*. For example, three of the initial pairs of preferences in Jung's typology are extraversion and introversion, sensing and intuition, and thinking and feeling. After studying them, Briggs Myers added a fourth pair, judging and perceiving. His work has been influential in psychiatry and in the study of religion, literature, and related fields (Jung, 1988). Haggbloom and colleagues (2002) conducted a survey that was published in the journal titled, *Review of General Psychology*. The results indicated that Jung was considered to be the 23rd most cited psychologist of the 20th century.

Henry Alexander Murray (1893–1988)

Henry Alexander Murray was an American psychologist at Harvard University. He had a great understanding of Carl Jung's technique of psychoanalysis, which made him well qualified to direct the Harvard Psychological Clinic in the School of Arts and Sciences from 1928–1937. Murray established the theory of personality termed "personology," that was systematized in relation to motives, presses, and needs. This term describes how persons are different as individuals. Murray described a need as a "potentiality or readiness to respond in a certain way under certain given circumstances" (Murray, 1938, p. 124). His five principles consisted of the following:

1. Personality is imbedded in the brain. The individuals' cerebral physiology directs and oversees each feature of the personality. Personality relies on the brain for any responses such as feeling states, conscious and unconscious memories, beliefs, attitudes, fears, and values.
2. The concept of reducing tension that is satisfying but must reduce some degree of tension. Individuals need excitement, activity, and movement to increase rather than decrease tension. They create tension to have the satisfaction of reducing it.
3. The individuals' experiences develop their personality, which means that their past and present experiences are important.
4. Personality transforms and develops.
5. Individuals are unique but have some similarities (Schultz & Schultz, 2014).

Murray (1938) thought that human nature consisted of a collection of worldwide basic needs, but these needs differ for each individual and determine the distinctive personality for each individual. Everybody possesses the identical basic set of needs but their importance varied among each individual's needs. Several needs are short-lived and transitory, while others are extremely settled in the individuals' nature (Shneidman, 1996). Murray (1938) classified each need as distinctive but acknowledged mutual characteristics among the needs, which reflect the personalities' behaviors. Murray (1938) used the individuals' needs and motives to create the theory of personality. Although certain needs are temporary and transforming, other needs are more intensely embedded in the individuals' nature. Murray assumes that such psychogenic needs function generally on the unconscious level but assume an important function in their personality (Cherry, 2017c).

In 1934, Murray and Christina Morgan, an artist/nurse, developed the Thematic Apperception Test (TAT), a projective test used to assess an individual's personality and self-understanding. Morgan was an artist, writer, and lay psychoanalyst who was captivated by the complexity of psychology. The TAT is composed of a sequence of pictures that are presented to an individual who creates a story about each picture. The initial measure had many of Morgan's personal drawings. She became the first author (Morgan & Murray, 1935) and in 1941 the measure was referred to as the "Morgan-Murray Thematic Apperception Test." In the later versions, Morgan's pictures and her name were deleted. The TAT has been used and continues to be used in many studies in personality and motivation and as a screening tool. Henry A Murray was considered a very creative and prominent personality theorist who made a significant contribution with his book on *Explorations in Personality* (Murray, 1938) and his TAT test.

CONCLUSION

Motivation is a valuable and transforming discipline that has observed considerable improvement in its fairly brief period of time. Innovative theories, principles, and research directions continue to emerge. Since 1930 several foremost movements in the scientific study of motivation have emerged. Primarily and principally appropriate to this review, an overall change from the formation of comprehensive, general theories to an emphasis on more compact, narrower, and confined "mini"-theories and the assessment of precise features of motivated behavior has occurred for both general and educational psychologists. The progress of motivational theory has had dissimilar influence at various places in the past. Consequently, the summary of general theories of motivation indicates its evolution in a wide-ranging historical framework. Previously, theory development has been a productive procedure where theorists differ in their support for different psychological theories; therefore, researchers differ in their interpretations based on their educational background (Graham & Weiner, 1996).

Most motivation theorists recognize that motivation contributes to the performance of all learned responses; that is, a learned behavior will only occur when it is recharged. It is unknown if motivation is a primary or secondary stimulus on behavior. Specifically, modifications in behavior are better justified by principles of environmental/ecological effects, perception, memory, cognitive development, emotion, explanatory style, or personality. However, theories exclusive to motivation may be more appropriate (Huitt, 2011). For instance, researchers have found that to some extent individuals progressively react to complicated or new situations (or stimuli) in their environment and then the rate to respond decreases. This inverted-U-shaped curve of behavior is famous and considerably recognized (e.g., Yerkes & Dodson, 1908). Nevertheless, the leading concern is one of justifying this phenomenon. Is this (1) type of conditioning (previous classical or operant conditioning affected the person's behavior), (2) another kind of external motivation like social or ecological, and (3) an internal motivational procedure (e.g., cognition, emotion, or self-regulation)? Or is there a different and better reason? (Huitt, 2011).

The information in this chapter is only the beginning but it should be enough to attract the readers' interest and motivate them to continue reading more theoretical and empirical information. However, more extensive and rigorous work needs to be continued for motivating researchers to rely on a theory that can be used to conduct their studies (Huitt, 2011).

REFERENCES

Abramson, L. Y., Seligman, M. E. P., & Teasdale, J. D. (1978). Learned helplessness in humans: Critique and reformulation. *Journal of Abnormal Psychology, 87,* 49–74.

Adler, A. (1938). *Social interest: A challenge to mankind.* London, England: Faber & Faber.

Allport, G. W. (1937). *Personality: A psychological interpretation.* New York: Holt, Rinehart, & Winston.

Allport, G. W. (1955). *Becoming: Basic considerations for a psychology of personality.* New Haven, CT: Yale University Press.

Allport, G. W., Vernon, P. E., & Lindzey, G. (1970). *Study of values.* New York, NY: Houghton Mifflin.

Austin, J. T., & Klein, H. J. (1996). Work motivation and goal striving. In K. R. Murphy (Ed.), *Individual differences and behavior in organizations* (pp. 209–257). San Francisco, CA: Jossey-Bass.

Bandura, A. (1989). Human agency in social cognitive theory. *American Psychologist, 44,* 1175–1184.

Blodgett, H. C. (1929). The effect of the introduction of reward upon the maze performance of rats. *University of California Publications in Psychology, 4,* 113–134

Carver, C. S., & Scheier, M. F. (1998). *On the self-regulation of behavior.* New York, NY: Cambridge University Press.

Cherry, K. (2017a). *Drive-reduction theory definition and examples.* Retrieved from https://www.verywell.com/drive-reduction-theory-2795381

Cherry, K. (2017b). *Motivation: psychological factors that guide behavior.* Retrieved from https://www.verywell.com/what-is-motivation-2795378

Cherry, K. (2017c). *Murray's theory of psychogenic needs: How needs might influence personality*. Retrieved from https://www.verywell.com/murrays-theory-of-psychogenic-needs-2795952

Friedman, H., & Schustack, M. (2015). *Personality classic theories and modern research*. New York, NY: Pearson.

Freud, S. (1925). Instincts and their vicissitudes. In *Collected Papers: Papers on metapsychology; papers on applied psycho-analysis* (O. Riviere, Trans.). (pp. 60–83). London, England: Hogarth Press. (Original work published 1915)

Freud, S. (1925). *Negation* (The Standard edition). New York, NY: W. W. Norton & Company.

Freud, S. (1933). *New introductory lectures on psychoanalysis*. New York, NY: W. W. Norton.

Gellatly, I. R. (1996). Conscientiousness and task performance: Test of cognitive process model. *Journal of Applied Psychology, 81*(5), 474–482.

Goldstein K. (1939/1934). *The organism: A holistic approach to biology derived from pathological data in man*. New York, NY: American Book Company. (Originally Der Aufbau des Organismus. Einführung in die Biologie unter besonderer Berücksichtigung der Erfahrungen am kranken Menschen. Den Haag, Nijhoff, 1934 [The structure of the organism. Introduction to biology with special emphasis on the experience of the sick. The Hague, Nijhoff, 1934]

Graham, S., & Weiner, B. (1996). Theories and principles of motivation. In D. C. Berliner & R. C. Calfee (Eds.), *Handbook of educational psychology* (pp. 63–84). New York, NY: Macmillan Library Reference

Graham, S., & Weiner, B. (2012). Motivation: Past, present, and future. In K. R. Harris, S. Graham, T. Urdan, C. B. McCormick, G. M. Sinatra, & J. Sweller (Eds.), *APA educational psychology handbook: Theories, constructs, and critical issues* (Vol. 1., pp. 367–397). doi:10.1037/13273-013

Haggbloom, S. J., Warnick, Jason E., Jones, Vinessa K., Yarbrough, Gary L., Russell, Tenea M., Borecky, Chris M., … Monte, E. (2002). The 100 most eminent psychologists of the 20th century. *Review of General Psychology, 6*(2), 139–152. Doi: 10.1037/1089-2680.6.2.139

Hilgard, E. R., & Bower, G. H. (1975). *Theories of learning*. Englewood Cliffs, NJ: Prentice-Hall.

Holt, E. B. (1931). *Animal drive and the learning process*. New York, NY: Holt.

Hovland, C. I. (1952). Clark Leonard Hull: 1884–1952. *Psychological Review, 59*(5), 347–350. doi:10.1037/h0056239

Huitt, W. (2011). Motivation to learn: An overview. *Educational Psychology Interactive*. Valdosta, GA: Valdosta State University. Retrieved from http://www.edpsycinteractive.org/topics/motivation/motivate.html

Hull, C. L. (1935). The conflicting psychologies of learning—a way out. *Psychological Review, 42*(6), 491–516. doi:10.1037/h0058665

Johnston, C. S. (1995). The Rokeach Value Survey: underlying structure and multidimensional scaling. *The Journal of Psychology, 129*(5), 583–597. doi:10.108 0/00223980.1995.9914930

Judge, T. A., & Ilies, R. (2002). Relationship of personality to performance motivation: A meta-analytic review. *Journal of Applied Psychology, 87*(4), 797–807.

Jung, C. G. (1903). *On the psychology and pathology of so-called occult phenomena* (Unpublished doctoral dissertation). University of Basel, Basel, Switzerland. (Later published in & extracted from *The collected works of C.G. Jung* (Vol. 1). Princeton, NJ: Princeton University Press.)

Jung, C. G. (1973). *The reaction time ratio in the association experiment. The Collected Works of C.G. Jung* (Vol. 2). Princeton, NJ: Princeton University Press. (Original work published 1905)

Jung, C. G. (1923). *Psychological types*. London, England: Kegan Paul.

Jung, C. G. (1934). Archetypes of the collective unconscious. In *The archetypes and the collective unconscious: Collected works of C.G. Jung* (Vol. 9). Princeton, NJ: Princeton University Press.

Jung, C. G. (1988). *Psychology and Western religion*. London, England: Ark Paperbacks

Jung, C. G. (1971). Psychological Types, *Collected Works of C.G. Jung*, Volume 6, Princeton, N.J.: Princeton University Press. (Original German version Jung, C. G. (1921). *Psychologische Typen* was first published by Rascher Verlag, Zurich.)

Kanfer, R. (1990). Motivation theory and industrial and organizational psychology. In M. D. Dunnette & L. M. Hough (Eds.), *Handbook of industrial and organizational psychology* (Vol. 1, pp. 75–170). Palo Alto, CA: Consulting Psychologists Press.

Kanfer, R., & Heggestad, E. D. (1997). Motivation traits and skills: A person-centered approach to work motivation. *Research in Organizational Behavior, 19*, 1–5.

Kasser, T., & Ryan, R. M. (1993). A dark side of the American dream: Correlates of financial success as a central life aspiration. *Journal of Personality and Social Psychology, 65*, 410–422.

Kremer, W., & Hammond, C. (2013, September 1). Abraham Maslow and the pyramid that beguiled business. *BBC World Service*. Retrieved from http://www.bbc.com/news/magazine-23902918

Leo, E. L., & Galloway, D. (1996). Evaluating research on motivation: Generating more heat than light? *Evaluation and Research in Education, 10*(1), 35–47.

Lewin, K. (1936). *Principles of topological psychology*. New York, NY: McGraw-Hill.

Maslow, A. H. (1943a) A preface to motivation theory". *Psychosomatic Medicine, 5*(1), 85–92.

Maslow, A. H. (1943b). A theory of human motivation. *Psychological Review, 50*(4), 370–396. doi:10.1037/h0054346

Maslow, A. H. (1954). *Motivation and personality*. New York, NY: Harper.

Maslow, A. H. (1987). *Motivation and personality* (3rd ed.). New York, NY: Longman.

McClelland, D. C. (1961). *The achieving society*. Princeton, NJ: Van Nostrand.

McClelland, D. C. (1988). *Human motivation*. New York, NY: Cambridge University Press.

McDougall, W. (1908). *An introduction to social psychology*. London, England: Methuen & Co. Retrieved from https://archive.org/stream/introductiontoso020342mbp#page/n9/mode/2up

McDougall, W. (1923). *Outline of psychology*. New York, NY: Scribner.

McLeod, S. A. (2017). *Maslow's hierarchy of needs*. Retrieved from www.simplypsychology.org/maslow.html

Morgan, C. D., & Murray, H. A. (1935). A method of investigating fantasies: The Thematic Apperception Test. *Archives of Neurology and Psychiatry*, *34*(2), 289–306. doi:10.1001/archneurpsyc.1935.02250200049005

Murray, H. A. (1938). *Explorations in personality*. New York, NY: Oxford University Press.

Myers, I. B., & Myers, P. B. (1995) *Gifts differing: Understanding personality type*. Mountain View, CA: Davies-Black Publishing. (Original work published 1980)

Myers, I. B., & Myers, P. B. (2014). *The Myers-Briggs Type Indicator* (MBTI). Menlo Park, CA: CPP. https://www.cpp.com/

Nicholson, N. (2003). How to motivate your problem people. *Harvard Business Review*, *81*(1), 56–65.

Pavlov, I. P. (1902). *The work of the digestive glands*. London, England: Griffin. (Original work published 1897)

Pavlov, I. P. (1927). *Conditioned reflexes: An investigation of the physiological activity of the cerebral cortex*. New York, NY: Oxford University Press.

Pintrich, P. R. (2003) A motivational science perspective on the role of student motivation in learning and teaching context. *Journal of Educational Psychology*, *95*(4), 667–686. doi:10.1037/0022-0663.95.4.667

Rennie, D. (2008). Two thoughts on Abraham Maslow. *Journal of humanistic psychology*. *48* (4), 445–448. doi:10.1177/0022167808320537

Rotter, J. (1966). Generalized expectancies for internal versus external control of reinforcement. *Psychological Monographs*, *80*(1, Whole No. 609), 1–28.

Sabir, M. G. (2014). Effectance motivation: A practical outcome of attachment-focused integrative reminiscence. *The International Journal of Reminiscence and Life Review 2*(1), 16–30.

Schultz, D. P., & Schultz, S. E. (2012). *A history of modern psychology*. Belmont, CA: Wadsworth.

Schultz, D. P., & Schultz, S. E. (2014). *Theories of personality*. Belmont, CA: Wadsworth.

Shneidman, E. S. (1996). *The suicidal mind*. New York, NY: Oxford University Press.

Skinner, B. F. (1953). *Science and human behavior*. New York, NY: Macmillan.

Theodotou, E. (2014). Early years education: are young students intrinsically or extrinsically motivated towards school activities? A discussion about the effects of rewards on young children's learning. *Research in Teacher Education*, *4*(1), 17–21.

Thorndike, E. L. (1898). *Animal intelligence: An experimental study of the associative processes in animals*. Psychological Review, Monograph Supplements, No. 8. New York, NY: Macmillan.

Thorndike, E. L. (1911). *Animal intelligence*. New York, NY: Macmillan.

Tolman, E. C. (1920). Instinct and purpose. *Psychological Review*, *27*(3), 217–233. doi:10.1037/h0067277

Tolman, E. C. (1932). *Purposive behavior in animals and men*. New York, NY: Appleton-Century.

Tolman, E. C. (1949). There is more than one kind of learning. *Psychological Review*, *56*(3), 144–155. doi:10.1037/h0055304

Tolman, E. C. (1952). A theoretical analysis of the relations between sociology and psychology. *The Journal of Abnormal and Social Psychology, 47*(2, Suppl), 291–298. doi:10.1037/h0054466

Vroom, V. H. (1964). *Work and motivation.* New York, NY: Wiley.

Wade, C., & Tavris, C. (1997). *Psychology in perspective* (2nd ed.). New York, NY: Longman.

Watson, J. B. (1913). Psychology as the behaviorist views it. *Psychological Review, 20*(2), 158–177.

Watson, J. B., & Rayner, R. (1920). Conditioned emotional reaction. *Journal of Experimental Psychology, 3*, 1–14.

Weiner, B. (1995). Lessons from the past. *Psychological Inquiry, 6*(4), 319–321.

Wertheimer M (1920). *Über Schlussprozesse im produktiven Denken* [About final processes in productive thinking]. Berlin, Germany: De Gruyter.

Wertheimer, M. (1945). *Productive thinking.* New York and Evanston: Harper & Row. (First published in 1920 under the title *Über Schlussprozesse im produktiven Denken* [About final processes in productive thinking.]

White, R. W. (1948). *Origins of abnormal psychology.* New York, NY: Ronald Press.

White, R. W. (1952). *Lives in progress; A study of the natural growth of personality.* New York, NY: Dryden Press.

White, R. W. (1959). Motivation reconsidered: The concept of competence. *Psychological Review 66*(5), 297–333. doi:10.1037/h0040934

Yerkes, R., & Dodson, J. (1908). The relation of strength of stimulus to rapidity of habit-formation. *Journal of Comparative Neurology and Psychology, 18*, 459–482.

PART II

ACADEMIC ACHIEVEMENT

CHAPTER 3

UNDERSTANDING MOTIVATION IN PRESCHOOL-AGED CHILDREN AND ITS EFFECT ON ACADEMIC ACHIEVEMENT

Sandy L. R. Dietrich and Robert Pasnak

There is an abundant amount of research that confirms the impact of motivation on academic achievement. However, most of the research has focused on motivation and learning behaviors and achievement in older children and adolescents (Gottfried, Fleming, & Gottfried, 1998; Wentzel & Wigfield, 1998; Steinmayr & Spinath, 2009). One study depicts how motivation at kindergarten has lasting effects throughout children's educational years, leading to educational attainment in adulthood. The Perry Preschool Study (Weikart & Hohmann, 1993) had teachers report kindergarten children's levels of motivation on the Pupil Behavior Inventory (PBI; Vinter, Sarri, Vorwaller, & Shafer, 1966). The children's motivation scores were divided into three groups (lowest, middle, highest); 33% of the children in the lowest group, 55% of children in the middle group, and 68% of children in the highest group graduated from high school (Luster & McAdoo, 1996). This study indicates the importance of motivation in early schooling, and there is an increasing interest in examining motivation

Contemporary Perspectives on Research on
Motivation in Early Childhood Education, pp. 47–74
Copyright © 2019 by Information Age Publishing
All rights of reproduction in any form reserved.

as early as in kindergarten. Yet, recent studies have found that children's motivation in preschool, before they have begun formal schooling, has an impact on later academic achievement and success. Researchers are aware of this and have stressed the need for more research in early childhood before school entry (Stipek & Greene, 2001; Turner & Johnson, 2003). The present chapter aims to review the current literature on motivation and academic achievement in preschoolers, highlighting contextual factors that influence the relationship. The ultimate goal is to emphasize the importance, for later academic achievement, of motivation *before* formal school entry and to provide implications and recommendations that enhance motivation in the early educational years and beyond. Although the focus of the chapter is on research done with preschool age children, we will incorporate findings reported for older students because (1), it provides a reference to what has been studied thoroughly in older children and (2), it provides contextual information on how motivation is similar and different in preschool versus later in formal school. But before delving into this literature, it is important to understand the unique characteristics of preschool age children and why it is critical to examine motivation and its effect on academic success at this developmental period.

THE PRESCHOOL YEARS

The preschool years are considered to be the period between ages 3 and 5. It is the period when most children first encounter academic experiences in an environment known as preschool. As a matter of fact, it has been reported that more than 80% of American children participate in preschool the year prior to kindergarten (Barnett et al., 2010). The federally funded program, Head Start, and state funded preschool programs (e.g., universal preschool) make preschool education accessible to most families across the United States, regardless of income. This investment in early childhood education is a result of mounting evidence of the positive impact preschool education has on school readiness, including the reduction of achievement gap at kindergarten and beyond (Karoly, Kilburn, & Cannon, 2005) and the long term benefits reported in adolescent and adult years (e.g., higher rates of graduating from high school, less involvement in criminal activities, higher earnings; Arteaga, Humpage, Reynolds, & Temple, 2013; Campbell et al., 2012). The question is: what motivates children this young to excel and master early academic concepts, while adjusting to the novelty of being in a classroom setting? Research has shown that the concepts and skills learned in preschool are precursors to mastering higher level skills in later grades. Aunola, Leskinen, Lerkkanen, and Nurmi (2004) conducted a longitudinal study in which they found counting skills learned in preschool predicted future arithmetic skills. Similar results were found for reading; letter knowledge and rapid naming learned at age five predicted later reading performance in Grade 2 (Lyytinen et al., 2004; Pennington & Lefly, 2001). However, preschool entails more than just learning what is being taught; it also requires the child to learn to monitor and address (or ignore) competing stimuli in the classroom setting, while maintaining the motivation to learn. The preschool environment is constantly presenting children with novel situations (e.g., working with peers and teachers) which elicit cognitive development as well as the development of other skills, such as socialization, self-regulation, and emotion recognition, to name a few. The preschool environment stimulates the development across domains (cognitive, emotional, behavioral, social) which is fundamental when entering into kindergarten and the years beyond (Goble et al., 2017; Rimm-Kaufman & Pianta, 2000; Stipek 2006). With the rapid developmental growth and maturation that occurs during the preschool period and with the introduction to the academic environment that supports development, it is important to understand the relationship between motivation and academic achievement that is cultivated during this time period.

Another factor to consider when conducting research with this age group, is the limited availability of methods to assess preschool children's motivation. Motivation is a difficult concept to define for the scientific community, which is reflected in the multiple interpretations and theories proposed (discussed in the following section). Therefore, it is not surprising that young children are not able to identify or verbalize the motivation they experience. Consequently, the assessment of motivation in preschool age children is dependent on adults' assessment and/or observations of behaviors that have been identified to operationalize motivation.

MOTIVATION THEORIES AND DEFINITION

Many theories and definitions have been proposed in the study of motivation. Most research examining motivation in the academic context cite White's (1959) concept of motivation, which refers to motivation as a drive and human need; the need to master and influence the environment (Stipek & Greene, 2001; Turner & Johnson, 2003). Other theories have emerged since 1959, suggesting different components for and concepts of motivation in the academic setting. Motivation in that setting has been referred to with different terms (e.g., academic intrinsic motivation, learning motivation, achievement motivation, mastery motivation). For this chapter, motivation and achievement motivation will be used interchangeably. In general, the definitions and theories of motivation used in research in the context of academics are based on or derived from the concepts proposed by the self-determination theory (SDT; Deci & Ryan, 1985), followed by the expectancy and value theory (Eccles et al., 1983, Eccles & Wigfield, 2002), and the achievement goals theory (Dweck & Leggett, 1988; Pintrich, 2000). See Eccles and Wigfield, (2002), for a review of theories per se. The SDT framework proposes that motivation is based on the fulfillment of three innate psychological needs: the need for autonomy; the need for competence; and the need for relatedness. According to this approach, motivation is based on the experience of attaining a goal and the satisfaction and fulfillment to the self, focusing on the motivational factors of interest and enjoyment. It is believed that when one truly wants to attain a goal (versus being pressured from an external factor), autonomy is promoted, which leads to higher levels of motivation and thus accomplishment. Two components of motivation were proposed; intrinsic and extrinsic motivation. Intrinsic motivation refers to attaining a goal for the purpose of self-satisfaction or pleasure, whereas, extrinsic motivation alludes to attaining a goal for the purpose of an external factor (e.g. reward, avoidance of punishment, pressure from others, etc.). Intrinsic motivation has been widely reported to having a positive effect on academic achievement (Deci & Ryan, 1985; Gottfried, 1990). Most recently, Lemos and Verissimo (2014) confirmed that intrinsic and extrinsic motivation are qualitatively different from each other, on two separate dimensions (rather than two poles on one dimension), that coexist in the school setting. Lemos and Verissimo found intrinsic motivation to have a consistently positive effect on academic achievement (based on teacher's ratings of students' academic performance) throughout the elementary years. In contrast, extrinsic motivation was found to work well with intrinsic motivation and have a positive effect on achievement in the early elementary years, but then had a negative effect on achievement in the later years of elementary schooling.

The expectancy and value theory further describe the self-element in motivation proposed in the SDT framework, and introduces the components of expectancy and value. Expectancy refers to the perceived self-belief or evaluation of one's competency to complete or accomplish a task or goal. This is also referred to as self-efficacy (Bandura, 1997; Schunk & Pajares, 2002). The value component refers to the incentive received or reason for wanting to complete or accomplish a goal (Wigfield & Eccles 2000). Different types of value have been identified in the literature; two types often examined in the school context are intrinsic and extrinsic motivation, which were discussed earlier.

Then there is the achievement goal theory, which further delves into the reason for an individual wanting to attain a goal or the value component to the expectancy and value theory. The achievement theory identifies two distinct goals: mastery and performance goals, which are also referred to as mastery-oriented and performance-oriented goals (Dweck, 1998; Maehr & Zusho, 2009). The mastery goals approach focuses on the task and self-representation to the private self. Someone who has a mastery goal approach is willing to complete a task, even if it is challenging and failure occurs, and displays persistence until achieving competency. In contrast, the performance goals approach focuses on the self and how the individual is perceived by others, rather than on accomplishing the task. Someone with a performance goals framework avoids challenges because of the possibility of failure and often fails to complete the task when the likelihood of incompetency is present. The mastery goal approach is most preferred and results in more adaptive outcomes versus the performance goal perspective (Dweck, 1998; Maehr & Zusho, 2009).

In summary, although these theories were developed based on research with older children, they have been referenced to, and at times been the basis for, motivational studies with preschool-aged children. The theories encompass many of the motivational factors and variables used to operationalize motivation. Some studies examine a single factor of motivation, whereas others examine more than one motivational factor. Because of the different variables and factors used to operationalize motivation across studies, there is an inconsistency in the methods used to assess motivation, which makes interpretation of results across literature a challenge. This inconsistency is further exacerbated in studies with preschool children, due to their limited ability to describe their thoughts and feelings and the reliance on others (e.g., parents, teachers) to report on their motivation (Berhenke, Miller, Brown, Seifer, & Dickstein, 2011). Furthermore, preschoolers' motivation and their cognitive process of the self may not be exhibited in the same ways and/or as developed as those of the older, elementary-aged children on whom researchers based their theories.

THE DEVELOPMENT OF MOTIVATION

There is a body of research on the development of motivation in children as young as infants and toddlers, providing evidence that motivation is present in the first years of life. It can be seen in young children's engagement in activities, their goal-directed actions, and their persistence in getting others' attention to assist with achieving a goal (Liszkowski, Carpenter, & Tomasello, 2008; Meltzoff, 1995; Over & Carpenter, 2009). Additionally, it has been reported that at the preschool age, children start to develop a preference for a type of goal approach, for example, a mastery goal approach or a performance goal approach, and also have a perception of self-competency and self-evaluation on performance, although it is inflated (Butler, 1990; Turner & Johnson, 2003). Also, based on Nicholls's (1990) findings on children's level of reasoning, preschoolers do not have the ability to distinguish causes of outcomes due to effort, ability, and performance. In young children (before preschool attendance), research focuses on the relationship between motivation and cognitive development (Stipek & Greene, 2001). Once children enter formal schooling, the literature tends to shift focus to motivation and its effect on academic achievement, but the studies are primarily on older elementary aged children and beyond (Hornstra, van der Veen, Peetsma, & Volman, 2013; Luster, Lekskul, & Oh, 2004). Only recently, since the increased attention from the U.S. government to making preschool universal, and the increased reports of preschool attendance having a robust effect on children's education, has more and more research emerged examining the effect of motivation on academic achievement *before* formal school entry (Stipek, 2006).

Longitudinal studies are a powerful tool for examining the development of processes and mechanisms. Longitudinal studies provide a temporal dimension to findings that allow researchers to make inferences on causality and directionality among constructs. The longer the timeframe of a study the more information it provides on the long-term effects and the developmental trajectories of processes. However, that all comes at an expense (i.e., it is costly to manage a study over years, and participant retention is a challenge). With that said, longitudinal studies are best in providing information on the temporal relationship between motivation and academic achievement in preschool children. However, the currently published longitudinal studies that have examined the relationship between motivation and academic achievement in early education start with kindergarteners (Howse, Lange, Farran, & Boyles, 2003; Luster & McAdoo, 1996). Only a few longitudinal studies start at the preschool period. From those few studies, we have learned that there may be a bidirectional relationship between motivation and academic achievement, in which the constructs affect each other's development equally over time (Luster et al., 2004). This is similar to what has been reported for older children (Marsh, Trautwein, Lüdtke, Köller, & Baumert, 2005; Wigfield & Cambria, 2010). In other words, greater levels of motivation result in greater achievement which influences greater motivation and so forth. If this is so, then we can assume that motivation affects academic achievement first, (because academic achievement would not be present in the beginning of preschool), followed by the bidirectional relationship over time as found in older children. However, there is contradicting evidence on the temporal relationship between motivation and academic achievement. Goble et al. (2017) found preschool achievement to predict the motivational factor, school engagement, but not vice versa (i.e., preschool school engagement did not predict kindergarten academic achievement). This does not support the bidirectional relationship found in other studies.

Further research is needed to examine the development of the relationship between preschoolers' early motivation, later academic achievement, and the subsequent development of motivation.

Another benefit of longitudinal studies is that researchers are able to identify the developmental trajectories of processes and to group similar trajectories into profiles. In the motivation literature, there are a few longitudinal studies that have examined the stability of motivation and changes in it over time starting at the preschool years and have identified motivational profiles in children as young as the preschool age. In general, these studies have found that children tend to enter preschool having high levels of motivation, regardless of economic status (Stipek & Ryan, 1997). However, at the transition period, between preschool and kindergarten, their motivation, such as school engagement, seems to change (i.e., school engagement in preschool does not predict school engagement in kindergarten), but then it positively predicts motivation the following year (i.e., kindergarten to first grade; Goble et al., 2017). Possible explanations for the difference in motivation during the transition from preschool to elementary school include cognitive changes (i.e., the development of a more realistic self-competency perspective; increase of social comparison) and contextual changes (i.e., no longer a play focus in elementary school, more structured classroom setting) experienced. One study, Gilmore, Cuskelly, and Purdie (2003), reported motivation, specifically task persistence—children's persistence in completing a challenging task—to be stable from age 2 to 8 years, however, this was true only for girls. Caution needs to be used when interpreting these results, due to the wide span of time between the two assessment points, which could have missed changes in the trajectory (e.g., the transition between preschool and kindergarten). This study, though, introduces the finding that gender may have an effect on motivation trajectory which future researchers should consider when examining motivation development.

Researchers have further identified motivational profiles that originate before formal school entry. Laitinen, Lepola, and Vauras (2017) identified three motivational profiles in 4-year-olds based on cognitive (stay on task), social (social dependency), and emotional (affect while doing task) factors. One factor, task-oriented, refers to children who display on-task and engagement behaviors and independence and enjoyment while doing task. A second factor, task-avoidance, refers to children who are non-task oriented, highly dependent on others, and experience negative thoughts and feelings when doing a task. The third factor, undifferentiated, includes children who display behaviors from the other two profiles. Children in this profile are task-oriented at times and nontask oriented at other times. Laitinen et al. found that the majority of children belonged to the same motivational profile from ages 4 to 6. However, when changes in motivational profiles occurred, they were usually in the direction of a more favorable motivational tendency (e.g., from undifferentiated to task-oriented). Further research is needed to provide additional knowledge of the different profiles of motivation present in children before entry into formal schooling.

There is an increasing number of studies that have examined the trajectory of motivation post-school entry, that is, early elementary years and beyond, supporting a consensus that motivation decreases after entering the elementary school context (Jacobs, Lanza, Osgood, Eccles, & Wigfield, 2002; Spinath & Steinmayr, 2008). However, more longitudinal research is necessary with multiple assessment points before and after the transition period of preschool to kindergarten to understand the origination of the decline and to connect the trajectory of motivation before and after formal school entry. Like the development of all processes, the development of motivation is dependent on individual differences and the influence of environmental factors before school entry (Stipek & Greene, 2001; Eccles & Wigfield, 2002).

For the next sections of this chapter, we will adopt the ecological model of development (Bronfenbrenner & Morris, 1998), to provide a conceptual framework in understanding the mechanisms and factors that affect the relationship between motivation and academic achievement. The theory posits mechanisms of centrality to the child, starting with the child's own unique characteristics and extending out to contextual factors and social interactions that influence the child's development. For motivation and academic achievement development, we review the effects of the individual's characteristics of cognitive abilities and gender, followed by the contextual factors, home and classroom environment, with attention on the social interactions that occur at each context.

EFFECTS OF INDIVIDUAL CHARACTERISTICS

Cognitive Abilities

It has been documented that general cognitive abilities are highly correlated to academic achievement in preschool children, yet they are separate constructs (Kaufman, Reynolds, Liu, Kaufman, & McGrew, 2012). Researchers attribute the difference between cognitive abilities and academic achievement to noncognitive constructs, such as motivation, that have a positive effect on academic achievement (Kaufman et al., 2012). Academic abilities refer to the knowledge children gain from concepts taught in the classroom, whereas cognitive abilities entail the capabilities or abilities attained naturally from brain maturation and the nonacademic environment. Intelligence and cognitive abilities are terms used interchangeably in this chapter. Positive relationships between motivation and academic achievement have been found independent of cognitive abilities in high school youths (Steinmayr & Spinath, 2009), young elementary school students (Hornstra et al., 2013) and in preschool age children (Greene, Pasnak, & Romero, 2007). Greene et al. (2007) examined the relationship among the three constructs in preschool children, by assessing each construct with two direct child performance measures at two time points, 11 weeks apart. Piagetian measures of cognitive development (understanding of the oddity principle[1] and of seriation[2]), two measures of intrinsic motivation (bag toss[3] and marble drop[4]), and two Woodcock-Johnson scales were administered (e.g., the Letter-Word Identification and the Applied Problems Scale). Motivation was found to be positively associated with later cognitive development (but not vice versa; cognitive abilities were not associated with later motivation). Motivation was also found to predict later achievement in numeracy (but not vice versa). There was no temporal relationship between motivation and later achievement in literacy. Similarly, Stipek and Ryan (1997) also found that motivation, specifically expectancy and glances—a measure of dependency—assessed in the fall predicted the cognitive variables of puzzle solving, number memory, and conceptual grouping achievement in numeracy which were assessed in the spring of the same school year. Specific motivational factors were associated with specific achievement domains. For instances, worrying was associated with numbers achievement and enjoyment was found to predict spring number achievement. Gilmore et al. (2003), also found the motivation, specifically persistence, as reported by parents at age two predicted cognitive ability and achievement in spelling and reading (not math) at age 8 as reported on the Wechsler Abbreviated Scale of Intelligence (WASI; The Psychological Corporation, 1999), however, these findings were present only for girls. No predictive relationships were found for boys.

Many other preschool studies have examined the relationship between motivation and cognitive abilities by using receptive language as an indicator of cognitive abilities. Luster et al. (2004) found children's cognitive abilities at 18 months, assessed with the Bayley Mental Development Index (MDI; Bayley, 1969) and at the preschool age, assessed with the Peabody Picture Vocabulary Test—Revised (PPVT-R: Dunn & Dunn, 1981), a measure of receptive vocabulary, to be positively associated with academic motivation, reported by teachers on two assessments (the Pupil Behavior Inventory, PBI, and a rating scale on the child's level of academic motivation relative to the other children in the same grade) at the end of first grade. Laitinen et al. (2017) also found receptive language, assessed on a standardized comprehension of instruction test (NEPSY: Kemp, Korkman, & Kirk, 2001) to have a positive relationship with motivational behaviors (e.g., task orientation, task-avoidance, and social dependence) as reported by teachers and categorized into profiles. They reported that children with higher language comprehension skills were more likely than the children with lower language comprehension skills to be in the task-oriented group (willing to take a challenge, display independence and persistence) and less likely to be in the task-avoidance group (not interested in the task, socially dependent) the following year. A possible explanation of such a finding is that children who excel in language comprehension are able to understand the directions and instructions for a task and therefore, can focus on the task, whereas those who experience language comprehension difficulties or deficits may not understand all or part of the directions and instructions, thus experiencing frustration and stress, which results in them giving up and/or avoiding the task.

Within the domain of language, private speech, an aspect of cognition, in which children engage in self-regulation via audible speech to themselves, has been found to be related to the development of motivation in preschool children (Winsler, 2009). It is a window that allows us to see the thought processing that occurs during cognitive activities such as motivation. Private speech emerges and is used the most in preschool-aged children. Later it evolves into inner/internalized speech. Researchers have reported that different types of private speech are related to different components of motivation. Sawyer (2017) found that in preschool-aged children, performance motivation was positively related to metacognitive private speech, whereas persistence was positively related to playful private speech. Private speech has also been found to be associated with different motivational orientations in preschool children (Chiu & Alexander, 2000; Day & Burns, 2011). Positive self-talk (e.g., "I can do this") has been found to occur mostly with mastery-oriented children whereas, negative self-talk (e.g., "This is too hard") tends to occur with performance-oriented children (Chiu & Alexander, 2000). Although no differences were found in motivational orientation patterns in preschool children of low- and middle-income families, there was a significant difference in their self-talk. Children of middle-income families displayed more positive private speech than children of low-income families, and children of low-income families displayed more negative private speech than their counterparts from middle-income families. This could eventually lead to the establishment of different motivational patterns: e.g. positive private speech with mastery orientation and negative private speech with performance orientation. (Day & Burns, 2012). In summary, it is important to take into account the influence of cognitive processing and abilities on the development of motivation, which in turn has an effect on academic achievement.

Gender

Gender differences across the different components of motivation (e.g., task value, perception of ability) have been documented in older children in academic contexts (Eccles, Wigfield, Harold, & Blumenfeld, 1993; Jacobs et al., 2002). However, the effect of gender on younger children's motivation development is ambiguous. As aforementioned, Gilmore et al. (2003) found the motivational factor, task persistence, to be stable in girls between ages 2 and 8, but in boys, it changed over time, becoming significantly less than girls' persistence at age 8. As for the relationship between motivation and academic achievement, girls' persistence reported by parents at age 2 on the Object Persistence Scale of the Dimensions of Mastery Questionnaire (DMQ; Morgan et al., 1992) was related to achievement in the area of reading and spelling assessed by the Wechsler Individual Achievement Test Screener (WIATScreener; The Psychological Corporation, 1992) at age 8. No predictive relationships were found for boys (Gilmore et al., 2003). Goble et al. (2017) also found significant gender differences across teachers' ratings on two motivational factors, positive social interaction skills and school engagement, such that girls received higher ratings than boy across both motivational factors and across 3 years (e.g., preschool, kindergarten, and first grade). Possible explanations for the gender difference are that environmental factors differ for boys and girls (e.g., the expectations teachers or parents or both have for boys may differ from those they have for girls). Alternatively, the environment can be the same but the environmental factors may affect boys and girls differently because they have different interests. However, there are other studies that have not found gender differences in motivation in preschoolers. Stipek and Ryan (1997) did not find systematic gender differences across thirteen motivational measures in a sample of preschool-aged children, and consequently suggested that gender differences emerge after kindergarten. Similarly, Berhenke and colleagues (2011) observed Head Start graduates during the completion of a puzzle and trivia task and found no gender differences in the motivational factors, emotional and task engagement.

Another way gender can affect motivation in young children is through the language that is used with them. Cimpian (2010) examined the effect of generic versus non-generic language on preschool-aged children's motivation, based on children's reports on emotion, enjoyment, and competence before and after playing a game. Cimpian found that children's motivation tends to decrease when generic language and own-gender (e.g., "boys are good at this") or other-gender (e.g., "girls are good at this) references are used. This is because generic language with own-gender reference sets an expectation that imposes additional pressure for the study participant to meet, whereas, the generic language with other-gender reference implies stability in ability, and therefore discourages the study participant to try.

Either way, there is evidence that gender differences may be present in motivation at the preschool age which seems to continue after entry into elementary and beyond (Eccles et al., 1983; Jacobs et al., 2002). Additional research is necessary to confirm the effect of gender on motivation and academic achievement.

EFFECTS OF FAMILY CHARACTERISTICS

It is important to take into consideration family characteristics when examining motivation development and its effect on academic achievement. Researchers have found that socioeconomic status (SES) has an effect on children's development due to the different environmental influences across SES. Children of low-income families experience an environment consisting of more stressors and fewer resources than that experienced by their higher income counterparts. This difference has been associated with developmental delays and negative academic outcomes (Barbarin et al., 2006; Chang & Burns, 2005). Less than a handful of comparative studies have been conducted that compare motivation in preschool children from low-and middle-income families (Day & Burns, 2011; Stipek & Ryan, 1997; Malakoff, Underhill, & Zigler, 1998) and the findings contradict each other. Stipek and Ryan (1997) and Day and Burn (2011) found no difference in levels of motivation (e.g., self-confidence, attitude toward school, expectations for success, dependency, and preference for challenge) and patterns of motivation orientation (performance-oriented and mastery-oriented), respectively, at the time low- and middle-income children entered preschool. Malakoff et al. (1998), on the other hand, found families' SES to have an effect on preschool-aged children's effectance motivation, based on children's curiosity for novel stimuli, preference for challenging tasks, persistence, preference for intrinsic reinforcement, such that children from middle-income families who attended private preschool had higher levels of effectance motivation than children in Head Start. However, children with Head Start experience had higher levels of effectance motivation than children of low-income families with no preschool experience. In the following section we will review parental and family characteristics that have been found to vary across SES and have an effect on motivation and academic achievement.

Parental Influences

Researchers have consistently reported that family characteristics (e.g. parents' education, parenting practices, parents' attitudes, mother-child relationships) have an influence on preschool children's academic skills (Burchinal, Peisner-Feinberg, Pianta, & Howes 2002; Pianta, Nimetz, & Bennett, 1997). It has been documented in older elementary school children that parental characteristics (e.g., parental motivational practice, parenting styles) are related to motivation and academic achievement (Doctoroff & Arnold, 2017; Gottfried, Fleming, & Gottfried, 1994). Eccles et al.'s (1983) motivational theory of expectancy and value even includes a parent socialization component, describing parents' actions and beliefs (e.g., parent's beliefs about their children's competency, parents' interests, parents' perceptions and the values they place on tasks) that influence children's motivation development.

Few studies have extended findings to younger children and examined the effects of parental characteristics on motivation and academic achievement in preschool children. Luster et al. (2004) conducted a longitudinal study of children born to teen mothers, in which they followed children from infancy to first grade, examining the relationship of various parent and home characteristics to motivation in the academic setting. These researchers found both home experiences prior to school entry, as assessed by the Home Observation for Measurement of the Environment (HOME: Caldwell & Bradley, 1984) when children were 36 months old, and parenting practice as reported by family advocates at 54 months of age, to be positively related to motivation at first grade. The latter was assessed by the children's teachers on the PBI and an overall rating on the child's level of academic motivation. Luster et al., also examined the relationship of maternal education to children's academic achievement at first grade, and found them not be related. Early home environment and the children's' cognitive abilities based on their score on the PPVT-R in preschool had an indirect effect on motivation at the end of first grade. This was mediated by academic achievement as assessed by the Peabody Individual Achievement Test—Revised (PIAT-R; Markwardt, 1989) in the beginning of first grade. A limitation to this study is that most constructs were assessed at one time point, restricting interpretation of effects to one temporal order, which precludes the examination of concurrent effects or change of construct development over time or a different sequence of effect (e.g., motivation assessed at the end of preschool predicting achievement at the end of first grade).

Turner and Johnson (2003) also examined the relationship of parental characteristics (parent education, parent income, self-efficacy, parenting belief, and parent-child relationship) to 4-year-old African American children's motivation orientation. All of these measures were based on parent reports and a measure of academic achievement, assessed with a standardized test, was also obtained. The researchers found that children with higher mastery motivation tended to have parents with high levels of efficacy and positive parent-child relationships. Parents' education predicted parenting beliefs, parenting beliefs predicted parent-child relationships, parent-child relationships predicted mastery motivation, and lastly, mastery motivation predicted academic achievement. Additionally, these researchers found a positive correlation between mastery motivation and parenting beliefs—but the predictive effect was not significant independently of parent-child relationships. Instead, parent-child relationships were the only significant predictor of mastery motivation, which implies the possibility of parent-child relationships mediating the effect of parenting beliefs and mastery motivation.

Researchers have further examined parent-child relationships, identifying characteristics that support motivation development. For instance, parent involvement was found to mediate the effect of motivation, and parents who provided a structure that is autonomy-supportive were found to elicit competence, greater levels of engagement, and better grades in their children (Grolnick, 2016). However, these findings are based on older children, after school entry. There is not much research that provides information on the characteristics of parent-child relationships that promote motivation and academic success for preschool-aged children.

One study (Harris, Robinson, Chang, & Burns, 2007) reported the interaction of the temperament, effortful control, and motivation to be associated with attention regulation in a parent-child task such that children with higher levels of effortful control and mastery motivation scored higher in attention regulation which allowed them to perform successfully in the parent-child task. In addition, it was found that the children with high levels of effortful control during parent-child interactions were likely to perform a task on their own without external motivation. Motivation orientation (e.g., mastery and performance) was assessed in this study by observing children's behavior during the completion of a puzzle task jointly with parent and then a week later independently. Harris et al (2007) suggested that motivation may be involved indirectly, through its interaction with parent-child interactions, however, further research is needed to confirm this idea.

Other studies have examined the effect of adult feedback during parent-child interactions on preschoolers' motivation (Cimpian, Arce, Markman, & Dweck, 2007; Kamins & Dweck; 1999). Cimpian et al. (2007) found that adult feedback has an effect on motivation which subsequently affects achievement in preschool age children. The findings demonstrate that children who received praises and criticisms that entailed their own attributes (also referred to as generic) tend to display more helpless behavior and exhibit less persistence than those who received praises or criticisms based on the process they engaged in (e.g., focusing on the effort and behavior the child engaged in; also referred to as nongeneric). Cimpian et al., explained that evaluations of the person's trait or ability tend to make the outcome more permanent than when the evaluations are based on the process or strategies used. Furthermore, criticism of the process and strategy is associated with more mastery-orientated motivation than criticism of the person (Cimpian et al., 2007; Kamins & Dweck; 1999). Gunderson et al. (2013) further confirmed this with a longitudinal study that examined the form of parents' praise to their children when they were 1 to 3 years old and the effect it had on the children's motivational framework (assessed at 8 years old). It was found that children whose parents used praise focused mostly on process and procedural when they were a toddler tended to have an incremental framework of motivation, whereas children whose parents used mostly trait-focused type of praises tended to have a fixed-ability framework of motivation 5 years later. Consideration needs to be taken on the time gap between the last assessment of the parents' praise (at age 3) and the one assessment of the children's motivational framework. There are many factors that could have occurred during the 5-year gap that could have influenced children's motivational framework at 7 and 8 years old (e.g., praises from teachers and other family members, parents' praise changing as the child got older, etc.). Also, additional assessments of children's motivational frameworks are necessary across different time periods and contexts to confirm the robustness of the motivational framework.

In sum, such researcher as exists suggests that the home environment and the interactions that occur in it are important for the development of motivation in preschool-aged children, and thus for academic success, however, more research is necessary to confirm and identify mechanisms that support motivational development in the home environment.

EFFECTS OF CLASSROOM CHARACTERISTICS

There is a growing body of evidence that suggests that classroom characteristics (e.g., teacher-child relationship, peer interactions, instructional strategies) have an effect on children's motivation (Pakarinen et al., 2010; Patrick, Mantzicopoulos, Samarapungavan, & French, 2008) and academic success (Burchinal et al., 2002; Hamre & Pianta, 2000). This evidence supports the concept that teachers' behavior (evaluation of children's performance, expectation of children's performance), their belief in the children's competence, and the environment teachers create in their classroom (e.g., promoting autonomy, providing opportunities to master challenging tasks, social interaction, availability of support) can have an effect on the development of children's motivation (Stipek, 1996). However, as mentioned before, most of the evidence has been found for older children, after entry into elementary school and not so much for preschool children.

Teacher Influences

Teacher characteristics including instructional strategies, have been found to have an influence on motivation and academic achievement. Stipek, Feiler, Daniels, and Milburn (1995) examined the relationship of different instructional approaches (child-centered programs versus didactic, highly academic programs) on motivation and achievement in preschool and kindergarten children from low- and middle-class income families. Children in the didactic programs had higher scores than children in the child-centered programs in the letters and reading achievement domain, but not in the numbers domain, as assessed on an adapted version of the Woodcock-Johnson Achievement test (Woodcock & Johnson, 1989) in combination with supplemental items from the Peabody Individual Achievement Test (PIAT; Dunn & Markwardt, 1970). However, preschoolers in the didactic programs had lower ratings across various motivation components than those in the child-centered programs (e.g., lower expectations for academic success, lower confidence in abilities, more dependency on adults, less pride in their accomplishments). Program effects were robust across income levels and grades (preschool and kindergarten). Later, Stipek et al. (1998), examined the two instructional strategies across both preschool children and kindergartners, but also added a social component to it (i.e., a basic skills strategy with a didactic approach that uses less positive social climate versus a de-emphasized basic skills strategy with a child-centered approach that emphasized positive social climate). Letters and reading achievement and numbers and math achievement and motivation (perceptions of competence, attitudes toward school, anxiety, affect, risk-taking, expectations for success, independence, and persistence) assessed with self-report measures and direct task assessments (e.g., puzzle task), were the outcome measures for the study. The classroom environment that emphasized basic skills and less positive social climate, following a structured didactic approach, did not result in favorable outcomes for motivation or achievement in preschool-aged children. However, in kindergarten, the program effect was mixed for achievement and motivation; showing gains in some achievement areas (i.e., reading in the didactic structured, language skills in child-centered) and the development of positive motivation for some factors (e.g., preference for challenge, greater persistence for didactic structured, performance in the child-centered) and negative effect on other motivational factors (e.g., mostly factors related to negative affect for the didactic structure, less persistence and preference for challenge for the child centered) across both programs. A possible reason for the different effects across grades of the programs with the social component added could be that preschool aged children are used to the preschool context, which is high in social climate. In contrast, the elementary school context has fewer social opportunities for learning and instead engages in a more structured didactic approach to instruction. Therefore, when preschool children are confronted with a structured didactic approach program that has a less positive social climate, it has a negative effect on preschool achievement and motivation. Kindergarteners, on the other hand, are used to the structured didactic approach of instruction, because it is similar to what they experience in the formal schooling context. This can be the reason why they showed some gains with the structured didactic approach that emphasized basic skills and a less positive social climate.

Bonawitz et al. (2011) further examined how approaches to teaching affected preschool children's motivation to explore and discover. The researchers conducted two experiments with different teaching scenarios to teach the functioning of a toy. In experiment one, the child was the direct recipient of the different types of teaching (direct teaching-teacher explained and demonstrated the function of the toy, interrupted teaching-partial explanation of the function of the toy was given, and no teaching-no explanation about the functions of the toy was given). In experiment two, the child was the direct and indirect recipient of the teaching. The teaching scenarios included: direct recipient of teaching, indirect recipient of teaching-teaching was directed to another child, indirect recipient of teaching—teaching was directed to an adult, and no teaching. Results indicated that direct teaching whether to the child or to another child (with the target child listening to the teaching) decreases a preschool child's motivation to explore and discover. Whereas, in situations where no teaching occurred, or the teaching was directed at an adult, children displayed high levels of exploratory motivation and discovery and learning the functions of a novel toy. Bonawitz and colleagues suggested that the possible reason for this finding was the children's perception of the information and source providing the teaching. It seems likely that when children receive information from a reliable source they assume that all possible information has been shared and that there is nothing more to discover. Therefore, there is no need to further explore. Children may also apply this conception when they witness a teaching directed to another child. Again, they believe that all information has been divulged even though it was not directly to them but rather to a child similar to them. However, that does not hold true if the recipient of the teaching is an adult. Preschool children may not pay attention or relate to teaching done to an adult, so in such situations, children believe that they have not been taught and have the need to learn or obtain information on their own. This may be why higher levels of exploratory and discovery motivation was observed. Bonawitz et al.'s study provides important information on preschool children's perception of learning and the effect of teaching on motivation. The right teaching environment implemented in the preschool context is one that elicits motivation but also provides guidance and knowledge.

Another factor to consider when examining teacher's influence on the development of motivation in preschool-aged children is the feedback characteristic received from teachers. This is similar to that mentioned earlier when discussing the effect of parent-child relationships on motivation development. Like that of parents, teachers' feedback can have an effect on preschool children's motivation. Cimpian et al. (2007) demonstrated this thru a role play scenario with puppets in which the experimenter acted as the teacher puppet, giving "generic" versus "nongeneric" praises to the student puppet, which was played by the child. The children tended engage more in mastery motivation (versus taking a helpless approach) when given "nongeneric" phrases than "generic" phrases.

In summary, longitudinal studies with a long-time span that include assessments as early as the preschool years are necessary so that the long-term effects of instructional programming and classroom/teacher characteristics, including teacher-child relationships, on motivation development and academic achievement can be examined.

Before discussing peer influences and the effect peer interactions has on motivation, it is important to discuss the importance of play in the preschool setting and the effect it has on motivation development. "Vygotsky regarded sociodramatic play (pretend role-play) as the most beneficial, or 'leading' activity for preschoolers' overall development, and a key source for the development of motivation and agency" (Sawyer, 2017, p. 85). Sawyer most recently confirmed the importance of play on motivation when he found preschool children to display higher levels of mastery motivation, performance and persistence, in a playful context. These types of motivation were higher in a fishing game that entailed pretend role-play and emphasized intrinsic motivation and prosocial behavior, versus a fishing activity that emphasized the extrinsic motivation of work production in a nonplayful context of earning stickers. Such a finding posits the importance of play opportunities in the preschool setting to enhance motivation. However, further research is need to replicate Sawyer's study with a larger sample (> 40 children) and to identify mechanisms relating play, motivation, and academic achievement.

Peer Influences

Peer influences on motivation and academic achievement has been examined mostly in older children (e.g., Masland & Lease, 2016). However, there are a few studies that have examined the effect of peer influence on the relationship between preschool children's motivation and academic achievement. Goble et al. (2017), found that social interaction, reported by kindergarten teachers on the Penn Interactive Peer Play Scale (PIPPS; Fantuzzo, Mendez, & Tighe, 1998), mediated the effect of preschool academic achievement on school engagement, a motivational factor, as reported by first grade teachers on the Teacher Rating Scale of School Adjustment (Birch & Ladd, 1997; Ladd, Birch, & Buhs, 1999). In this study, academic achievement was assessed by the WJ-III (Woodcock, McGrew, & Mather, 2001; Spanish equivalent, Batería-III Woodcock-Muñoz; Muñoz-Sandoval, Woodcock, McGrew, & Mather, 2005. Furthermore, the findings suggested that social interaction skills and school engagement had a bidirectional relationship which carried over from preschool to elementary school. Evaluation of such constructs over a longer time period (instead of the 3 years examined in this study) and assessment of all constructs (e.g., social interaction, motivation, and academic achievement at every time point (instead of assessing different constructs at different time points) would provide further information about the temporal and directionality characteristics of the relationship among the constructs.

Social interaction is an important skill, which quickly emerges when children start preschool. For most children, preschool is their first encounter with a classroom and having many children of the same age around. Therefore, it may not be surprising to learn that collaboration with peers to complete a challenging task can increase motivation. Butler and Walton (2013) found greater motivation, longer persistence and increased liking of the task, when preschool children believed they were doing a task (completing a puzzle) with someone else versus alone. The finding was based on the preschoolers' belief that they were collaborating and not on actual collaboration with peers.

IMPLICATIONS FOR RESEARCH

A common thread across all contexts is that more research on motivation is needed with younger, preschool-aged children. Most motivational studies are done with older children, after entry into formal schooling. Having an understanding of the development of motivation when children first encounter the academic world would be helpful because it sets up the foundation to future motivation and academic experiences. More research is needed to examine factors that influence the development of motivation and its relation to academic achievement and to examine the mechanisms among variables that result in positive outcomes. Replication studies are also needed to confirm current findings and for generalizability. More longitudinal studies are needed to make causal inferences and predictions of how motivation develop in preschool and beyond and the effect it has on academic achievement and learning behaviors concurrently and over time (preferably over years). Research is also needed to examine the effect of motivation in preschool on the transition to kindergarten and other future transitions (e.g., to middle school and high school). Current research suggests that motivation continuously declines after school entry; however, research is needed to identify factors that contribute to the decline and to examine if the motivation in preschool can change the trajectory of later motivation.

Lastly, it is important for researchers to consider the complexity of motivation and the different components of motivation when doing motivational research; making sure that the assessments and interpretation of findings are specific to the component of motivation studied. Furthermore, when assessing motivation in young children like preschoolers, researchers need to take into account the unique developmental characteristics for this age group, including cognitive limitations, that can restrict the type assessments that can be used.

IMPLICATIONS FOR PRACTICE

There are many implications from the literature which educators and parents can implement profitably with preschool children. The most important implication would be to be observant of children's level of motivation constantly, and to not assume a child's motivation will remain stable or that the first assessment of a child's motivation will predict child's motivation for the entire academic year or over a longer time. Multiple assessments/observations are needed to fully understand a child's level of motivation. Children's motivation can change as the contextual variables including family, classroom, relationships with others (parents, teachers, peers) and the child's own characteristics (e.g., brain maturation) change, which is why frequent assessment of children's motivation is necessary. Below is a list of additional implications to consider for enhancing motivation in preschool children:

- Support children's autonomy, providing structure but yet choices and independence when completing a task
- Provide tasks and activities that offer the right level of challenge for the child to develop mastery on his or her own or with minimal assistance
- Encourage parental involvement and positive display of motivational behavior and beliefs

- Provide praises and criticisms that focus on the process and strategies the child engaged in (e.g., nongeneric responses)
- Provide opportunities for children to collaborate with peers during challenging tasks
- Listen to children's private speech when they are working on a task and encourage the use of positive speech (e.g., "I can do this")
- Provide a learning environment that is child-centered and playful
- Provide support to children that show indications of delay or deficit in language comprehension

Lastly, it is necessary to take into account that there are different components and factors that make up motivation and that each component develops and affects learning differently. Thus, we recommend that educators and parents develop and implement activities that will target specific motivational factors, so all components of motivation can be enhanced.

CONCLUSION

There is no doubt that skills developed in preschool are critical for concurrent and future academic achievement (Gardner-Neblett, DeCoster, & Hamre, 2014; Nguyen et al., 2016) and motivation is no exception. Although the literature on achievement motivation in preschool children is scarce compared to literature on the motivation of older children, there is sufficient evidence to show that motivation is present in preschool and that it has an effect on academic achievement concurrently and predictively. As in all research literature, mixed findings are reported, which can be clarified with additional innovative or replicative studies. A possible explanation for the mixed findings in the motivation literature for preschool children is the various factors and variables being used to operationalize motivation. Many of the motivational factors overlap with cognitive, emotional, behavioral, and social constructs. Furthermore, the identification of various motivational factors has resulted in methodological inconsistency in the assessment of motivation (task performance, teacher/parent report, observation measures, self- report). Again, only more research will be able to tease apart the influences of interrelated factors and identify and streamline the methodological assessment of motivation for this young age group. Even with its methodological limitations, the present literature provides an in-depth insight into the impact motivation has on academic achievement *before* elementary school entry, and also how its development is influenced by contextual factors that interact with the child's own characteristics. Thus, it is imperative for educators, parents, and researchers to provide early interventions and opportunities to enhance motivation before school entry, so that by the time children start elementary school they will be better equipped to attain academic achievement.

NOTES

1. The oddity principle was tested with problems that used everyday objects to see if the child was able to detect the object that was different from other objects based on form, size, or orientation.
2. The seriation principle was tested with problems that consisted of lining up ordinary objects from smallest to largest. The number of objects varied across problems and there were some problems in which an additional object was inserted into the series after it was already ordered.
3. The bag toss assessment entailed throwing ten bags to a hole that was cut out from clown's picture. The child chose how close they wanted to be to the hole when they threw. Researchers record the degree of difficulty, the child chose, whether the bag went in the hole, and the difficulty of the next attempt.
4. The marble toss task entailed watching an adult drop five marbles into a wooden box with six holes on top and the having the children do the same thing with 500 marbles. Children were allowed to play as long as the wanted. Total time played and the number of marbles dropped in the box were recorded.

REFERENCES

Arteaga, I. A., Humpage, S., Reynolds, A. J., & Temple, J. A. (2013). One year of preschool or two? Is it important for adult outcomes? Results from the Chicago Longitudinal Study of the Chicago Parent-Child Centers. *Economics of Education Review*, 115–157.

Aunola, K., Leskinen, E., Lerkkanen, M.-K., & Nurmi, J.-E. (2004). Developmental dynamics of math performance from preschool to grade 2. *Journal of Educational Psychology, 96*, 699–713.

Bandura, A. (1997). *Self-efficacy: The exercise of control*. New York, NY: W.H. Freeman.

Barbarin, O., Bryant, D., McCandies, T., Burchinal, M., Early, D., Clifford, R., & Howes, C. (2006). Children enrolled in public pre-K: The relation of family life, neighborhood quality, and socioeconomic resources to early competence. *American Journal of Orthopsychiatry, 76*, 265–276.

Barnett, W. S., Epstein, D. J., Carolan, M. E., Fitzgerald, J., Ackerman, D. J., & Friedman, A. H. (2010). *The state of preschool 2010*. Rutgers, NJ: The National Institute for Early Education Research.

Bayley, N. (1969). *Bayley Scales of Infant Development*. New York, NY: Psychological Corporation.

Berhenke, A., Miller, A. L., Brown, E., Seifer, R., & Dickstein, S. (2011). Observed emotional and behavioral indicators of motivation predict school readiness in Head Start graduates. *Early Childhood Research Quarterly, 26*(4), 430–441.

Bonawitz, E., Shafto, P., Gweon, H., Goodman, N. D., Spelke, E., & Schulz, L. (2011). The double-edged sword of pedagogy: Instruction limits spontaneous exploration and discovery. *Cognition, 120,* 322–330.

Bronfenbrenner, U., & Morris, P. A. (1998). The ecology of developmental processes. In W. Damon & R. M. Lerner (Eds.), *Handbook of child psychology: Theoretical models of development* (Vol. 1., pp. 993–1028). New York, NY: Wiley.

Burchinal, M. R., Peisner-Feinberg, E., Pianta, R., & Howes, C. (2002). Development of academic skills from preschool through second grade: Family and classroom predictors of developmental trajectories. *Journal of School Psychology, 40*(5), 415–436.

Butler, R. (1990). The effects of mastery and competitive conditions on self-assessment at different ages. *Child Development 61,* 201–210.

Butler, L. P., & Walton, G. M. (2013). The opportunity to collaborate increases preschoolers' motivation for challenging tasks. *Journal of Experimental Child Psychology, 116*(4), 953–961.

Birch, S. H., & Ladd, G. W. (1997). The teacher-child relationship and children's early school adjustment. *Journal of School Psychology, 35*(1), 61–79.

Caldwell, B. M., & Bradley, R. H. (1984). *Home observation for measurement of the environment.* Little Rock, AR: University of Arkansas at little Rock.

Campbell, F. A., Pungello, E. P., Burchinal, M., Kainz, K., Pan, Y., Wasik, B. H., ... & Ramey, C. T. (2012). Adult outcomes as a function of an early childhood educational program: An Abecedarian Project follow-up. *Developmental Psychology, 48*(4), 1033.

Chang, F., & Burns, B. M. (2005). Attention in preschoolers: Associations with effortful control and motivation. *Child Development, 76*(1), 247–263.

Chiu, S., & Alexander, P. A. (2000). The motivational function of preschoolers' private speech. *Discourse Processes, 30*(2), 133–152.

Cimpian, A. (2010). The impact of generic language about ability on children's achievement motivation. *Developmental Psychology, 46,* 1333–1340.

Cimpian, A., Arce, H. M. C., Markman, E. M., & Dweck, C. S. (2007). Subtle linguistic cues affect children's motivation. *Psychological Science, 18*(4), 314–316.

Day, C. A., & Burns, B. M. (2011). Characterizing the achievement motivation orientation of children from low-and middle-income families. *Early Education & Development, 22*(1), 105–127.

Deci, E. L., & Ryan, R. M. (1985). *Intrinsic motivation and self-determination in human behavior.* New York, NY: Plenum Press.

Doctoroff, G. L., & Arnold, D. H. (2017). Doing homework together: The relation between parenting strategies, child engagement, and achievement. *Journal of Applied Developmental Psychology, 48,* 103–113.

Dunn, L. M., & Dunn, L. (1997). *Peabody picture vocabulary test* (3rd ed.). Circle Pines, MN: American Guidance Service

Dunn, L. M., & Markwardt, F. C. (1970). *Peabody individual achievement test.* American Guidance Service.

Dweck, C. S. (1998). The development of early self conceptions: Their relevance for motivational processes. In J. Heckhausen & C. S. Dweck (Eds.), *Motivation and self-regulation across the life span* (pp. 257–280). Cambridge, England: Cambridge University Press.

Dweck, C. S., & Leggett, E. L. (1988). A social-cognitive approach to motivation and personality. *Psychological Review, 95*(2), 256–273.

Eccles, J., Adler, T. F., Futterman, R., Goff, S. B., Kaczala, C. M., Meece, J. L., & Midg-ley, C. (1983). Expectancies, values, and academic behaviors. In J. T. Spence (Ed.), *Achievement and achievement motivation* (pp. 75–146). San Francisco, CA: W. H. Freeman.

Eccles, J. S., & Wigfield, A. (2002). Motivational beliefs, values, and goals. *Annual review of psychology, 53*(1), 109–132.

Eccles, J., Wigfield, A., Harold, R. D., & Blumenfeld, P. (1993). Age and gender differences in children's self- and task- perceptions during elementary school. *Child Development, 64* (3), 830–847.

Fantuzzo, J., Mendez, J., & Tighe, E. (1998). Parental assessment of peer play: Development and validation of the parent version of the Penn Interactive Peer Play Scale. *Early Childhood Research Quarterly, 13*(4), 659–676.

Gardner-Neblett, N., DeCoster, J., & Hamre, B. K. (2014). Linking preschool language and sustained attention with adolescent achievement through classroom self-reliance. *Journal of Applied Developmental Psychology, 35*(6), 457–467.

Gilmore, L., Cuskelly, M., & Purdie, N. (2003). Mastery motivation: Stability and predictive validity from ages two to eight. *Early Education and Development, 14*, 411–424.

Goble, P., Eggum-Wilkens, N. D., Bryce, C. I., Foster, S. A., Hanish, L. D., Martin, C. L., & Fabes, R. A. (2017). The transition from preschool to first grade: A transactional model of development. *Journal of Applied Developmental Psychology, 49*, 55–67.

Gottfried, A. E., Fleming, J. S., & Gottfried, A. W. (2001). Continuity of academic intrinsic motivation from childhood through late adolescence: A longitudinal study. *Journal of Educational Psychology, 93*(1), 3.

Gottfried, A. E. (1990). Academic intrinsic motivation in young elementary school children. *Journal of Educational psychology, 82*(3), 525.

Gottfried, A. E., Fleming, J. S., & Gottfried, A. W. (1994). Role of parental motivational practices in children's academic intrinsic motivation and achievement. *Journal of Educational Psychology, 86*(1), 104.

Gottfried, A. E., Fleming, J. S., & Gottfried, A. W. (1998). Role of cognitively stimulating home environment in children's academic intrinsic motivation: A longitudinal study. *Child Development, 69*(5), 1448–1460.

Greene, M. R., Pasnak, R., & Romero, S. L. (2009). A Time Lag Analysis of Temporal Relations Between Motivation, Academic Achievement, and Two Cognitive Abilities. *Early Education and Development, 20*(5), 799–825.

Grolnick W.S. (2016) Parental Involvement and Children's Academic Motivation and Achievement. In W. Liu, J. Wang, R. Ryan (Eds.), *Building autonomous learners* (pp. 169–183). Singapore, Malaysia: Springer.

Gunderson, E. A., Gripshover, S. J., Romero, C., Dweck, C. S., Goldin-Meadow, S., & Levine, S. C. (2013). Parent praise to 1- to 3-year-olds predicts children's motivational frameworks 5 years later. *Child Development, 84*(5), 1526–1541.

Hamre, B. K., & Pianta, R. C. (2001). Early teacher-child relationships and the trajectory of children's school outcomes through eighth grade. *Child Development, 72*(2), 625–638.

Harris, R C., Robinson, J. B., Chang, F., & Burns, B. M. (2013). Characterizing preschool children's attention regulation in parent-child interactions: The role of effortful control and motivation. *Journal of Applied Developmental Psychology, 28*, 25–39.

Hornstra, L., van der Veen, I., Peetsma, T., & Volman, M. (2013). Developments in motivation and achievement during primary school: A longitudinal study on group-specific differences. *Learning and Individual Differences, 23*, 195–204.

Howse, R. B., Lange, G., Farran, D. C., & Boyles, C. D. (2003). Motivation and self-regulation as predictors of achievement in economically disadvantaged young children. *The Journal of Experimental Education, 71*(2), 151–174.

Jacobs, J. E., Lanza, S., Osgood, D. W., Eccles, J. S., & Wigfield, A. (2002). Changes in children's self competence and values: Gender and domain differences across grades one through twelve. *Child Development, 73*(2), 509–527.

Kamins, M. L., & Dweck, C. S. (1999). Person versus process praise and criticism: implications for contingent self-worth and coping. *Developmental Psychology, 35*(3), 835.

Karoly, L., Kilburn, M. R., & Cannon, J. S. (2005). *Early childhood interventions: Proven results, future promise*. Santa Monica, CA: RAND Corporation.

Kaufman, S. B., Reynolds, M. R., Liu, X., Kaufman, A. S., & McGrew, K. S. (2012). Are cognitive g and academic achievement g one and the same g? An exploration on the Woodcock–Johnson and Kaufman tests. *Intelligence, 40*(2), 123–138.

Kemp, S. L., Korkman, M., & Kirk, U. (2001). *Essentials of NEPSY assessment* (Vol. 6). New York, NY: John Wiley & Sons.

Ladd, G. W., Birch, S. H., & Buhs, E. S. (1999). Children's social and scholastic lives in kindergarten: Related spheres of influence? *Child Development, 70*(6), 1373–1400.

Laitinen, S., Lepola, J., & Vauras, M. (2017). Early motivational orientation profiles and language comprehension skills: From preschool to Grade 3. *Learning and Individual Differences, 53*, 69–78.

Lemos, M. S., & Verissimo, L. (2014). The relationships between intrinsic motivation, extrinsic motivation, and achievement, along elementary school. *Procedia-Social and Behavioral Sciences, 112*, 930–938.

Liszkowski, U., Carpenter, M., & Tomasello, M. (2008). Twelve-month-olds communicate helpfully and appropriately for knowledgeable and ignorant partners. *Cognition, 108*(3), 732–739.

Luster, T., Lekskul, K., & Oh, S. M. (2004). Predictors of academic motivation in first grade among children born to low-income adolescent mothers. *Early Childhood Research Quarterly, 19*(2), 337–353.

Luster, T.,&McAdoo, H. (1996). Family and child influences on educational attainment: A secondary analysis of the High/Scope Perry Preschool data. *Developmental Psychology, 32*, 26–39.

Lyytinen, H., Ahonen, T., Eklund, K., Guttorm, T., Kulju, P., Laakso, & Viholainen, H. (2004). Early development of children at familiar risk for dyslexia—Follow-up from birth to school age. *Dyslexia, 10*, 146–178.

Maehr, M. L., & Zusho, A. (2009). Achievement goal theory: The past, present, and future. In K. R. Wentzel & A. Wigfield (Eds.), *Handbook of motivation at school* (pp. 77–104). New York, NY: Routledge.

Malakoff, M. E., Underhill, J. M., & Zigler, E. (1998). Influence of inner-city environment and Head Start experience on effectance motivation. *American Journal of Orthopsychiatry, 68*(4), 630.

Markwardt, F. C. (1989). *Peabody individual achievement test-revised*. Circle Pines, MN: American Guidance Service.

Marsh, H.W., Trautwein, U., Lüdtke, O., Köller, O., & Baumert, J. (2005). Academic self-concept, interest, grades, and standardized test scores: Reciprocal effects models of causal ordering. *Child Development, 76*, 397–416.

Masland, L. C., & Lease, A. M. (2016). Characteristics of academically-influential children: achievement motivation and social status. *Social Psychology of Education, 19*(1), 195–215.

Meltzoff, A. N. (1995). Understanding the intentions of others: Re-enactment of intended acts by 18-month-old children. *Developmental Psychology, 31*(5), 838.

Morgan, G. A., Harmon, R. J., Maslin-Cole, C. A., Busch-Rossnagel, N. A., Jennings, K. D., Hauser-Cram, P., & Brockman, L. M. (1992). *Assessing perceptions of mastery motivation: The Dimensions of Mastery Questionnaire, its development, psychometrics and use*. Ft. Collins, Colorado State University, Human Development and Family Studies Department.

Muñoz-Sandoval, A. F., Woodcock, R. W., McGrew, K. S., & Mather, N. (2005). *Batería III Woodcock-Muñoz*. Itasca, IL: Riverside Publishing.

Nicholls, J. G. (1990). What is ability and why are we mindful of it? A developmental perspective. R. J. Sternberg & J. Kolligian (Eds.), *Competence considered* (pp. 11–40). New Haven, CT: Yale University Press.

Nguyen, T., Watts, T. W., Duncan, G. J., Clements, D. H., Sarama, J. S., Wolfe, C., & Spitler, M. E. (2016). Which preschool mathematics competencies are most predictive of fifth grade achievement? *Early Childhood Research Quarterly, 36*, 550–560.

Over, H., & Carpenter, M. (2009). Eighteen-month-old infants show increased helping following priming with affiliation. *Psychological Science, 20*(10), 1189–1193.

Pakarinen, E., Kiuru, N., Lerkkanen, M. K., Poikkeus, A. M., Siekkinen, M., & Nurmi, J. E. (2010). Classroom organization and teacher stress predict learning motivation in kindergarten children. *European Journal of Psychology of Education, 25*(3), 281–300.

Patrick, H., Mantzicopoulos, P., Samarapungavan, A., & French, B. F. (2008). Patterns of young children's motivation for science and teacher-child relationships. *The Journal of Experimental Education, 76*(2), 121–144.

Pennington, B. F., & Lefly, D. L. (2001). Early reading development in children at family risk of dyslexia. *Child Development, 72,* 816–833.

Pianta, R. C., Nimetz, S. L., & Bennett, E. (1997). Mother-child relationships, teacher-child relationships, and school outcomes in preschool and kindergarten. *Early Childhood Research Quarterly, 12*(3), 263–280.

Pintrich, P. R. (2000). Multiple goals, multiple pathways: The role of goal orientation in learning and achievement. *Journal of Educational Psychology, 92*(3), 544.

Psychological Corporation. (1992). *Wechsler Individual Achievement Test.* San Antonio, CA: Author.

Psychological Corporation. (1999). *Wechsler Abbreviated Scale of Intelligence.* San Antonio: Author.

Rimm-Kaufman, S. E., & Pianta, R. C. (2000). An ecological perspective on the transition to kindergarten: A theoretical framework to guide empirical research. *Journal of Applied Developmental Psychology, 21*(5), 491–511.

Sawyer, J. (2017). I think I can: Preschoolers' private speech and motivation in playful versus non-playful contexts. *Early Childhood Research Quarterly, 38,* 84–96.

Schunk, D. H., & Pajares, F. (2002). The development of academic self-efficacy. In A. Wigfield, & J. S. Eccles (Eds.), *Development of achievement motivation* (pp. 15–31). San Diego, CA: Academic Press.

Steinmayr, R., & Spinath, B. (2009). The importance of motivation as a predictor of school achievement. *Learning and Individual Differences, 19*(1), 80–90.

Stipek, D. (2006). No child left behind comes to preschool. *The Elementary School Journal, 106*(5), 455–466.

Stipek, D. J. (1996). Motivation and instruction. *Handbook of Educational Psychology,* 85–113.

Stipek, D. J., & Greene, J. K. (2001). Achievement motivation in early childhood: Cause for concern or celebration? In S. L. Golbeck (Ed.), *Psychological perspectives on early childhood education* (pp. 64–91). Mahwah, NJ: Erlbaum.

Stipek, D. J., Feiler, R., Byler, P., Ryan, R., Milburn, S., & Salmon, J. M. (1998). Good beginnings: What difference does the program make in preparing young children for school? *Journal of Applied Developmental Psychology, 19*(1), 41–66.

Stipek, D., Feiler, R., Daniels, D., & Milburn, S. (1995). Effects of different instructional approaches on young children's achievement and motivation. *Child Development, 66*(1), 209–223.

Stipek, D. J., & Ryan, R. H. (1997). Economically disadvantaged preschoolers: ready to learn but further to go. *Developmental Psychology, 33*(4), 711.

Spinath, B., & Steinmayr, R. (2008). Longitudinal analysis of intrinsic motivation and competence beliefs: Is there a relation over time? *Child Development, 79*(5), 1555–1569.

Turner, L. A., & Johnson, B. (2003). A model of mastery motivation for at-risk preschoolers. *Journal of Educational Psychology, 95*(3), 495.

Vinter, R. D., Sarri, R. S., Vorwaller, D. J., & Shafer, W. E. (1966). *Pupil Behavior Inventory: A manual of administration and scoring.* Ann Arbor, MI: Campus.

Wentzel, K. R., & Wigfield, A. (1998). Academic and social motivational influences on students' academic performance. *Educational Psychology Review, 10*(2), 155–175.

Weikart, D. P., & Hohmann, M. N. (1993). Organizing principles of the High/Scope curriculum. In R. Pasnak & M. Howe (Eds.), *Emerging themes in cognitive development: Competencies* (Vol II, pp. 188–216). New York, NY: Springer-Verlag.

White, R. W. (1959). Motivation reconsidered: The concept of competence. *Psychological Review, 66,* 297–333.

Wigfield, A., & Cambria, J. (2010). Students' achievement values, goal orientations, and interest: Definitions, development, and relations to achievement outcomes. *Developmental Review, 30*(1), 1–35.

Wigfield, A., & Eccles, J. S. (2000). Expectancy–value theory of achievement motivation. *Contemporary Educational Psychology, 25*(1), 68–81.

Winsler, A. (2009). Still talking to ourselves after all these years: A review of current research on private speech. In A. Winsler, C. Fernyhough, & I. Montero (Eds.), *Private speech, executive functioning, and the development of verbal self-regulation* (pp. 3–41). New York, NY: Cambridge University Press.

Woodcock, R., & Johnson, M. (1989). *Woodcock-Johnson Psycho-Educational Battery, revised*. Allen, TX: DLM.

Woodcock, R. W., McGrew, K. S., & Mather, N. (2001). *Woodcock-Johnson III tests of cognitive abilities* (pp. 371–401). Itasca, IL: Riverside Publishing.

CHAPTER 4

PARENTS' SOCIALIZATION OF THEIR YOUNG CHILDREN'S INTEREST IN MATH

Susan Sonnenschein and Rebecca Dowling

Increasing U.S. children's math skills is an important means of improving their academic and subsequent vocational well-being. U.S. school children routinely earn lower scores on math tests than do children from other industrialized countries. For example, on the 2015 Test of International Math and Science Studies (TIMSS, National Center for Education Statistics [NCES], 2015a), U.S. fourth graders ranked 14th in math among children from 49 different industrialized countries. Within the United States, many children fail to demonstrate age-appropriate math skills. According to test scores from the 2015 National Assessment of Educational Progress (NAEP), 60% of fourth graders, the youngest age the test is administered, scored below the proficient range (NCES, 2015b). There also were significant differences across demographic groups in the percentage of children receiving scores in the proficient range. Sixty-five percent of Asian and 51% of White fourth graders received proficient scores compared to 26% of Latino and 19% of Black fourth graders. Differences in attainment between boys and girls were smaller but still present with 42% of fourth grade boys versus 38% of fourth grade girls scoring in the proficient range. Children from low-socioeconomic status (SES) backgrounds, on average, start school with scores on math standardized tests at least one-half standard deviation

Contemporary Perspectives on Research on
Motivation in Early Childhood Education, pp. 75–100
Copyright © 2019 by Information Age Publishing
All rights of reproduction in any form reserved.

lower than children from higher-SES backgrounds (DeFlorio & Beliakoff, 2015; Galindo & Sonnenschein, 2015). On the 2015 NAEP, only 22% of fourth graders eligible for free or reduced lunch, an index of low-SES, received proficient scores in math compared to 45% of those not eligible for free or reduced lunch (NCES, 2015b).

The math skills children display during their first few years of school are critical for their subsequent development throughout school (Duncan et al., 2007; Jordan, Kaplan, Ramineini, & Locuniack, 2009; Siegler et al., 2012), and for obtaining jobs in STEM fields (Blevins-Knabe, 2016; National Mathematics Advisory Panel, 2008). Thus, we need to look for ways to improve children's math skills starting at the time they begin formal schooling or even before (Aunola, Leskinen, Lerkkanen, & Nurmi, 2004). One such way is to consider the important role played by parents in the development of young children's math skills (Ramani & Siegler, 2014; Sonnenschein, Metzger, & Thompson, 2016). Parents' involvement in their children's education is called parents' academic socialization.

Most of the research on parents' academic socialization focuses on how such beliefs and practices are associated with children's academic development. Far less research has addressed how parents' socialization practices impact children's motivation for learning academic skills. This chapter examines available research on that topic (Jacobs, Davis-Kean, Bleeker, Eccles, & Malanchuk, 2005).

Children's motivation is positively associated with their learning and academic development (e.g., Aunola, Leskinen, & Nurmi, 2006; Fisher, Dobbs-Oates, Doctoroff, & Arnold, 2012). The limited research on this topic shows that parents' socialization practices are associated with children's motivations (including their interest in learning) which, in turn, are associated with their academic skill development (e.g., Cheung & Pomerantz, 2012, 2015). A focus on the importance of using home-based activities to foster children's interest in math is consistent with a recent joint position statement by the National Association for the Education of Young Children and the National Council of Teachers of Mathematics (2002) which emphasized the importance of building upon children's natural interest in math to foster their math development.

Children's interest in academically-relevant tasks is positively associated with their subsequent academic performance (e.g., Jacobs et al., 2005; see Wigfield, Eccles, Schiefele, Roeser, & Davis-Kean, 2006; Wigfield, Rosenweig, & Eccles, 2017). The positive association between children's interest in a topic and their academic achievement may stem from their interest in a topic promoting deeper levels of processing, increasing time spent on a task, and/or increasing effort and practice devoted to a task (Fisher et al., 2012). It is also important to acknowledge that the relation between children's interest and achievement is bidirectional: interest predicts skills and skills predict interest (Denissen, Zarrett, & Eccles, 2007; Fisher et al., 2012). However, the processes through which interest fosters learning have not been well-investigated but, as noted, there is believed to be an association between children's interest in a topic and their engagement in related activities

Research on young children's math development shows a positive relation between their interest in math and their math skills. For example, Fisher et al. (2012), using an ethnically diverse low-income sample of preschoolers ($N = 166$), found that children's interest in math was moderately associated with how well they performed on a math test administered at that time. In addition, children's math scores positively predicted their interest in math five months later (see also Doctoroff, Fisher, Burrows, & Edman, 2016). Aunola et al. (2006) studied 196 children from Estonia as they transitioned from preschool through the first 2 years of elementary school. Children's math skills were assessed in preschool; measures of motivation were added in elementary school. Children's initial math skills positively predicted their subsequent interest in math which, in turn, predicted their subsequent math skills. Similar results have been found with older children (e.g., Cheung & Pomerantz, 2012, 2015). Despite a positive association between children's interest and their academic achievement, such interest unfortunately decreases with age (e.g., Gottfried, Fleming, & Gottfried, 2001; Mazzocco, Hanich, & Noeder, 2012). Thus, it is particularly important to find ways to maximize children's early interest in math (Gottfried et al., 2001).

This chapter will review the literature on parents' academic socialization of young children's math skills by addressing how socialization practices foster children's interest and engagement in math activities. We take the view that parents' beliefs and practices foster their children's interest in math which, in turn, is associated with the frequency of their engagement in activities and the type of activities engaged in. Such engagement then is associated with children's math development. Our conceptualization is consistent with the theoretical framework and research by Eccles and her colleagues (e.g., Wigfield et al., 2017). The body of research on this topic which is directly relevant is small. Of that which is relevant, more research has focused on reading than math, and has used children older than the focal age-group (ages 3–8) in this chapter. Accordingly, research on reading *and* math, where relevant, will be included. Most of the research has been conducted with children in the United States. As appropriate, however, research with children from outside the U.S. will be included. Note that findings with children outside of the U.S. reveal a similar pattern of associations to findings with children in the United States (e.g., Neuenschwander, Vida, Garrett, & Eccles, 2007).

We begin this chapter with a brief review of theories relevant for understanding how parents may influence their children's motivation and learning. We then present research on parents' academic socialization and its relation to children's academic development followed by a review of how parents' practices foster children's interest and engagement in math. We next compare beliefs and practices and patterns of development across demographic groups, focusing specifically on race/ethnicity, SES, and gender. We conclude with a section on future directions for research and how to help parents foster their children's interest in math.

RELEVANT THEORIES AND THEORETICAL APPROACHES

Parents' academic socialization and motivational theories are two important theoretical views or approaches for understanding how children's math skills develop. Both are discussed further in the remainder of this section on theories. As we discuss in this chapter, there are important racial/ethnic and income group-based differences in children's math development. Therefore, it is critical to keep in mind sociocultural theories that stress the importance of heritage influences and the larger social structure when examining family practices (Vygotsky, 1978; Wong & Hughes, 2006).

Parents' Socialization of Their Children's Interest and Academic Development

Parents' academic socialization includes parents' attitudes, values, goals, expectations, and beliefs about education, as well as the opportunities and activities parents make available to their children (Puccioni, 2015; Taylor, Clayton, & Rowley, 2004). Such socialization by parents can be expressed through beliefs explicitly or implicitly conveyed to their children, differential rewards for certain behaviors, parents' reactions to children's academic successes and failures, provision of artifacts and opportunities to engage in activities, and children's observation of parents as role models of positive engagement in academic endeavors (Jacobs et al., 2005; Sonnenschein et al., 2016). Such socialization beliefs and practices not only provide children with learning opportunities, they also convey to children the importance parents attach to their children's education and academic progress (Sonnenschein, 2002). As will be discussed in subsequent sections, parents' socialization is associated with children's academic development (Puccioni, 2015; Sonnenschein & Galindo, 2015) through children's interest and engagement in activities. The nature of parents' academic socialization is grounded in cultural models shared by members of a cultural group (Keels,

2009), although some socialization beliefs and practices also may reflect family income and parents' educational level (Sonnenschein, 2002).

Children's Motivation

Although there are many theories of motivation that are germane for children's development (see Wigfield et al., 2006 for review), we summarize here two key theories most pertinent for how parents socialize their children's interest in math development: Eccles's parent socialization model and Pomerantz' motivational development model.

Eccles parent socialization model. The overarching motivational model by Eccles and her colleagues (e.g., Fredricks & Eccles, 2002; Wigfied et al., 2006) focuses on children's expectancy to succeed and subjective task-values. The model addresses whether and why a child would want to engage in a task. As shown in Figure 4.1, the parent socialization component of the model is multifaceted. Characteristics of the parents, family, and the child are associated with parents' general beliefs and behaviors as well as those specific to the child. Parents' behaviors and beliefs, in turn, are associated with children's behaviors and motivation. The model has been extensively explored with research on children's academic motivation and engagement in academic (reading, math) and leisure activities (sports, music). For example, Simpkins, Frederick, and Eccles (2012), using data from the Childhood and Beyond Study, a longitudinal investigation starting when children were in kindergarten and going through 12th grade, found that mothers' beliefs predicted their behaviors which, in turn, predicted their children's subsequent motivational beliefs and behaviors. In addition, mothers' behaviors mediated the association between mothers' and children's beliefs. Similarly, children's beliefs mediated the association between mothers' and children's behaviors (see also Simpkins, Fredricks, & Eccles, 2015).

Unfortunately, most of the research coming from Eccles and colleagues' lab has been conducted primarily with White families. The model may well apply to other racial/ethnic groups but it is important to explore whether, in fact, it does. The research exploring Eccles's model also typically does not include preschool children. We return to this point later in the chapter.

Pomerantz' motivational development model. Pomerantz and her colleagues have discussed how parents' involvement in their children's education fosters children's skills and motivational development (e.g., Pomerantz & Grolnick, 2017; Pomerantz & Moorman, 2010). Although the two components are related, we focus here on their motivational model. The motivational model draws heavily upon the self-determination theory of Deci and Ryan (e.g., Grolnick, Deci, & Ryan, 1997) which highlights the

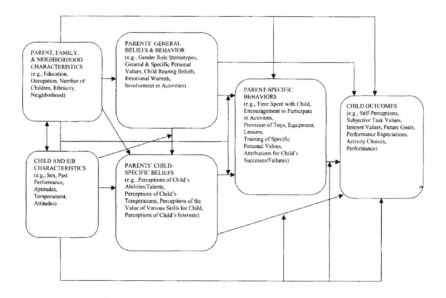

Figure 4.1. Eccles et al.'s (1983) Model of Parent Socialization. Reprinted from 'I can, but I don't want to': The impact of parents, interests, and activities on gender differences in math (p. 249), by J. E., Jacobs, P., Davis-Kean, M., Bleeker, J. S., Eccles, & O. Malanchuk, 2005. In A. M. Gallagher & J. C. Kaufman (Eds.), *Gender differences in mathematics: An integrative psychological approach* (pp. 246–263). New York, NY: Cambridge University Press.

importance of children's feelings of competence, autonomy, and relatedness. Pomerantz and colleagues suggest that parents provide their children with a context to foster motivation and learning through the opportunities they provide their children and the nature of interactions when choosing and engaging in activities. Through engagement in certain activities children develop feelings of competence and the belief that they exert autonomy in choosing their activities. Pomerantz and Grolnick (2017) described four ways that parents can interact with their children to promote motivation for engaging in activities: Supporting children's autonomy, providing them with a structured rather than chaotic environment, being affectively positive rather than negative or critical, and focusing on the process of learning (e.g., the child's efforts) rather than performance outcomes (e.g., whether the child succeeded or not). Such interactive patterns not only increase children's motivation but also increase children's learning and academic outcomes.

Pomerantz's motivational model is a more recent one than Eccles' model and there has been far less research done on it. Although Pomerantz and her colleagues discuss what parents can and should do to foster their children's motivation, much of their empirical work has addressed how parent involvement fosters adolescent engagement and academic success. Their studies have included children of middle school age and older. Using Chinese and U.S. adolescents, they have shown how parents' involvement facilitates children's academic achievement through children's internalizing their parents' views which, in turn, fosters children's self-regulation and academic achievement (e.g., Cheung & Pomerantz, 2012, 2015). Whether these findings apply to younger children is still an empirical question.

RESEARCH ON PARENTS' SOCIALIZATION OF CHILDREN'S ACADEMIC SKILLS

There is a large body of research showing that parents' academic socialization predicts the frequency of children's engagement in academic activities and their subsequent reading and math skills (e.g., Sénéchal & LeFevre, 2002; Serpell, Baker, & Sonnenschein, 2005; Sonnenschein et al., 2016). Much of the earlier research focused on children's reading development but the corpus of work on children's math development has grown substantially over the past few years. We present research from both domains because many of the findings from research on reading may be relevant for our understanding of the socialization of math. Both math and reading can be considered forms of language; therefore, similar socialization practices may be relevant for each. Given that both math and reading are important academic domains, parents may emphasize the two more than other non-academic domains. Finally, children can have significant exposure to both math and reading through engagement in daily living activities. We first present research on reading and then turn to research on math.

Research on parents' socialization has shown that parents' beliefs, the types of activities they provide to their children, and the nature of their interactions with their children are positively associated with children's reading development. For example, Serpell et al. (2005) conducted a 5-year longitudinal investigation of literacy development with low- and middle-income Black and White families in Baltimore, MD starting when children were in prekindergarten. There were three particularly interesting findings. One, parents' views of how to facilitate their children's reading development was related to the type of activities made available to children, children's frequency of engagement in activities, the nature of the interactions when engaging in literacy tasks, and children's literacy development. A view that learning to read was best facilitated by an approach that engaged the child's interest was positively associated with their literacy skills. An approach that focused on skills inculcation was either negatively related or not related. Two, the frequency with which children engaged in literacy-related activities, and the range of activities in which they engaged, was positively related to their subsequent literacy skills (see also Huntsinger, Jose, & Luo, 2016). Three, using data from the same longitudinal study, Baker, Mackler, Sonnenschein, and Serpell (2001) found that the nature of the reading interaction (affective quality and the amount of talk that goes beyond the immediate context) in first grade was associated with the frequency of children's reading age-appropriate chapter books in second grade.

Sonnenschein et al. (2016) assessed academic socialization beliefs and practices of Black and Latino parents of Head Start preschoolers as well as measured the children's language, early reading, and math skills. Consistent with findings by Serpell et al. (2005), parents' endorsement of an approach that fostered their children's engagement was positively associated with children's early literacy skills. In addition, parents' serving as role models of engagement in literacy activities was positively associated with children's engagement in such activities and, in turn, was positively associated with their receptive and expressive language skills. We discuss the pattern for math found by Sonnenschein et al. (2016) when we discuss parents' socialization of their children's math development.

Sénéchal and LeFevre (2002) considered the type of activity children engaged in and its relation to children's literacy development. They conducted a 5-year longitudinal study of children and their families beginning when the children were in kindergarten. Most of the families in the study were White and came from middle- to upper-middle income backgrounds. There were different patterns of association depending upon the type of activity children engaged in and the language or literacy outcome being assessed. Children's exposure to books was related to their vocabulary and listening comprehension. In contrast, parents' reports of purposely teaching children to read and write was positively related to their children's early literacy skills.

Parents emphasize and value reading more than math (Sonnenschein et al., 2016), with the differences in emphasis across domains greater for Black than Latino parents. Given such an emphasis by parents, it is not surprising that children engage in reading more than math activities (e.g., Anders et al, 2012; Sonnenschein et al., 2016). Findings showing associations between the frequency of children's engagement in math-related activities at home and their early math scores are mixed. On the one hand, many researchers do find such a pattern. For example, Sonnenschein and Galindo (2015), using the 1998 ECLS-K dataset, found that engaging in a broad array of math-related activities at home was positively associated with kindergarteners' math scores (see also Kleemans, Peeters, Segers, & Verhoeven, 2012; Niklas & Schneider, 2013). On the other hand, some researchers do not find such a pattern (see Blevins-Knabe, 2016, for a review). Blevins-Knabe (2016) suggested the difference in findings may stem from variability in outcome measures and how early math skills are conceptualized, variability in how math-related activities are defined, and parents' lack of knowledge of what activities children engage in. Despite some variability in patterns across studies, Blevins-Knabe concluded that more studies find an association between parents' beliefs, practices, and children's math skills than do not.

Consistent with what has been shown for reading, parents' beliefs about how children learn math and their role in such learning is related to the frequency with which children engage in tasks and their math development. Sonnenschein et al. (2012) interviewed a racially/ethnically diverse group of parents of preschool through first graders. Parents' beliefs about math development and their role in fostering it were significantly related to the frequency with which children engaged in math activities. More specifically, the frequency of such engagement was related to the frequency with which children observed their parents do math activities, to parents' beliefs about using daily living activities to foster math learning, and their beliefs about the importance of children doing math at home. Sonnenschein et al. (2016) used a previously described dataset of low-income Black and Latino parents of preschoolers to explore components of parents' beliefs and children's math activities and math skills. They found that parents as role models of math engagement, based on how much they enjoyed engaging in math activities and how frequently their children saw them doing so, predicted children's engagement in math activities and their early math skills. Some interesting differences occurred in how parents described the best ways to socialize their children's reading and math development. About 20% of the parents discussed the importance of using daily living activities to foster their children's math skills. No one mentioned using daily living activities for fostering reading.

As previously noted, many researchers, although not all, find positive associations between the frequency of children's engagement in math activities and their math skills (e.g., Huntsinger et al., 2016; Kleemans et al., 2012; LeFevre et al., 2009; Vandermaas-Peeler & Pittard, 2014). Several researchers have explored the types of math-related activities children engage in or the quality of the interactions they have with their parents when they do engage in such activities. For example, LeFevre and colleagues (e.g., LeFevre et al., 2009; Skwarchuk, Sowinksi, & LeFevre, 2014) explored children's engagement in what they called formal and informal math activities. Formal activities involved direct instruction in numbers or some form of numerical knowledge. Informal activities were board games or activities that could involve numbers but that was not the main purpose of the activity. Engagement in formal activities predicted subsequent math knowledge but engagement in informal activities did not. It is quite possible, however, that it is not the type of activity (formal or informal) children engage in but what takes place during the activity that is relevant. Metzger, Sonnenschein, Galindo, and Patel (2015) asked first through fourth graders to describe what they did when engaging in cooking and grocery shopping, two activities thought to have opportunities for fostering math development. Most of the children reported they engaged in nonmath activities (reading labels, picking out items) when they assisted their parents with cooking or grocery shopping.

Other research shows that playing math board games can be an effective tool for acquiring math skills. Ramani and Siegler (2008) used math board games that they created to successfully train children's early numeracy skills (see also Cheung & McBride, 2017). Ramani and Siegler (2008) trained children to count the spaces in a specific way on a linearly arranged board game. Not only did children show growth from pre- to post-training in their early math skills, but low-income children in the training condition improved their early math skills to the level displayed by middle-income children. Additional evidence about the importance of the nature of the interactions rather than just the type of activities comes from the work of Vandermaas and her colleagues (Vandermaas-Peeler, Boomgarden, Finn, & Pittard, 2012; Vandermaas-Peeler, Ferretti, & Loving, 2012) who found that without specific instruction on the importance of using math language when playing math-related games with their children, and guidance on what to say, most mothers did not highlight the math content of games or activities for their children.

Ramani, Rowe, Eason, and Leech (2015) using a low-income sample of preschoolers, found that the nature of mothers' math-related talk was positively associated with the specific types of math that children learned. That is, mothers whose talk included more advanced math concepts had children who displayed more advanced math knowledge. Levine, Suriyakham, Rowe, Huttenlocher, and Gunderson (2010) found a similar pattern with preschoolers whose understanding of cardinal numbers was associated with the nature of the math talk they heard from their parents.

In sum, research shows that the beliefs parents have about how their children learn and their role in such learning, the type and amount of activities engaged in, and the nature or quality of the interactions are related to the frequency of children's engagement in activities and their subsequent math development. Parents also emphasize reading more than math and children engage less frequently in math than reading activities. Equally importantly, parents often report not knowing what to do to facilitate their children's math development (Cannon & Ginsburg, 2008). They also seem not to know how to highlight the pertinent math content in math-related activities, at least without specific instruction (Vandermaas-

Peeler, Boomgarden et al., 2012; Vandermaas-Peeler, Ferretti et al., 2012). We turn next to how parents socialize their children's interest in learning, specifically their interest in learning and engaging in math activities. Such socialization is critical for increasing children's engagement in math activities and their acquisition of math skills (Wigfield et al., 2006).

RESEARCH ON PARENTS' SOCIALIZATION OF CHILDREN'S INTEREST IN MATH

Parents can socialize their children's interest in learning by providing a cognitively stimulating environment (Gottfried, Fleming, & Gottfried, 1998) and by the nature of their interactions with their children (e.g., Doctoroff & Arnold, 2017; Sonnenschein & Munsterman, 2002). Unfortunately, this is still a relatively understudied topic, particularly for math development. However, as discussed before, the principles that apply to reading also may apply to math. Similarly, the research described in prior sections that addressed how parents socialize their children's engagement with tasks should be applicable. That is, expressing a set of beliefs about the importance of engaging the child's interest in learning and providing opportunities for engagement in a broad array of activities (Serpell et al., 2005) was relevant for children's reading development. Focusing on math, Sonnenschein et al. (2016) found that low-income Black and Latino parents who enjoyed engaging in math activities and whose preschool children frequently saw them engage in such activities had children who themselves more frequently engaged in such activities.

Sonnenschein and Munsterman (2002) used data from the Early Childhood Project to study reading interactions. The sample of 30 dyads in the Sonnenschein and Munsterman study came mostly from low-income backgrounds. Of particular interest was the affective quality of the reading interactions that children experienced. The reading interactions were observed the summer before the children entered kindergarten and children's motivations for reading were assessed at the start of first grade. The affective quality of the reading interactions was the strongest predictor of children's reading motivation a year later. Children's reading motivation was associated with the frequency with which children subsequently chose to read (Serpell et al., 2005). In another study focusing on reading development, Doctoroff and Arnold (2017) found that mothers who used an approach to doing homework with their children that fostered feelings of autonomy by offering them choices (e.g., which task do you want to do now) was positively associated with the nature of children's engagement. Such engagement, in turn, predicted children's scores on a standardized measure of reading.

Few studies have focused on how parents and children interact when doing math tasks. Much of the relevant research on factors that foster children's motivation comes from the work of Eccles and her colleagues (see Jacobs et al., 2005; Wigfield et al., 2006 for reviews). This research will be discussed more extensively in the section on gender issues. However, in brief, Eccles' research shows that parents' beliefs are associated with the environment they create for their children which, in turn, is related to children's engagement in activities and subsequent math development. Relevant components of the environment include a positive climate for learning, provision of artifacts to encourage and facilitate children's engagement in math activities, and parents who serve as role models of math engagement.

Aunola, Viljaranta, Lehtinen, and Nurmi (2013) studied Finnish first graders and their mothers to assess the relation between children's interest in math and the nature of the interactions they had with others. Children's interest in math was assessed in the fall and the spring. Mothers kept a diary for a week in the fall and again in the spring about the nature of their interactions with their children on math homework tasks. There was a positive relation between mothers' reports of supporting their children's sense of competence and autonomy, two key aspects of self-determination theory, and their children's subsequent interest in math after the homework task was completed.

In a study with 11- year-old U.S. children, Else-Quest, Hyde, and Jejmadi (2008) had mothers and their children complete a math homework task together. They found a positive association between parents' and children's displays of interest in the homework task. In addition, children's interest in the homework task predicted their scores on a math test administered after the homework task engaged in by mothers and their children.

In sum, there has been limited research that directly addresses how parents socialize their children's interest in math. The available research, as well as that conducted with reading, shows that providing a cognitively stimulating environment (Gottfried et al., 1998), pleasant interactions (Aunola et al., 2013; Sonnenschein & Munsterman, 2002), role models of parents enjoying and being interested in math tasks (Else-Quest et al., 2008; Sonnenschein et al., 2016), and encouraging children's feeling of autonomy in choosing tasks (Aunola et al., 2013) are related to children's interest in learning and engaging in academically-relevant tasks.

Race/Ethnicity Differences in Parents' Academic Socialization of Children's Math Interest and Skills

Demographic group differences in children's math skills are a well-established finding in the literature. Black and Latino children, on average, earn lower scores than White or Asian children (Sonnenschein & Sun, 2016; see Cross, Woods, & Schweingruber, 2009 for review) although there is some evidence that the size of the gaps recently have decreased (Reardon & Portilla, 2016). These group-related differences in math scores are evident by the start of kindergarten or even earlier (Burchinal et al., 2011; Sonnenschein & Sun, 2016). Although influences on children's math skills are multi-determined, an increasing number of studies have focused on parents' beliefs and practices as one means of understanding group-based differences. However, little research has addressed whether there are racial/ethnic differences in how parents socialize children's motivation to engage in math activities or whether the associations between children's interest and outcomes differ across racial/ethnic groups.

Most parents, including those from different demographic groups, highly value education for their children (Sonnenschein, 2002) and express high aspirations for their children's future academic success (Sonnenschein & Galindo, 2015). Nevertheless, children from Asian and White families engage in academically-relevant activities more than do children from Black and Latino families (e.g., Cheadle & Amato, 2011; Sonnenschein & Sun, 2016). Sonnenschein and Galindo (2015), using data from the nationally representative 1998 Early Childhood Longitudinal Study-Kindergarten cohort (1998 ECLS-K), found that Black and Latino kindergartners engaged in math-relevant activities less frequently than White children, whereas Parmar, Harkness, and Super (2008) found that White children (N = 24), ages 3–6 years, engaged in academic types of activities less than Asian children (N = 24). Similarly, using the 1998 ECLS-K, a much larger data set, Sy and Schulenberg (2005) found that White parents emphasized academic skills for their kindergartners significantly less than Asian parents.

The differences in academically relevant experiences across groups may reflect differences in cultural beliefs. Chinese parents emphasize the importance of children earning high grades in school (Zhou & Lee, 2014) and the relevance of effort for school success (Hsin & Xie, 2014). They also engage in more systematic or direct instruction at home (Huntsinger & Jose, 2009; Sy & Schulenberg, 2005). These socialization practices are positively associated with children's math skills (Huntsinger & Jose, 2009).

Sonnenschein et al. (2018) compared the socialization beliefs and practices of non-U.S. born Chinese and Latino immigrants who were parents of children in prekindergarten through first grade. Consistent with what has been reported by others, Chinese parents reportedly engaged in more systematic instruction. They also discussed the need to modify the nature of children's instruction as their skills changed. Latino parents stressed the importance of children engaging in math activities at home but did not report the same systematic, planned nature of engagement as Chinese parents.

Despite the extensive research comparing and contrasting parents' socialization practices across different racial/ethnic groups, little research has addressed group-related differences in parents' socialization of children's motivation for engaging in academic activities. Some theorists have suggested that Latino parents' socialization focuses on motivational practices by telling their children about the sacrifices they have made for them to do well in school (see Sonnenschein et al., 2018 for review). However, research has not investigated whether such a focus is related to children's academic motivation, specifically their interest in math. Sonnenschein et al. (2018) did not find that Latino parents discussed such motivational practices or their children's interest in learning. In contrast, the Chinese parents in that study, while emphasizing the importance of children practicing math skills, also emphasized the need to make tasks interesting or their children would not want to do the tasks.

With few exceptions, there has been little research investigating whether the pattern of associations between parents' socialization and children's outcomes vary across demographic groups, and even fewer studies that consider children's motivation (cf. Cheung & Pomerantz, 2012, 2015). The more general research on associations between parents' socialization and children's outcomes shows a mixed pattern of findings. Keels (2009) found group-based differences in the strengths of associations between White, Black, and Latino parents' beliefs and practices and children's outcomes using data from the Early Head Start Research and Evaluation study. Sonnenschein and Galindo (2015), using the 1998 ECLS-K dataset, found similar differences in group-related associations between White, Black, and Latino parents' beliefs and practices and their kindergarten children's math skills (see also Sonnenschein & Sun, 2016). Associations between Latino parents' socialization of their children's math skills and children's outcomes were weaker than associations found with Black and White families. These patterns may reflect limitations in the set of beliefs and activities assessed by the datasets. That is, there may not have been questions pertinent for Latino families. Sy and Schulenberg (2005), also using the 1998 ECLS-K, did not find group-related differences in the associations between Asian and White parents' beliefs/practices and their kindergarteners reading and math scores.

In sum, there are clear demographic group-based differences in how parents socialize their children's math development. Research linking these group-based differences in practices to children's skill development is more limited; however, such research generally shows a positive association between practices and children's outcomes. There is even less of a focus on the association between parents' socialization practices and children's motivation. Future research is needed on this topic.

SES-Related Differences in Parents' Academic Socialization of Children's Math Interest and Skills

There is a fairly large literature documenting SES-related differences in children's math skills (see DeFLorio & Baliakoff, 2015 for a review). Given that these differences are evident at the start of school, it is reasonable to assume they may be due in part to the amount, type, or nature of home-based experiences. However, research has not found a consistent pattern of such SES-related differences in the frequency with which children engage in math-related activities. For example, neither Tudge and Doucet (2004) nor DeFlorio and Beliako (2015) found a difference in the number of math-related activities children engaged in. On the other hand, Saxe, Guberman, and Gearhart (1987) and Ramani and Siegler (2008) did. Research focusing on SES has not sufficiently addressed the nature of the interactions nor has it considered how parents socialize their children's interest in math.

Gender Differences in Parents' Academic Socialization of Children's Math Interest and Skills

Whether there are gender-related differences in children's math skills has long been a focus of inquiry with research revealing mixed findings (see Cross et al., 2009, for a review). On the one hand, as noted previously in this chapter, the 2015 NAEP math scores, consistent with those from past years, show that a slightly higher percentage (about 4%) of fourth grade boys than girls scored in the proficient range. Girls are still less likely than boys to enroll in more advanced math courses and pursue STEM careers (Ceci, Williams, & Barnett, 2009; Sadler, Sonnert, Hazari, & Tai, 2012), however, such differences may be decreasing (Kena et al., 2015). On the other hand, some researchers do not find such a pattern of differences or find them only for certain math skills (Jacobs et al., 2005; Jordan, Kaplan, Olah, & Locuniak, 2006). For example, Lachance and Mazzocco (2006) found no gender difference in children's math skills with a group of children ($N = 200$) followed from kindergarten through third grade. In a 1990 meta-analysis, Hyde, Fennema, and Lamon (1990) found what they called trivial differences favoring boys. In a more recent set of analyses, however, Hyde, Lindberg, Linn, Ellis, and Williams (2008) found no such differences.

A separate line of research has addressed whether there are differences in boys' and girls' motivational beliefs about math. There do appear to be differences, with boys exhibiting more positive views about their competency and displaying greater interest in math than girls in first grade. However, these gender-related differences decrease as the children proceed through school (Frederick & Eccles, 2002; Ganley & Lubienski, 2016; Simpkins et al., 2012).

Given the mixed pattern of findings on gender-related differences in math beliefs and skills, and its developmental trajectory, it is important to consider whether there are differences in how parents socialize their sons' and daughters' math development. This is a particularly important, although somewhat understudied topic, given that gender-related differences in STEM vocational choices continue despite decreasing gender-related differences in children's actual math skills (Jacobs et al., 2005).

An early line of research addressed whether parents differentially viewed their sons' and daughters' success in math. For example, Yee and Eccles (1988) asked 48 parents of boys and girls in junior high to attribute the source of their children's success in their math classes. Mothers were more likely to attribute their sons' success to talent and their daughters' success to effort. Such attributions may be associated with implicit or explicit messages that parents give their children or with different practices which, in turn, may be associated with children's beliefs about themselves and their math competencies (Jacobs & Bleeker, 2004).

Jacobs and Bleeker (2004) used data from the Childhood and Beyond dataset to investigate whether parents differentially socialized their children's math skills depending upon the gender of the child, and whether such practices were associated with children's subsequent interest in math. Almost all the families in the study were White. Parents were more likely to provide their sons than daughters math toys and artifacts. Parents' provision of math-related toys and other artifacts as well their participation in math-related activities in early elementary school were positively associated with children's interest in math in middle school.

Using the same longitudinal dataset, Jacobs et al. (2005) found that parents were more likely to provide an environment associated with boys' than girls' interest in math. That is, they provided their sons with more math toys and artifacts and spent more time on math activities with their sons. They also made more positive attributes about their sons' interest and skills. These practices and attributions were positively associated with their children's later math beliefs/motivation and math skills.

In sum, research on gender differences in the association between parents' practices and young children's motivation is limited. The available research has focused primarily on relations starting when children enter elementary school and has not sufficiently addressed children's interest in math but has included a wider array of motivational beliefs. That said, there appear to be gender-related differences in parents' socialization of their children's math interest and engagement. By differentially serving as role models of positive engagement and by differential provision of activities, opportunities, and artifacts, parents may stimulate more of an interest in math for boys than for girls.

CONCLUSION

Parents' beliefs about how their children learn and their role in such learning, the opportunities and activities they make available to their children, and the nature of their interactions are associated with children's interest in learning, their engagement in academic activities and their learning. Although there are many theories about children's motivation and its relations to learning (see Wigfield et al., 2006 and Wigfield et al., 2017 for reviews), far less theory or research addresses how parents socialize their children's interest, particularly their young children's interest, in engaging in math activities. Two pertinent exceptions are models presented by Eccles and colleagues (e.g., Wigfield et al., 2006) and Pomerantz and colleagues (e.g., Pomerantz & Grolnick, 2017). Both theories discuss the role of parent involvement in fostering children's motivation and engagement in math. However, there are still significant limitations in what we know, as is discussed below. Understanding the role that parents can play in fostering their children's math interest and engagement is important because math instruction is a large part of children's schooling. Children's success in math in the early grades is associated with their subsequent academic success; math, as one of the STEM fields, plays an increasingly important role in children's future vocational opportunities (Blevins-Knabe, 2016; Cross et al., 2009). Relatedly, children's interest in math and engagement in math activities is associated with their math development (Wigfield et al., 2006)

Research into children's math development is a burgeoning field. Nevertheless, research on how parents facilitate their children's interest in math, particularly their young children's interest, is still limited. Thus, this review included relevant research that was based on an older age group than the focal group in this chapter (children ages 3–8). It also included research on reading. Even though there are some differences in parents' views of the importance of reading and math and children's frequency of engagement in activities in the two domains (Anders et al., 2012; Sonnenschein et al., 2016), it was assumed that many aspects of parents' socialization of reading would be applicable to math (Sonnenschein et al., 2016). On the other hand, it is important for future research to document similarities and differences in parents' socialization across the two domains.

The review of the relevant literature highlights the importance of certain components for fostering children's interest in math and their participation in math activities. These components include: parents' beliefs about math, provision of a broad-array of math-related activities for their children, and interactions that occur in a pleasant climate. Parents who themselves enjoyed math and were role models of positive engagement had children more likely to engage in math activities. Giving children a choice of activities to engage in and taking an approach that focuses on enjoying interactions also is related to children's interest in and engagement in math activities. Despite the increase in research on children' math development and ways to foster such development, there are still clear limitations to our knowledge that future research should address. These are discussed below.

Expanding Eccles's Parents' Academic Socialization Model

Much of what we have learned about parents' socialization of children's motivation comes from the work of Eccles and her colleagues (Jacobs et al., 2005). That research is based on the findings from one longitudinal dataset. It is important that other samples confirm these findings. Relatedly, the Eccles sample included a mostly White sample of which kindergartners were the youngest group of children.

Generalizing findings to a more diverse sample. As discussed, there are many studies documenting racial/ethnic differences in children's math skills (Cross et al., 2009; Sonnenschein & Galindo, 2015). There are also some studies showing group-related differences in home learning opportunities, however, this corpus of work should be expanded given inconsistencies in findings across studies (Blevins-Knabe, 2016). There are two key limitations to work considering racial/ethnic diversity issues. One, little of the work on children's math development has focused on what different groups of parents do to foster their children's interest in learning math. Two, there has been very limited research testing whether the associations between parents' socialization of children's math, their interest, engagement in activities, and their math outcomes is similar across demographically different groups. There seems to be an implicit assumption that it is, but such an assumption is unwarranted without empirical evidence.

Generalizing findings to younger children. Differences in children's math skills are evident upon school entry and before. This has caused researchers to emphasize the importance of the home in fostering children's early math skills. However, little research has focused on parents' socialization practices with preschool children, especially for math development and for fostering children' interest in math during those early years. Although the processes that are applicable during elementary school and beyond may well be applicable during the preschool period, we need additional research with this age group to confirm the notion.

Expanding Pomerantz's Motivational Model

Many of the concerns noted above with Eccles's model are pertinent for Pomerantz's. That is, empirical research on the model has been limited to Chinese and U.S. adolescents. Also, although Pomerantz suggests ways that parents can increase children's interest in math, she and her colleagues have not directly assessed the relative effectiveness of these means.

Increasing Our Knowledge of What Mothers and Fathers Are Doing With Their Children

Most of the research on parents' socialization, including how parents foster their children's interest in math, has been based on the role that mothers play with their children. However, the few studies that have included both mothers and fathers have shown some gender-related differences in socialization (e.g., Jacobs et al., 2005). Additional research on this topic is clearly needed.

Improving Parents' Knowledge of How to Facilitate Their Children's Math Development

As discussed earlier in the chapter, parents do not necessarily know what to do to facilitate their children's math development (Cannon & Ginsburg, 2008). They need information about the type of tasks to do with their children and even how to highlight the math aspects of tasks that seem relevant for math development (Vandermaas-Peeler, Boomgarden, et al., 2012; Vandermaas-Peeler, Ferretti, et al., 2012). Educators who work with parents need to inform them about ways to foster their children's math skills, and devise scenarios for what parents should do and say when engaged in such activities.

Research by Sonnenschein et al. (2012, 2016) showed that parents who enjoyed math and provided their children opportunities to observe them engage in math tasks served as good math role models for their children. Being such role models was associated with children's engagement which was associated with their math development. It is not surprising that parents who enjoy math may be better role models for their children's math development. However, researchers and educators should look for ways to assist parents who do not particularly enjoy math to provide positive and appropriate math environments for their children. Providing more detailed scenarios for these parents could be beneficial.

SUMMARY

Providing a stimulating home environment for children is associated with their interest in learning and their subsequent academic development. Parents who serve as positive role models of math engagement and who provide their children with a range of opportunities to engage in math tasks as well as have pleasant interactions with their children when engaging in such tasks have children who express more interest in math and engage more frequently in math tasks. Such engagement, in turn, is related to children's math development.

This chapter focused on the important role that the home environment plays in young children's math development, particularly in fostering their interest and engagement in math. Despite the importance of a home environment that supports and facilitates children's engagement in math activities, the role that teachers and schools play is also extremely important and should not be undervalued. Not only do teachers provide direct instruction in math, they can compensate when children are not getting sufficient math experience at home, and can provide suggestions for what parents can do at home to foster their children's interest and engagement in math.

REFERENCES

Anders, Y., Rossbach, H. -G., Weinert, S., Ebert, S., Kuger, S., Lehrl, S., & von Maurice, J. (2012). Home and preschool learning environments and their relations to the development of early numeracy skills. *Early Childhood Research Quarterly, 27*, 231–244. doi:10.1016/j.ecresq.2011.08.003

Aunola, K., Leskinen, E., Lerkkanen, M. -K., & Nurmi, J. -E. (2004). Developmental dynamics of math performance from preschool to grade 2. *Journal of Educational Psychology, 96*, 699–713. doi:10.1037/0022-0663.96.4.699

Aunola, K., Leskinen, E., & Nurmi, J.-E. (2006). Developmental dynamics between mathematical performance, task motivation, and teachers' goals during the transition to primary school. *British Journal of Educational Psychology, 76*, 21–40. doi:10.1348/000709905X51608

Aunola, K., Viljaranta, J., Lehtinen, E., & Nurmi, J.-E. (2013). The role of maternal support of competence, autonomy, and relatedness in children's interests and mastery orientation. *Learning and Individual Differences, 25*, 171–177. doi:10.1016/j.lindif.2013.02.002

Baker, L., Mackler, K., Sonnenschein, S., & Serpell, R. (2001). Parents' interactions with their first grade children during storybook reading activity and home achievement. *Journal of School Psychology, 39*, 415–438. doi:10.1016/S0022-4405(01)00082-6

Blevins-Knabe, B. (2016). Early mathematical development: How the home environment matters. In B. Blevins-Knabe & A. M. Berghout (Eds.), *Early childhood mathematics skill development in the home environment* (pp. 7–28). Cham, Switzerland: Springer International. doi:10.1007/978-3-319-43974-7_2

Burchinal, M., McCartney, K., Steinberg, L., Crosnoe, R., Friedman, S. L., McLoyd, V., . . . the NICHD Early Child Care Research Network. (2011). Examining the Black-White achievement gap among low income children using the NICHD study of early child care and youth development. *Child Development, 82*, 1404–1420. doi:10.1111/j.1467-8624.2011.01620.x

Cannon, J., & Ginsburg, H. P. (2008). "Doing the math": Maternal beliefs about early mathematics versus language learning. *Early Education and Development, 19*, 238–260. doi:10.1080/10409280801963913

Ceci, S. J., Williams, W. M., & Barnett, S. M. (2009). Women's underrepresentation in science: Sociocultural and biological considerations. *Psychological Bulletin, 135*, 218–261. doi:10.1037/a0014412

Cheadle, J. E., & Amato, P. R. (2011). A quantitative assessment of Lareau's qualitative conclusions about class, race, and parenting. *Journal of Family Issues, 32*, 679–706. doi:10.1177/0192513X10386305

Cheung, C., & Pomerantz, E. M. (2012). Why does parents' involvement in children's learning enhance children's achievement? The role of parent-oriented motivation. *Journal of Educational Psychology, 104*, 820–832. doi:10.1037/a0027183

Cheung, C. S., & Pomerantz, E. M. (2015). Value development underlies the benefits of parents' involvement in children's learning: A longitudinal investigation in the United States and China. *Journal of Educational Psychology, 107*, 309–320. doi:10.1037/a0037458

Cheung, S. K., & McBride, C. (2017). Effectiveness of parent-child number board game playing in promoting Chinese kindergartners' numeracy skills and mathematic interest. *Early Education and Development, 28*, 572–589. http://dx.doi.org/10.1080/10409289.2016/

Cross, C. T., Woods, T. A., & Schweingruber, H. (Eds.). (2009). *Mathematics learning in early childhood: Paths toward excellence and equity.* Washington, DC: National Academies Press. doi:10.17226/12519

DeFlorio, L., & Beliakoff, A. (2015). Socioeconomic status and preschoolers' mathematical knowledge: The contribution of home activities and parent beliefs. *Early Education and Development, 26*, 319–341. doi:10.1080/1040928 9.2015.968239

Denissen, J. J. A., Zarrett, N. R., & Eccles, J.S. (2007). I like to do it, I'm able, and I know I am: Longitudinal couplings between domain-specific achievement, self-concept, and interest. *Child Development, 78*, 430–447. doi:10.1111/j.1467-8624.2007.01007.x

Doctoroff, G. L., & Arnold, D. H. (2017). Doing homework together: The relation between parenting strategies, child engagement, and achievement. *Journal of Applied Developmental Psychology, 48*, 103–113. doi:10.1016/j.appdev.2017.01.001

Doctoroff, G. L., Fisher, P. H., Burrows, B. M., & Edman, M. T. (2016). Preschool children's interest, social–emotional skills, and emergent mathematics skills. *Psychology in the Schools, 53*, 390–403. doi:10.1002/pits.21912

Duncan, G. J., Dowsett, C. J., Dlaessens, A., Magnuson, K., Huston, A. C., Klebanov, P., ... Japel, C. (2007). School readiness and later achievement. *Developmental Psychology, 43,* 1428–1446. doi:10.1037/0012-1649.43.6.1428

Else-Quest, N. M., Hyde, J. S., & Hejmadi, A. (2008). Mother and child emotions during mathematics homework. *Mathematical Thinking and Learning, 10,* 5–35. doi:10.1080/10986060701818644

Fisher, P. H., Dobbs-Oates, J., Doctoroff, G. L., & Arnold, D. H. (2012). Early math interest and the development of math skills. *Journal of Educational Psychology, 104,* 673–681. doi:10.1037/a0027756

Fredricks, J. A., & Eccles, J. S. (2002). Children's competence and value beliefs from childhood through adolescence: Growth trajectories in two male-sex-typed domains. *Developmental Psychology, 38,* 519–533. doi:10.1037/0012-1649.38.4.519

Galindo, C., & Sonnenschein, S. (2015). Decreasing the SES math achievement gap: Initial math proficiency and home learning environments. *Contemporary Educational Psychology, 43,* 25–38. doi:10.1016/j.cedpsych.2015.08.0030361-476X/c 2015

Ganley, C. M., & Lubienski, S. T. (2016). Mathematics confidence, interest, and performance: Examining gender patterns and reciprocal relations. *Learning & Individual Differences, 47,* 182–193. doi:10.1016/j.lindif.2016.01.002

Gottfried, A. E., Fleming, J. S., & Gottfried, A.W. (1998). Role of cognitively stimulating home environment in children's academic intrinsic motivation: A longitudinal study. *Child Development, 69,* 1448–1460. doi:10.2307/1132277

Gottfried, A. E., Fleming, J. S., & Gottfried, A. W. (2001). Continuity of academic intrinsic motivation from childhood through late adolescence: A longitudinal study. *Journal of Educational Psychology, 93,* 3–13. doi:10.1037/0022-0663.93.1.3

Grolnick, W. S., Deci, E. L., & Ryan, R. M. (1997). Internalization within the family: The self-determination theory perspective. In J. Grusec & L. Kuczynski (Eds.), *Parenting and children's internalization of values: A handbook of contemporary theory* (pp. 135–161). New York, NY: Wiley.

Hsin, A., & Yie, Y. (2014). Explaining Asian Americans' academic advantage over Whites. *Proceedings of the National Academy of Science, 111,* 8416–8421. doi:10.1073/pnas.1406402111

Huntsinger, C. S., & Jose, P. E. (2009). Parental involvement in children's schooling: Different meanings in different cultures. *Early Childhood Research Quarterly, 24,* 398–410. doi:10.1016/j.ecresq.2009.07.006

Huntsinger, C., Jose, P., & Luo, Z. (2016). Parental facilitation of early mathematics and reading skills and knowledge through encouragement of home-based activities. *Early Childhood Research Quarterly, 37,* 1–15. doi:10.1016/j.ecresq.2016.02.005

Hyde, J. S., Fennema, E., & Lamon, S. J. (1990). Gender differences in mathematics performance: A meta-analysis. *Psychological Bulletin. 107,* 139–155. doi:10.1037/0033-2909.107.2.139

Hyde, J. S., Lindberg, S. M., Linn, M. C., Ellis, A. B., & Williams, C. C. (2008). Gender similarities characterize math performance. *Science, 321,* 494–495. doi:10.1126/science.1160364

Jacobs, J. E., & Bleeker, M. M. (2004). Girls' and boys' developing interests in math and science: Do parents matter? *New Directions for Child & Adolescent Development, 106,* 5–21. doi:10.1002/cd.113

Jacobs, J. E., Davis-Kean, P., Bleeker, M., Eccles, J. S., & Malanchuk, O. (2005). 'I can, but I don't want to': The impact of parents, interests, and activities on gender differences in math. In A. M. Gallagher, & J. C. Kaufman (Eds.), *Gender differences in mathematics: An integrative psychological approach* (pp. 246–263). New York, NY: Cambridge University Press.

Jordan, N. C., Kaplan, D., Olah, L. N., & Locuniak, M. N. (2006). Number sense growth in kindergarten: A longitudinal investigation of children at risk for math difficulties. *Child Development, 77,* 153–175. doi:10.1111/j.1467-8624.2006.00862.x

Jordan, N. C., Kaplan, D., Ramineini, C. & Locuniak, M. N. (2009). Early math matters: Kindergarten number competence and later mathematics outcomes. *Developmental Psychology, 45,* 850–867. doi:10.1037/a0014939

Keels, M. (2009). Ethnic group differences in early head start parents' parenting beliefs and practices and links to children's early cognitive development. *Early Childhood Research Quarterly, 24,* 381–397. doi:10.1016/j.ecresq.2009.08.002

Kena, G., Musu-Gillette, L., Robinson, J., Wang, X., Rathbun, A., Zhang, J., ... Dunlop Velez, E. (2015). *The Condition of Education 2015* (NCES 2015-144). U.S. Department of Education, National Center for Education Statistics. Washington, DC. Retrieved from http://nces.ed.gov/pubs2015/2015144.pdf

Kleemans, T., Peeters, M., Segers, E., & Verhoeven, L. (2012). Child and home predictors of early numeracy skills in kindergarten. *Early Childhood Research Quarterly, 27,* 471–477. doi:10.1016/j.ecresq.2011.12.004

Lachance, J. A., & Mazzocco, M. M. M. (2006). A longitudinal analysis of sex differences in math and spatial skills in primary age children. *Learning and Individual Differences, 16,* 195–216. doi:10.1016/j.lindif.2005.12.001

LeFevre, J.-A., Skwarchuk, S.-L., Smith-Chant, B. L., Fast, L., Kamawar, D., & Bisanz, J. (2009). Home numeracy experiences and children's math performance in the early school years. *Canadian Journal of Behavioural Science, 41,* 55–66. doi.org/10.1037/a0014532.

Levine, S. C., Suriyakham, L., Rowe, M., Huttenlocher, J., & Gunderson, E. A. (2010). What counts in the development of young children's number knowledge? *Developmental Psychology, 46,* 1309–1319. doi:10.1037/a0019671

Mazzocco, M. M. M., Hanich, L., & Noeder, M. M. (2012). Primary school age students' spontaneous comments about math reveal emerging dispositions linked to later math achievement. *Child Development Research, 2012,* Article ID 170310, doi:10.1155/2012/170310.

Metzger, S., Sonnenschein, S., Galindo, C., & Patel, H. (2015, March). *Children's beliefs about the utility of math and how these beliefs relate to their home math engagement.* Poster presented at SRCD, Philadelphia, PA.

National Association for the Education of Young Children and National Council of Teachers of Mathematics. (2002). Position statement. Early childhood mathematics: Promoting good beginnings. Retrieved from: http://www.naeyc.org/about/positions/psmath.asp

National Mathematics Advisory Panel. (2008). Foundations for Success: The Final Report of the National Mathematics Advisory Panel, U.S. Department of Education: Washington, DC.

National Center for Education Statistics. (2015a). Trends in International Mathematics and Science Study (TIMSS), report prepared by International Association for the Evaluation of Educational Achievement. Retrieved from https://nces.ed.gov/timss/timss2015/timss2015_table01.asp

National Center for Education Statistics. (2015b). The Nation's Report Card: Mathematics, report prepared for the U.S. Department of Education (Washington: Institute of Education Sciences, 2015). Retrieved from: https://www.nationsreportcard.gov/reading_math_2015/#mathematics?grade=4

Neuenschwander, M. P., Vida, M., Garrett, J. L., & Eccles, J. S. (2007). Parents' expectations and students' achievement in two western nations. *International Journal of Behavioral Development, 31*, 594–602. doi:10.1177/0165025407080589

Niklas, F., & Schneider, W. (2013). Casting the die before the die is cast: The importance of the home numeracy environment for preschool children. *European Journal of Psychology of Education, 29*, 327–345. doi:10.1007/s10212-013-0201-6

Parmar, P., Harkness, S., & Super, C. M. (2008). Teacher or playmate? Asian immigrant and Euro-American parents' participation in their young children's daily activities. *Social Behavior and Personality, 36*, 163–176. doi:10.2224/sbp.2008.36.2.163

Pomerantz, E. M., & Grolnick, W. S. (2017). The role of parenting in children's motivation and competence: What underlies facilitative parenting? In A. Elliot, C. S. Dweck, & D. Yeager (Eds.), *Handbook of competence and motivation: Theory and application* (2nd ed., pp. 566–586). New York, NY: Guilford Press

Pomerantz, E. M., & Moorman, E. A. (2010). Parents' involvement in children's schooling. In J. L. Meece & J. S. Eccles (Eds.). *Handbook of research on schools, schooling, and human development* (pp. 398–416). New York, NY: Routledge.

Puccioni, J. (2015). Parents' conceptions of school readiness, transition practices, and children's academic achievement trajectories. *Journal of Educational Research, 108*, 130–147. doi:10.1080/00220671.2013.850399

Ramani, G. B., Rowe, M. L., Eason, S. H., & Leech, K. A. (2015). Math talk during informal learning activities in Head Start families. *Cognitive Development, 35*, 15–33. doi:10.1016/j.cogdev.2014.11.002

Ramani, G. B., & Siegler, R. S. (2008). Promoting broad and stable improvements in low-income children's numerical knowledge through playing number board games. *Child Development, 79*, 375–394. doi:10.1111/ j. 1467-8624.2007.01131.x

Ramani, G. B., & Siegler, R. S. (2014). How informal learning activities can promote children's numerical knowledge. In R. C. Kadosh & A. Dowker (Eds.), *Oxford handbook of mathematical cognition* (pp. 1135–1155). Oxford, England: Oxford University Press.

Reardon, S. F., & Portilla, X. A. (2016). Recent trends in income, racial, and ethnic school readiness gaps at kindergarten entry. *AERA Open, 2*(3), 1–18. doi:10.1177/2332858416657343

Sadler, P. M., Sonnert, G., Hazari, Z. & Tai, R. (2012). Stability and volatility of STEM career interest in high school: A gender study. *Science Education, 96,* 411–427. doi:10.1002/sce.21007

Saxe, G. B., Guberman, S. R., & Gearhart, M. (1987). Social processes in early number development. *Monographs of the Society for Research in Child Development, 52,* 162. doi: 10.2307/1166071

Sénéchal, M., & LeFevre, J.-A. (2002). Parental involvement in the development of children's reading skill: A five-year longitudinal study. *Child Development, 73,* 445–460. doi:10.1111/1467-8624.00417

Serpell, R., Baker, L. & Sonnenschein, S. (2005). *Becoming literate in the city: The Baltimore Early Childhood Project.* New York, NY: Cambridge University Press.

Siegler, R. S., Duncan, G. J., Davis-Kean, P. E., Duckworth, K., Claessens, A., Engel, M., . . . Chen, M. (2012). Early predictors of high school mathematics achievement. *Psychological Science, 23,* 691–69. doi:10.1177/0956797612440101

Simpkins, S. D., Fredricks, J. A., & Eccles, J. S. (2012). Charting the Eccles' expectancy-value model from mothers' beliefs in childhood to youths' activities in adolescence. *Developmental Psychology, 48,* 1019–1032. doi:10.1037/a0027468

Simpkins, S. D., Fredricks, J. A., & Eccles, J. S. (Eds., 2015). The role of parents in the ontogeny of achievement-related motivation and behavioral choices. *Monographs of the Society for Research in Child Development, 80* (2), 65–84. doi:10.1111/mono.12160

Skwarchuk, S.-L., Sowinski, C., & LeFevre, J.-A. (2014). Formal and informal home learning activities in relation to children's early numeracy and literacy skills: The development of a home numeracy model. *Journal of Experimental Child Psychology, 121,* 63–84. doi:10.1016/j.jecp.2013.11.006.

Sonnenschein, S. (2002). Engaging children in the appropriation of literacy: The importance of parental beliefs and practices. In O. Saracho & B. Spodek (Eds.), *Contemporary perspectives in early childhood education* (pp. 127–149). Greenwich, CT: Information Age Publishing.

Sonnenschein, S., & Galindo, C. (2015). Race/ethnicity and early mathematics skills: Relations between home, classroom, and mathematics achievement. *Journal of Educational Research, 108,* 261–277. doi:10.1080/00220671.2014.880394

Sonnenschein, S., Galindo, C., Metzger, S. R., Thompson, J. A., Huang, H. C., & Lewis, H. (2012). Parents' beliefs about children's math development and children's participation in math activities. *Child Development Research Journal Online.* doi:10.1155/2012/851657.

Sonnenschein, S., Metzger, S. R., & Thompson, J. A. (2016). Low-income parents' socialization of their preschoolers' early reading and math skills. *Research in Human Development, 13,* 207–224. doi:10.1080/15427609.2016.1194707

Sonnenschein, S., & Munsterman, K._(2002). The influence of home-based reading interactions on 5-year-olds' reading motivations and early literacy development. *Early Childhood Research Quarterly, 17,* 317–338. doi:10.1016/S0885-2006(02)00167-9

Sonnenschein, S., & Sun, S. (2016). Racial/ethnic differences in kindergartners' reading and math skills: Parents' knowledge of children's development and home-based activities as mediators. *Infant and Child Development, 26*(5), e2010. doi:10.1002/icd.2010

Sonnenschein, S., Galindo, C., Simons, C. L., Metzger, S.R., Thompson, J. A., & Chung, M. (2018). How do children learn mathematics? Chinese and Latino immigrant perspectives. In S. S. Chuang & C. Costigan (Eds.), *International perspectives on parenting and parent-child relations in immigrant families: Theoretical and practical implications*. (pp. 111–128). New York, NY: Springer.

Sy, S. R., & Schulenberg, J. E. (2005). Parent beliefs and children's achievement trajectories during the transition to school in Asian American and European American families. *International Journal of Behavioral Development, 29*, 505–515. doi:10.1080/01650250500147329

Taylor, L. C., Clayton, J. D., & Rowley, S. J. (2004). Academic socialization: Understanding parental influences on children's school-related development in the early years. *Review of General Psychology, 8*, 163–178. doi:10.1037/1089-2680.8.3.163

Tudge, J. H., & Doucet, F. (2004). Early mathematical experiences: Observing young Black and White children's everyday activities. *Early Childhood Research Quarterly, 19*, 21–39. doi:10.1016/j.ecresq.2004.01.007

Vandermaas-Peeler, M., Boomgarden, E., Finn, L., & Pittard, C. (2012). Parental support of numeracy during a cooking activity with four-year-olds. *International Journal of Early Years Education, 20*, 78–93. doi:10.1080/09669760.2012.66323

Vandermaas-Peeler, M., Ferretti, L., & Loving, S. (2012). Playing the Ladybug Game: Parent guidance of young children's numeracy activities. *Early Child Development and Care, 182*, 1289–1307. doi:10.1080/03004430.2011.609617

Vandermaas-Peeler, M., & Pittard, C. (2014). Influences of social context on parent guidance and low-income preschoolers' independent and guided math performance. *Early Child Development and Care, 184*, 500–521. doi:i1080/03004430.2013.799155.

Vygotsky, L. S. (1978). *Mind in society: The development of higher psychological processes*. Cambridge, MA: Harvard University Press.

Wigfield, A., Eccles, J. S., Schiefele, U., Roeser, R., & Davis-Kean, P. (2006). Development of
achievement motivation. In W. Damon, R. M. Lerner, & N. Eisenberg (Eds.), *Handbook of child psychology* (6th ed., Vol. 3, pp. 933–1002). New York, NY: Wiley.

Wigfield, A., Rosenzweig, E. Q., & Eccles, J. S. (2017). Achievement values: Interactions, interventions, and future directions. In A. J. Elliot, C. S. Dweck, D. S. Yeager, A. J. Elliot, C. S. Dweck, & D. S. Yeager (Eds.), *Handbook of competence and motivation: Theory and application* (pp. 116–134). New York, NY: Guilford Press.

Wong, S. W., & Hughes, J. N. (2006). Ethnicity and language contributions to dimensions of parent involvement. *School Psychology Review, 35*, 645–662.

Yee, D. K., & Eccles, J. S. (1988). Parent perception and attributions for children's math achievement. *Sex Roles, 19*, 317–333. doi:10.1007/BF00289840

Zhou, M., & Lee, J. (2014). Assessing what is cultural about Asian Americans' academic advantage. *Proceedings of the National Academic of Science, 111*, 8321–8322. doi:10.1073/pnas.1407309111

CHAPTER 5

MOTIVATION AND MATHEMATICS IN EARLY CHILDHOOD

Nicole R. Scalise, Jessica R. Gladstone, and Geetha B. Ramani

Early mathematics learning lays the foundation for children's achievement throughout their school years, which opens doors for later career pathways and predicts positive adulthood outcomes including college performance, career opportunities, rates of full-time employment, and annual income (Geary, 2011; National Mathematics Advisory Panel, 2008; Ritchie & Bates, 2013). As the development of the next generation of the science, technology, engineering, and mathematics (STEM) workers continues to be a national priority, having a strong foundation of mathematical knowledge is imperative for today's students. Children's mathematics achievement during early childhood predicts their long-term math achievement through high school (Duncan et al., 2007), which has led to efforts to promote children's math skills from a young age. However, even prior to the start of formal schooling, there is variability in children's mathematical knowledge (Klibanoff, Levine, Huttenlocher, Vasilyeva, & Hedges, 2006). This variability may be due in part to children's motivation. In order to identify the best methods of early math intervention, it is necessary to unpack sources of the observed variability in children's skills, including children's motivational beliefs about mathematics. The purpose of the present chapter is to discuss extant research on the relations between young children's motiva-

Contemporary Perspectives on Research on
Motivation in Early Childhood Education, pp. 101–129
Copyright © 2019 by Information Age Publishing
All rights of reproduction in any form reserved.

tion for math and their mathematics achievement, explore factors that influence early motivation by drawing from research on young children's interactions with parents and teachers, and recommend areas for future research, policy, and practice based on the findings. We begin the chapter with a brief overview of the types of children's motivational beliefs, honing in on the specific motivational constructs that serve as our focus. We next review each motivational construct and its relation to young children's mathematics achievement. Then, we describe how the social interactions children share with parents and early childhood educators may inform the development of their math-related motivational beliefs. In the final section, we describe ways in which future research could extend the rich knowledge about older students' math motivation to younger children, and provide suggestions for parents, teachers, and policymakers looking to promote young children's early motivational beliefs.

FRAMEWORK OF MOTIVATIONAL BELIEFS

One source of the variability in children's early mathematics achievement is their motivational beliefs about math. Motivational beliefs are broad and encompassing, defined as "beliefs about the self that explain the initiation, direction, intensity, persistence, and quality of behavior" (Wentzel, 2015, p. 302). In this chapter, we frame our discussion of children's motivational beliefs about math with a series of questions for motivational decision-making. According to Wentzel (2015), children's motivational beliefs can be conceptualized as the answers to six key questions: (1) What do I want to do? (2) What am I supposed to do? (3) Is this important and enjoyable to do? (4) Can I do it? (5) What causes success and failure? and, (6) Does anyone care if I do it? These six questions are relevant for understanding students' motivation for school, and different responses may lead to different types of learning behaviors and ultimately different levels of academic achievement. Although historical models of motivation have approached motivational beliefs broadly (e.g., academic self-concept), more contemporary work has argued for the domain-specificity of motivational beliefs. In particular, mathematics may serve as a context that requires higher levels of motivation for children to succeed, as it may be seen as more difficult than other disciplines (Mazzocco, Hanich, & Noeder, 2012).

The six questions for motivational decision-making frame three conceptual areas within motivation research, namely children's goals and values (Questions 1–3), children's beliefs about their own abilities, causality and control (Questions 4–5), and children's feelings of social belongingness (Question 6; Wentzel, 2015), and each can consist of multiple motivational constructs. Although each of these areas play an important role in developing a comprehensive picture of a student's academic motivation, some of the questions may be more appropriate to consider for young children (0 to 8 years old). Indeed, many key motivational constructs linked to the academic achievement of older students remain understudied in younger students, such as achievement goal orientation, attributional beliefs, and self-efficacy, and therefore will not be discussed in this chapter. In the present review, we focus on the constructs of children's interest in mathematics (Q1: What do I want to do?), children's mathematics anxiety (Q3: Is this important and enjoyable to do?), and children's mathematical ability beliefs (Q4: Can I do it?). Previous research has demonstrated that children younger than 8 years old do have these motivational beliefs, and that there are valid and reliable measures for assessing them (e.g., Fisher, Dobbs-Oates, Doctoroff, & Arnold, 2012; Fredricks & Eccles, 2002; Harari, Vukovic, & Bailey, 2013). Furthermore, although children base their responses to these motivational questions on both internal and external cues (Wentzel, 2015), these three constructs may be particularly susceptible to influence by external sources such as parents, teachers, and peers. These external sources can easily convey information about their perceptions of the child's ability and their own math interest and anxiety, which may in turn be internalized by the child. Thus, it is important to both examine the nature of the relations between these motivational beliefs and children's mathematics performance as well as how these beliefs may develop through social interactions with others in order to support children's positive development.

CHILDREN'S MOTIVATIONAL BELIEFS FOR MATHEMATICS

Although there is an extensive literature on students' motivational beliefs and their relation to math achievement, the vast majority focuses on older children and young adults. In the present section, we summarize the existing research on children from birth to 8 years old and their math ability beliefs, interest in math, and math anxiety. While the paucity of research on young children may be due to the metacognitive skills necessary to form cogent motivational beliefs and the traditional measurement of such beliefs (i.e., self-report questionnaires that are text heavy), the studies described below suggest that as early as preschool, children do hold these types of motivations and they can be reliably measured.

Children's Mathematical Ability Beliefs

Children's mathematical ability beliefs play an important role in their subsequent interest and achievement in math. Eccles and Wigfield (2002) define ability beliefs as an evaluation of one's competence in a domain. Given the power of ability beliefs to predict children's later interest and achievement in math, researchers have been concerned with how ability beliefs in math develop over time (for a review, see Wigfield et al., 2015). The development of math ability beliefs has primarily been examined with either short-term longitudinal data or cross-sectional data, and has tended to focus on older children. Studies using these methods have consistently found that ability beliefs in math begin to decline across middle childhood and early adolescence (Eccles, Wigfield, Harold, & Blumenfeld, 1993; Wigfield et al., 1997). However, less is known about mathematical ability beliefs in early childhood. Recent work by Arens and colleagues (2016) suggests that as early as preschool children can differentiate between their math ability beliefs and their affective responses to math (i.e., liking numbers and number games), and their math ability beliefs relate to their prior and future math achievement.

Eccles and colleagues have documented changes in children's ability beliefs in math across grades one through twelve, using a cross-sequential design that involved following three cohorts of children longitudinally (Fredricks & Eccles, 2002; Jacobs, Lanza, Osgood, Eccles, & Wigfield, 2002). They found that children have the highest beliefs about their math ability in first grade and these beliefs steadily decline during the elementary, middle, and high school years. Uncovering the mechanisms behind these changes in children's ability beliefs has been at the forefront of motivational research for over three decades. One potential explanation may be that young children tend to report unrealistically high ability beliefs compared to their actual performance (Wigfield et al., 1997), possibly because they have a less clear understanding of success and failure (Eccles, Midgley, & Adler, 1984). As children get older, they become better attuned to their teachers' assessment of their ability (Eccles et al., 1984; Nicholls, 1978). Children younger than 9 years old also have limited experience with social comparison. Therefore, when young children are asked to make ability judgments, such as rating who is the best at math in their class, the majority respond that they themselves are (Wigfield et al., 2015).

A second explanation for the decline in children's ability beliefs in math over time relates to children's understanding of effort, ability, and their relations to achievement. Nicholls (1978) described four phases of children's understanding of what ability is, beginning with children aged 6 and younger, who do not distinguish between effort and ability but instead believe that individuals who work harder are smarter. In the second phase, children 7 to 8 years old begin to separate effort and ability, and believe that greater effort leads to greater achievement. However, children in the second phase believe that if a student puts forth the same effort they should receive the same grade, regardless of who they think is smarter. During the third and fourth phases, children 9 years and older begin to recognize that both effort and ability can determine their achievement. These developmental changes in untangling effort and ability may also be a consequence of children becoming better able to understand their failures and participating more in social comparison as the classroom environment shifts to become more performance-oriented in late elementary school through high school (Eccles et al., 1984; Nicholls, 1978; Wigfield et al., 1997). Research on older students' beliefs about why they failed or succeeded suggests it is more adaptive to frame academic success as a result of hard work and effort as opposed to innate ability (Blackwell, Trzesniewski, & Dweck, 2007). Although Nicholls's (1978) framework suggests children younger than 9 years old have difficulty disentangling the effects of effort and ability on academic achievement, frequent praise of young children's effort on math tasks may help build a foundation of positive math ability beliefs.

In addition to providing a developmental picture of ability beliefs, some research has addressed potential gender differences in young children's math ability beliefs over time. The longitudinal patterns of children's math ability beliefs reveal that beginning in first grade boys report higher ability beliefs in math than girls, a trend that continues across elementary school grades. However, this gender gap essentially disappeared once the students entered high school (Eccles et al., 1993; Jacobs et al., 2002; Fredricks & Eccles, 2002).

Children's ability beliefs in mathematics relate significantly to their math achievement outcomes and other math motivational beliefs. Longitudinal studies of 6- to 18-year-old children have demonstrated that even when controlling for previous performance, students' ability beliefs in math predict their later performance in math (Eccles et al., 1983, Wigfield et al., 2015). Mathematics ability beliefs have also been linked to subsequent interest in math. Children who believe they are capable in math are also more likely to be interested in math (Parajes, 2005; Wang & Degol, 2013). Even younger children show developmental precursors to ability beliefs: children as young as 2 years old react positively (e.g., smiling) when they are successful at a task (Stipek, Recchia, McClintic, & Lewis, 1992), while some 5- and 6-year olds react negatively and report they are not good at a task, not smart, and not a good person after receiving critical feedback from a teacher (Heyman, Dweck, & Cain, 1992). Thus, fostering children's positive math ability beliefs at a young age can help students stay interested and motivated in mathematics as they progress through school.

Interest in Mathematics

Children's interest in mathematics and specific math activities may relate to their prior math ability beliefs and achievement, and may provide a foundation for their future beliefs and mathematics success. Definitions of interest differentiate individual interest, which describes a long-term, stable tendency to focus on particular content, versus situational interest, which signals temporary attraction and attention to something in the environment (Alexander & Grossnickle, 2016; Schiefele, 2009). Because individual interest relies heavily on self-report measures, much of the work focusing on young children's interest is situational, in which engagement and affect are assessed during particular tasks. Hidi and colleagues (2004) suggest that when young children maintain their situational interests over time, seek out information about the content of interest, and self-regulate and identify with the interest, their early situational interests blossom into individual interests. Interest is related to but separate from other motivational beliefs due to its specific focus on content or an activity as opposed to a general motivation to engage (Fisher et al., 2012; Hidi, 1990). Broadly, theories of interest and academic performance suggest that interest plays an important role in supporting learning experiences through mechanisms such as sustained attention, deeper processing of content, and increased time and effort through deliberate practice of particular content or activities (Ericsson, Krampe, & Tesche-Römer, 1993; Hidi, Renninger, & Krapp, 2004).

Young children's interest is related to both their concurrent and later mathematical achievement. Specifically, individual interest (as rated by their preschool teacher) and situational interest (assessed with behavioral observations of children playing with educational math materials) in math is correlated with concurrent measures of their math performance (Fisher et al., 2012; Edens & Potter, 2013). Researchers also have studied the predictive relations over time between math interest and ability. Reciprocal models of math interest and ability over time suggest that students' early math skills predict their later math interest because highly skilled students would have positive, efficacious experiences in math, and early interest in math would likely lead to more time and effort on math activities, which may translate to better math performance (Ma, 1997). Fisher and colleagues (2012) found support for bidirectional influences with a sample of preschoolers, such that children's initial interest in math in the fall of the school year predicted their math skills in the spring, controlling for fall math skills. In addition, children's initial math skills also predicted their interest in math in the spring, controlling for their fall math interest (Fisher et al., 2012). However, there is some evidence that the longitudinal relations between interest and math skills may differ depending on how interest is measured and the age of the children. In contrast to Fisher and colleagues, who assessed preschoolers' math interest using teacher reports and behavioral observations, Ganley and Lubienski (2016) found in their study of third grade students that math performance predicted students' self-reported individual math interest in fifth grade, but third grade math interest was not predictive of later math performance.

As with math ability beliefs, research has also investigated whether there are early differences in boys' and girls' math interest. Across early childhood, findings appear to be mixed. Preschool teachers reported that their female students were more interested in math activities than their male students, yet ratings of the same students' situational interest while playing with math toys showed no gender differences (Fisher et al., 2012). A 3-year longitudinal study of first, second, and fourth grade students found that elementary school male and female students did not differ significantly in their self-reported level of interest in math (Wigfield et al., 1997). However, other studies have shown that among third graders, girls report less interest in math than boys, although the gender gap in math interest decreases in later elementary and middle school (Ganley & Lubienski, 2016). These discrepancies may reflect age-related trends, as later elementary school students are exposed to more gender stereotypes and their domain-specific interests begin to solidify (Wang & Degol, 2013; Wigfield et al., 1997), as studies of older students tend to show gender gaps in students' math interest (e.g., Köller, Baumert, & Schnabel, 2001).

In general, there is evidence for children's early math interest predicting their later skills, as well as children's early math abilities predicting their later interest. Longitudinal data suggest that once formed, interest in math does not meaningfully decline throughout elementary school (Wigfield et al., 1997), underscoring the importance of fostering math interest in early childhood for boys and girls.

Mathematics Anxiety

Mathematics anxiety is consistently linked to math performance for older students and adults (Ashcraft, 2002); however, among younger children the relation between math anxiety and achievement is variable. Math anxiety is defined as negative emotions, such as feelings of tension, apprehension, or fear, to math or the idea of doing math (Ashcraft, 2002; Hembree, 1990). People who report high math anxiety tend to avoid engaging with math whenever possible, receive lower grades in math classes, and generally report negative attitudes toward math (Ashcraft, 2002). Math anxiety is related to but theoretically distinct from general anxiety and other negative attitudes, and uniquely predicts variance in math achievement in analyses controlling for general anxiety, test anxiety, and IQ (Haase et al., 2012; Wu, Amin, Barth, Malcarne, & Menon, 2012). Neuroimaging studies with children aged 7 to 9 years old suggest children with mathematics anxiety show different neural activation patterns in their amygdala (responsible for processing negative emotions), and these patterns are uniquely correlated with math anxiety and not general anxiety, intelligence, working memory, or reading ability (Young, Wu, & Menon, 2012). Compared to research on middle school, high school, and college students, there is relatively little research on math anxiety with samples of young children, and the relations with math performance are mixed (Dowker, Ashcraft, & Krinzinger, 2012). A meta-analysis of attitudes toward mathematics (defined as students' affective responses to math, encompassing math anxiety among other constructs) found that the relations between attitudes and achievement were the weakest among samples of early elementary school students (Grades 1–4), with much stronger effects seen among samples of older students (Ma & Kishor, 1997).

Some researchers have claimed that math anxiety emerges during late elementary school, as a confluence of factors: math curricula becoming sufficiently challenging to provoke anxiety, students having had several years to build up negative experiences with math, and children having the cognitive and self-reflective capacities to accurately complete self-report measures (e.g., Ashcraft, Krause, & Hopko, 2007). However, more recent work has shown that children as young as first graders do report math anxiety, at variable rates (Harari, Vukovic, & Bailey, 2013; Krinzinger, Kaufmann, & Willmes, 2009; Ramirez, Gunderson, Levine, & Beilock, 2013). Indeed, a study of first and second grade students found that nearly half of the students reported experiencing mid to high levels of math anxiety (Ramirez et al., 2013). Results from longitudinal designs suggest that children tend to start out with fairly low rates of math anxiety, but significantly increase in their math anxiety over time (Krinzinger, Kaufmann, & Willmes, 2009). It is unlikely that children would experience math anxiety prior to their entry into preschool, however negative experiences with math at home and math ability judgments about their own skills relative to peers could form a basis for the development of math anxiety in early elementary school.

Like math interest, there may theoretically be reciprocal influences between math performance and math anxiety that unfold over time, whereby math anxiety leads to poor math performance and poor math performance may lead to developing math anxiety (Ashcraft, 2002). Although there is little data so far to support bidirectional influences of math anxiety and performance among children 8 years old and younger, there are significant relations showing math anxiety predicting math performance (Vukovic, Kieffer, Bailey, & Harari, 2013).

Findings for the relations between math anxiety and young children's concurrent math performance are mixed. Several studies have found no significant relation between math anxiety and young children's concurrent math performance (Dowker, Bennett, & Smith, 2012; Hill et al., 2016; Krinzinger et al., 2009). In contrast, other studies have reported significant negative correlations between math anxiety and math achievement in early elementary school students (Harari et al., 2013; Wu et al., 2012), with larger effects for children with strong working memory (Ramirez et al., 2013; Vukovic et al., 2013). Studies of children in later elementary school (fourth, fifth, and sixth grade) tend to also report significant, negative relations between math anxiety and student math performance (Haase et al., 2012; Punaro & Reeve, 2012; Yüksel-Sahin, 2008). These differences in results may be due in part to measurement issues in assessing both math anxiety measures may not be developmentally appropriate for young children, as well as the use of standardized math achievement outcomes which include more conceptually challenging items, as opposed to measures of calculation abilities (Wu et al., 2012). Some theories of math anxiety propose that the pathway of influence on math performance is in part due to impairing working memory performance, which is key to solving more challenging problems (Ashcraft, 2002; Ashcraft & Krause, 2007). Similarly, data from seventh through ninth graders suggests math anxiety may impact math performance indirectly by decreasing students' perceived importance of math and their expectations for their math performance (Meece, Wigfield, & Eccles, 1990). Thus, future work could investigate whether the relation between math anxiety and math performance depends on other mediating variables such as working memory or perceived importance.

Gender differences in reports of math anxiety may follow age-related trends, like gender differences in mathematics ability beliefs and interest. In a study of first grade students, Harari and colleagues (2013) found no gender differences in math anxiety. Similarly, studies of second and third graders reported no correlation between students' gender and their math anxiety (Dowker et al., 2012; Jameson, 2014). However, several studies that included fourth and fifth grade students found that females reported more math anxiety than male students (Griggs, Rimm-Kaufman, Merritt, & Patton, 2013; Hill et al., 2016; Yüksel-Sahin, 2008), although the effect sizes were small. These findings may represent the beginning of a developmental trajectory, which results in persistent differences in female and male students' math anxiety throughout secondary school and adulthood (Hembree, 1990). Alternatively, these differences may reflect a pattern of gender stereotypes, such that female students both expect and are more willing to admit being anxious about math than male students (Dowker, Sarkar, & Looi, 2016).

Like math ability beliefs and math interest, math anxiety is relatively understudied among samples of young children. Math ability beliefs predict children's later math achievement and interest. Early math interest predicts later math achievement, and early math achievement also predicts later math interest. Math anxiety research is somewhat mixed, but suggests that there may be predictive relations between early math anxiety and math performance, particularly for children with high working memory skills. Longitudinal data suggest that young children's ability beliefs and math interest start out high and decline over time, while children's math anxiety may start lower and increase as children get older. These patterns of development suggest that life experiences can affect children's math motivational beliefs, including interactions with parents and teachers.

SOCIAL INFLUENCES ON CHILDREN'S MOTIVATIONAL BELIEFS

Children's mathematics motivation, including their math ability beliefs, math interest, and math anxiety, relate to their concurrent and future math achievement. However, it remains an open question as to how children develop their early motivational beliefs about math. Theories of sociocultural development propose that children learn from social interactions with other people, particularly through experiences that parents and teachers scaffold (e.g., Vygotsky, 1978). In this section, we describe the ways in which parents and teachers interact with young children in mathematical contexts, and the ways in which their interactions may influence children's motivation.

PARENTS' INFLUENCES ON CHILDREN'S MATH MOTIVATION AND ACHIEVEMENT

Although research has shown that general parenting practices affect children's motivational beliefs broadly, little is known about how parents affect young children's domain-specific motivational beliefs about mathematics (Rowe, Ramani, & Pomerantz, 2016). However, certain types of mathematical interactions, such as math activities and mathematical language at home, as well as certain types of parent beliefs, such as their beliefs about their child's math ability and their own math anxiety, are related to children's math learning. These interactions and parental beliefs may communicate important information about mathematics that influence young children's own developing ability beliefs, interest, and math anxiety.

Home Numeracy Environment

School-aged children spend only 20% of their waking time in classrooms, with younger children typically spending even more time at home and with parents (Bransford, Brown, & Cocking, 2000). Beyond the formal math instruction that occurs in classrooms, the home numeracy environment that parents and other family members create for young children is an important influence on their early numerical learning (Niklas & Schneider, 2014). Analogous to the home literacy environment, the home numeracy environment refers to the types of numerical information and activities available to the child at home, both formal (e.g., flashcards, worksheets) and informal (e.g., measuring while cooking, number card games). Formal and informal home numeracy activities have been found to differentially predict children's mathematical skills, as described by the home numeracy model (Skwarchuk, Sowinski, & LeFevre, 2014). For example, parental reports of the frequency with which they engage in directly teaching their preschool- and kindergarten-aged child about math are related to children's symbolic math skills, such as counting, identifying numerals, and making comparisons between numbers (LeFevre, Polyzoi, Skwarchuk, Fast, & Sowinski, 2010; Ramani, Rowe, Eason, & Leech, 2015; Skwarchuk et al., 2014).

Reports of formal math learning experiences at home correlate with young children's concurrent performance on numerical assessments (LeFevre et al., 2010; Ramani et al., 2015), as well as predict their numeracy skills 1 year later (Skwarchuk et al., 2014). Additionally, reports of more informal mathematics activities, such as playing numerical card and board games, also relate to children's non-symbolic number skills and more foundational numerical skills (Ramani et al., 2015; Skwarchuk et al., 2014). Research suggests that the relations between formal and informal math experiences and children's mathematical knowledge differs depending on the age of the child; for 3-year-olds children provision of more basic, informal math experiences relates to their math achievement, whereas for 4-year-old children only more formal math activities relate to math achievement (Thompson, Napoli, & Purpura, 2017).

Parents similarly influence children's numerical development through their mathematical language. There is wide variation in the amount of mathematical talk by parents when interacting with their young children (Levine, Suriyakham, Rowe, Huttenlocher, & Gunderson, 2010; Vandermaas-Peeler, Nelson, & Bumpass, 2007), and the variability in parents' math talk predicts differences in children's concurrent and later math skills. One study demonstrated that the number of times parents said number words across observation periods when there was child 14 to 30 months old predicted their child's cardinality knowledge in preschool (Levine et al., 2010); however, parents' talk involving counting or labeling sets of objects that were visible to the child was the most predictive (Gunderson & Levine, 2011). Similarly, preschoolers whose caregivers engaged in more advanced mathematical talk during a joint activity had more advanced numerical skills (Ramani et al., 2015). As with the types of activities, different types of parental math talk may be more important for children at different ages. A study of 5- and 6-year old children showed that parents' overall frequency of number talk did not significantly predict children's math skills, but parents' talk about numbers greater than 10 did (Elliott, Braham, & Libertus, 2017). This suggests that parent mathematical talk must be sufficiently complex and targeted at or above the child's skill level in order to best support their learning.

Exposure to numerical activities and mathematical language in the home may be both a source of variation in young children's early math skills as well as a foundation for children's mathematical motivation. Parents who provide children with frequent exposure to math and formal opportunities to practice math skills, like practice with arithmetic facts, may be helping their child develop positive math ability beliefs by allowing them to become more familiar with mathematics. Play-based math activities like numerical games may particularly help children develop early interest and positive associations with learning math. Indeed, mothers' purchases of math and science toys and frequency of engaging in math and science activities with their children in early elementary school predicted children's self-reported math interest 8 years later (Jacobs & Bleeker, 2004). Frequent, positive experiences with math activities in a low-stakes, supportive home context could also help prevent children from developing math anxiety and negative math ability beliefs.

Parent Beliefs About Ability

Parent socialization models suggest that the development of children's own ability beliefs about math are shaped by their parents' beliefs about them (e.g., Eccles, 2007). Research has shown that parents' beliefs about their child's math ability significantly predict the child's own math ability beliefs and expectations for success in his or her math class (Parsons, 1984). Furthermore, parent perceptions of their child's math ability were stronger predictors of children's ability beliefs than children's prior math grades (Fredricks & Eccles, 2002). Research on parental reports of math activities in the home has found that parents adjust their behavior based on children's achievement, such that mothers and fathers of lower performing students helped their child more (Silinskas, Leppänen, Aunola, Parrila, & Nurmi, 2010). However, parents' misperceptions of their child's ability may lead them to provide more or less challenging math contexts, which may in turn affect their child's math-related motivational beliefs. Indeed, parents who overestimate their preschool children's early math skills also report engaging in more advanced math activities with their child at home (Zippert & Ramani, 2017).

Studies that have separately measured mothers' and fathers' beliefs have found that beliefs of both parents predict their child's ability beliefs. Aunola, Nurmi, Lerkkanen, and Rasku-Puttonen (2003) found that both mothers' and fathers' beliefs of their 6- to 7-year-old children's math ability was directly related to the child's math performance, controlling for prior math ability. Similarly, Frome and Eccles (1998) found that both mothers' and fathers' perceptions of their elementary school aged child's math ability significantly predicted the child's self-reported math ability beliefs. These findings provide strong support for the notion that parents play a significant role in the development of a child's math ability beliefs.

Parents' Math Anxiety

In addition to parents' beliefs about their children's math ability, parents also hold beliefs about themselves and their own math abilities, which can in turn influence the types of math experiences they provide for their children. Although math anxiety negatively predicts math achievement, having math anxiety does not mean someone is bad at math—people with high math achievement can also have math anxiety (Foley et al., 2017). Despite not necessarily having poor math skills, math anxious adults tend to have negative emotions toward math and avoid engaging in math activities (Ashcraft, 2002; Hembree, 1990). Parents may communicate their math anxiety to their children during math interactions by both verbal (e.g., explicit statements) and nonverbal cues (e.g., expressions, body language), which may in turn affect children's motivational beliefs about math. A longitudinal study of first and second grade children found that when parents with high math anxiety reported frequently helping their child with their math homework, their child had lower math achievement at the end of the year (Maloney, Ramirez, Gunderson, Levine, & Beilock; 2015). However, the children of parents with high math anxiety who did not frequently help their child with math homework did not have lower math achievement. This suggests that parental math anxiety by itself may not affect children's math achievement, but rather the combination of parental math anxiety and repeated exposure to anxiety-inducing math interactions can undermine children's learning.

For parents with math anxiety, having clear guidance and support on how to engage with their children around math may mitigate some of the negative effects on children's achievement. For example, first grade students randomly assigned to practice mathematical story problems in an educational iPad app with their parents significantly improved their math skills across the school year (Berkowitz et al., 2015). However, these effects were even stronger for children who had math anxious parents and used the app at least once per week. By substituting potentially negative inter-actions with their math-anxious parents for highly scaffolded experiences with the math app, children's end-of-year math achievement was buffered from the negative effects of their parents' math anxiety.

As with parents' beliefs about their children's math abilities, parents' anxiety can influence the development of their children's math ability beliefs, interest, and anxiety. Parents' math anxiety likely influences their interactions with their children in mathematical contexts; because people with math anxiety tend to avoid math, parents with high math anxiety may provide less frequent and less complex home numeracy activities for their children. Children may be able to sense the discomfort of a parent with math anxiety, either through explicit statements (e.g., "Math isn't really my thing") or physical cues (e.g., nervous body language or unhappy expres-sions). If they realize their parent is anxious in mathematics situations, children may begin to model those behaviors themselves during math contexts, or simply be less likely to develop an interest in mathematics.

In sum, parents' interactions with children in mathematical contexts, including the math activities provided in the home numeracy environment and the frequency and quality of parents' mathematical language, can support both children's math skill building as well as provide a foundation (positive or negative) for their emerging motivation. Similarly, parents' beliefs about their child's math ability level and parents' own math anxiety are communicated to children in ways that affect their math motivation and achievement. However, children's social interactions with others are not limited to their parents; in the next section, we review relations between interactions with early education teachers, young children's math achieve-ment, and the influences on their motivational beliefs.

EARLY CHILDHOOD EDUCATORS' INFLUENCES ON CHILDREN'S MATH MOTIVATION AND ACHIEVEMENT

In addition to the important social learning contexts provided by parents, many young children also interact regularly with early childhood educa-tors. Rates of enrollment in preschool among 3, 4, and 5-year old children have increased dramatically from previous decades; in the 1960s, less than 30% of 4-year olds attended preschool, compared to nearly 70% in 2005 (National Institute for Early Education Research, 2007). Like parents, early childhood teachers' math-related interactions with students may influence children's learning and motivation. Below, we review research on teachers' pedagogical decisions, interactions with individual students, and student-teacher relationships, and describe how they may relate to children's math motivation and achievement. Although there are numerous ways in which early childhood educators influence children's math motivation and achievement, we chose to focus on these as three promising areas empirically related to mathematics, as demonstrated by the research reviewed in the subsequent sections.

Pedagogical Decisions

Early childhood educators' pedagogical choices can affect children's performance in and motivation for math. Although there is wide variability across classrooms, preschool and kindergarten teachers generally spend less than half as much instructional time on teaching mathematics as teaching language and literacy skills (Early et al., 2005; La Paro et al., 2009). However, time spent teaching mathematics, both in whole-class and small group activities, significantly predicts preschool children's math learning across the school year (Hofer, Farran, & Cummings, 2013). For instance, Hofer et al. (2013) found that teachers randomly assigned to a prekindergarten math intervention curriculum had students with larger math learning gains at the end of the school year compared to students in control group classrooms; however, the intervention effects on children's math learning were fully mediated by the frequency of participation in math activities. Similarly, a study assessing frequency of math instruction by sampling preschool teachers' mathematical talk during a one-hour observation found that the proportion of teachers' math talk predicted their students' math learning over the school year (Klibanoff et al., 2006). Thus, early childhood educators who spend more instructional time on math tend to have students with higher math learning gains.

The ways in which early childhood educators teach math to children during instructional time can also affect students' math learning and motivational beliefs. Kindergarten teachers who were rated as using more child-centered teaching practices (e.g., children are allowed to take responsibility to the degree that they are able) versus teacher-directed practices (e.g., children do not have opportunities to take responsibility) by independent observers had students with higher self-reported interest in mathematics at the end of the school year (Lerkkanen et al., 2012). Child-directed or constructivist teaching pedagogies allow children to play an active and exploratory role in their own learning, providing an element of autonomy that supports children's developing interests (Stipek, Feiler, Daniels, & Milburn, 1995; Stipek et al., 1998). Indeed, research on a math intervention that encouraged preschool teachers to introduce fun math activities that followed the students' lead found that students in the intervention classrooms had higher math achievement scores and higher ratings of math interest compared to students in control classrooms (Arnold, Fisher,

Doctoroff, & Dobbs, 2002). These findings suggest that teachers' pedagogical choices can affect students' math learning as well as their motivational beliefs about math, specifically their interest and enjoyment.

Beliefs About Individual Students

As the school year progresses, teachers form impressions of each of their students, including perceptions of their social, emotional, and academic abilities. Early work by Rosenthal and Jacobson (1968) demonstrated a "self-fulfilling prophecy" with regards to teachers' beliefs about students: if teachers were led to believe a student had strong academic ability, by the end of the school year the student's scores on standardized tests were greater than one would expect given their previous performance. Theoretical models of expectancy effects suggest that teachers' differential expectations for students may be communicated through their behavior, such as the provision of harder or easier tasks, paying more attention and interacting more frequently with certain students, and providing differential feedback to students depending on their perceived ability level (Brophy & Good, 1970). Children as young as elementary school students demonstrate awareness of their teachers' expectations for their individual performance, as well as teachers' differential treatment of high and low-achieving students (Weinstein, Marshall, Sharp, & Botkin, 1987). During early elementary school, children's own perceptions of their abilities grow to be increasingly similar to those reported by their teachers, suggesting teachers' beliefs about individual students in the early grades may be noticeably affecting them (Wigfield et al., 1997).

Research has shown that early elementary school teachers' beliefs about individual students significantly predicted their concurrent math achievement (Pesu, Viljaranta, & Aunola, 2016) as well as their long-term math achievement (Hinnant, O'Brien, & Ghazarian, 2009; Sorhagen, 2013; Upadyaya & Eccles, 2014, 2015). One likely reason that teacher beliefs about individual students are predictive is because of teachers' general accuracy in evaluating their students (i.e., the teachers' beliefs aligned well with students' previous math grades and standardized test scores; Helwig, Anderson, & Tindal, 2001). However, when discrepancies occurred, teachers' overestimation of students' math abilities led to better-than-expected math achievement in later grades, although the reverse was true for students whose abilities were underestimated (Hinnant et al., 2009; Sorhagen, 2013). Thus, like parents' beliefs about their children's math abilities, teachers' beliefs may provide information for the formation of children's own ability beliefs, interest, and later achievement.

Student-Teacher Relationships

The student-teacher relationship may play an important role in the development of math motivation in young children. Studies have shown that children as young as 3 years old can benefit from a positive relationship with their teacher (Choi & Dobbs-Oates, 2014). Choi and Dobbs-Oates (2014) found that when controlling for teacher education, experience, and child characteristics, teacher-child closeness was positively associated with preschoolers' math development. In a second study using the same data, Choi and Dobbs-Oates (2016) found that teachers report having closer relationships with children who had higher math abilities at the beginning of the school year. This finding raises questions about the nature of the relation between student-teacher relationships and student math achievement—do teachers have more close relationships with high achieving students, who tend to perform well in math throughout the school year? Or does the effect of a close student-teacher relationship help promote students' math development, regardless of their initial skill level? Additional research by Jones, Bub, and Raver (2013) supports the latter. They conducted an analysis of the impacts of the Chicago School Readiness Program, a preschool intervention for at-risk children, and found that children in the intervention condition significantly improved their early math skills. However, those gains were mediated by corresponding improvement in their student-teacher relationships (i.e., closeness and the student's interactive behavior with the teacher). Similarly, Crosnoe and colleagues (2010) found that children with lower skills prior to kindergarten entry, as compared to children with average and high math skills, learned the most over the early elementary school years and had increasing gains in their math achievement when their teacher provided them with challenging, inference-based instruction and their teacher reported having a positive (nonconflictual) relationship with the student.

Academically at-risk and low-performing children may benefit the most from a positive relationship with their teacher. A study of urban, low-income, racial and ethnic minority children found that high-quality student-teacher relationships in kindergarten predicted math achievement assessed in first grade (McCormick, O'Connor, Capella, McClowry, 2013). The authors speculate that early math learning requires complex thinking and higher-order reasoning, so struggling students may benefit both from instruction to support their skills as well as interpersonal support to persist through the challenging task at hand.

Some work suggests that the student-teacher relationship is also an important predictor of students' math motivation. Stephanou (2014) found that kindergarten students who reported a positive student-teacher relationship had higher competence beliefs and intrinsic interest in math, as well as higher math achievement. Hughes (2011) investigated the longitudinal effects of teacher and student perceptions of student-teacher relationship qualities on academic adjustment. Students' report of their relationship with their teacher in second and third grade significantly predicted math achievement and perceived academic ability beliefs, even when controlling for prior achievement. Teachers' report of their relationship with a student also predicted students' perceptions of their academic ability beliefs. Findings from this study indicate the importance of using both student and teacher reports of the student-teacher relationship.

Overall, teachers' pedagogical decisions, beliefs about individual students, and relationships with students can provide a strong foundation for encouraging math ability beliefs and interest, which may decrease math anxiety and ultimately promote math achievement. It is possible that in contexts with high quality mathematical instruction, when teachers accurately or overestimate students' math abilities, and provide close and supportive relationships, students may be more likely to adopt positive math ability beliefs and interest.

IMPLICATIONS FOR FUTURE RESEARCH, POLICY, AND PRACTICES

Students' motivation can affect behavior—what behavior is initiated, the intensity of the behavior and its persistence, and the overall quality of the behavior (Wentzel, 2015). Young children's motivational beliefs serve as answers to questions that decide their mathematical behaviors: What do I want to do (math interest)? Is this important and enjoyable to do (math anxiety)? Can I do it (math ability beliefs)? The existing research shows longitudinal patterns between children's mathematical motivational beliefs and later math achievement, and for some constructs, bidirectional influences from early math achievement to later math motivation. There is growing evidence that the developmental trends observed in adolescents and young adults begin in preschool and early elementary school, such as the steady decline in children's math ability beliefs and interest over time. In addition, there has been mixed evidence on early gender differences in children's math ability beliefs, interest, and anxiety; the existing research suggests there may not be differences very early on, but as children reach mid- to late elementary school, female students begin to report on average lower math ability beliefs, interest in math, and higher levels of math anxiety than male students. These findings point to the major challenge around motivation and mathematics in early childhood: promoting children's interest, positive ability beliefs, and low levels of anxiety.

The vast majority of research on children's early motivation and mathematics has focused on children aged three years and older. While children younger than three years old may show the beginnings of self-evaluations in their affective reactions to success and failure on tasks (e.g., Stipek et al., 1992), it is unlikely that children younger than three have the cognitive capabilities required to hold motivational beliefs. Research on preschool children aged 3 to 5 years old suggests they may hold rudimentary motivational beliefs (such as math ability beliefs; Arens et al., 2016), whereas children aged five and older begin to have distinct types of math motivation that can be reliably assessed. However, children's early experiences with mathematics from birth onward likely inform the development of their later math motivation.

Parents and early childhood educators play an important role in supporting young children's mathematical motivation, in addition to supporting their math skill development. Through their provision of mathematical activities at home, their numerical talk with their young children, and their beliefs about their child's math ability and their own math anxiety, parents communicate their own valuing, interest, and level of comfort with math. Similarly, early childhood educators' pedagogical choices for teaching math and beliefs about individual students' abilities provide children with information about their teacher's valuing of math and perceptions of their ability, while supportive student-teacher relationships may make students more likely to model their teachers' math-related behaviors and attitudes.

Based on the literature reviewed in the chapter, future research on the relations between motivation and math should consider two directions. First, research should focus on developing appropriate and reliable motivation measures for young children. Research on motivation includes myriad constructs for adolescents and adults; however, very few have been extended to children in preschool or elementary school. One barrier to studying younger children's motivation may be a lack of appropriate measures. Much of the research reviewed in the present chapter focused on studies of preschool through third grade students, often with self-report measures of their motivation. Although it is improbable that children hold consistent motivational beliefs prior to preschool, they likely demonstrate behaviors that precede later math ability beliefs, interest, and anxiety. Expanding the literature to even younger children may require more creative ways of assessing children's motivation indirectly, such as gauging their affective responses during math-specific activities (Stipek et al., 1992). Improved measures of young children's motivation would allow researchers to empirically investigate the origins and development of mathematics motivation, including how constructs such as ability beliefs, interest, and anxiety are related to mathematical interactions with parents and teachers.

A second direction for future research would be to better understand ways to promote young children's mathematical motivation. This research could have important implications for educators and policymakers. The existing literature has shown that the decline in students' math ability beliefs and interest, as well as the increase in their math anxiety, is a pattern that can begin as early as kindergarten (e.g., Jacobs et al., 2002). By developing programs or interventions for young children that capitalize on their positive math motivational beliefs, and either enhance or maintain their high levels of ability beliefs and interest and their low levels of anxiety, it may be possible to dampen the decline of children's math motivation over time. Early mathematics motivation interventions may be particularly important for female students and other groups at risk for poor math achievement (e.g., low socioeconomic status; racial/ethnic minority), who tend to see the largest declines in their math motivation over time (Wang & Degol, 2013). Such work could be informed by successful math motivation interventions for older students (for a review, see Rosenzweig & Wigfield, 2016) or by expanding on existing interventions for promoting preschoolers' math motivation (e.g., Arnold et al., 2002; Supekar, Iuculano, Chen, & Menon, 2015) to target children throughout their early childhood and elementary school years. Intervening in the early school years may be particularly effective, as young children's ability beliefs, interest, and anxiety are more malleable compared to students' motivation in the later school years. In addition, many existing interventions that target children's mathematics skills may similarly improve their math motivation; however, there is little empirical evidence to date. Future studies of early childhood math learning should include measures of math motivation such as ability beliefs, interest, and anxiety.

From a broader policy perspective, research on young children's mathematics motivational beliefs highlights the fact that in order to prepare the next generation of scientists, engineers, and mathematicians, we must attend to the STEM pipeline and children's motivation during early childhood. Since children's math motivational beliefs predict performance, and their math ability beliefs and interest begin to decline as early as elementary school, it is imperative for schools and practitioners to support early math learning with interesting and engaging activities. Playful learning activities such as games can promote children's motivation to learn by stimulating their curiosity and providing an interactive context, which in turn can increase children's attention to and retention of educational content (Hassinger-Das et al., 2017). Embedding high quality mathematical content in the form of playful activities such as numerical board games, card games, and tablet computer games can also lead to improvements in young children's math skills (Ramani & Siegler, 2008; Ramani, Jaeggi, Daubert, & Buschkuehl, 2017; Scalise, Daubert, & Ramani, 2017). The longitudinal patterns of children's motivational beliefs suggest that positive experiences with math learning early on may promote both positive motivational beliefs about math and later math achievement. Creating school-home partnerships around supporting math in formal and informal ways may be an effective option for children in preschool and early elementary school.

The implications for parents, early childhood educators, and adults in general, are that they play a role in children's development of math motivational beliefs. Young children notice when parents and teachers are excited about and interested in math activities, which likely supports their own math ability beliefs and interest. For those who suffer from math anxiety, it is important to realize that even young children may detect and be affected by an adult's negative reaction to math. However, seeking out high-quality, scaffolded math activities such as educational apps (parents), or professional development to support mathematics instruction (teachers), can serve to reduce math anxiety and limit the negative effects on the child's achievement. Young children's mathematical motivation relates to their current and future mathematics outcomes, thus warranting consideration from researchers, policymakers, practitioners, and parents alike.

ACKNOWLEDGMENT

The authors would like to thank Dr. Allan Wigfield, University of Maryland, for his valuable feedback on this chapter.

REFERENCES

Alexander, P. A. & Grossnickle, E. M. (2016). Positioning interest and curiosity within a model of academic development. In K. R. Wentzel & D. B. Miele (Eds.), *Handbook of motivation at school* (2nd ed., pp. 188–208). New York, NY: Routledge.

Arens, A. K., Marsh, H. W., Craven, R. G., Seeshing Yeung, A., Randhawa, E., & Hasselhorn, M. (2016). Math self-concept in preschool children: Structure, achievement relations, and generalizability across gender. *Early Childhood Research Quarterly, 36,* 391–403. doi:10.1016/j.ecresq.2015.12.024

Arnold, D. H., Fisher, P. H., Doctoroff, G. L., & Dobbs, J. (2002). Accelerating math development in Head Start classrooms. *Journal of Educational Psychology, 94*(4), 762. doi:10.1037/0022-0663.94.4.762

Ashcraft, M. H. (2002). Math anxiety: Personal, educational, and cognitive consequences. *Current Directions in Psychological Science, 11*(5), 181–185.

Ashcraft, M. H., & Krause, J. A. (2007). Working memory, math performance, and math anxiety. *Psychonomic Bulletin & Review, 14*(2), 243–248.

Ashcraft, M. H., Krause, J. A., & Hopko, D. R. (2007). Is math anxiety a mathematical learning disability? In D. B. Berch & M. M. Mazzocco (Eds.), *Why is math so hard for some children?* (pp. 329–348). Baltimore, MD: Brookes.

Aunola, K., Nurmi, J. E., Lerkkanen, M. K., & Rasku-Puttonen, H. (2003). The roles of achievement-related behaviours and parental beliefs in children's mathematical performance. *Educational Psychology, 23,* 403–421.

Berkowitz, T., Schaeffer, M. W., Maloney, E. A., Peterson, L., Gregor, C., Levine, S. C., & Beilock, S. L. (2015). Math at home adds up to achievement in school. *Science, 350*(6257), 196–198.

Blackwell, L. S., Trzesniewski, K. H., & Dweck, C. S. (2007). Implicit theories of intelligence predict achievement across an adolescent transition: A longitudinal study and an intervention. *Child Development, 78,* 246–263.

Bransford, J. D., Brown, A. L., & Cocking, R. R. (2002). Learning: From speculation to science. In J. D. Bransford, A. L. Brown, & R. R. Cocking (Eds.), *How people learn: brain, mind, experience, and school* (pp. 3–30), Washington, DC: National Academy Press.

Brophy, J. E., & Good, T. L. (1970). Teachers' communication of differential expectations for children's classroom performance: Some behavioral data. *Journal of Educational Psychology, 61(5)* 365–374.

Choi, J. Y., & Dobbs-Oates, J. (2014). Childcare quality and preschoolers' math development. *Early Child Development and Care, 184*(6), 915–932. doi:10.108 0/03004430.2013.829822

Choi, J. Y., & Dobbs-Oates, J. (2016). Teacher-child relationships: Contribution of teacher and child characteristics. *Journal of Research in Childhood Education, 30*(1), 15–28. doi:10.1080/02568543.2015.1105331.

Crosnoe, R., Morrison, F., Burchinal, M., Pianta, R., Keating, D., Friedman, S. L., & Clarke-Stewart, K. A. (2010). Instruction, teacher–student relations, and math achievement trajectories in elementary school. *Journal of Educational Psychology, 102*(2), 407–417. doi:10.1037/a0017762

Dowker, A., Ashcraft, M., & Krinzinger, H. (2012). Editorial: The development of attitudes and emotions related to mathematics. *Child Development Research, Volume 2012,* Article ID 238435. doi:10.1155/2012/238435

Dowker, A., Bennett, K., & Smith, L. (2012). Attitudes to mathematics in primary school children. *Child Development Research, Volume 2012,* Article ID 124939. doi:10.1155/2012/124939.

Dowker, A., Sarkar, A., & Looi, C. Y. (2016). Mathematics anxiety: What have we learned in 60 years? *Frontiers in Psychology, 7*(508), 1–16. doi:10.3389/fpsyg.2016.00508

Duncan, G. J., Dowsett, C. J., Claessens, A., Magnuson, K., Huston, A. C., Klebanov, P., Pagani, L., Feinstein, L., Engel, M., Brooks-Gunn, J., Duckworth, K., & Japel, C. (2007). School readiness and later achievement. *Developmental Psychology, 43*(6), 1428–1446.

Early, D., Barbarin, O., Bryant, D., Burchinal, M., Chang, F., Clifford, R., … Barnett, W. S. (2005). *Pre-kindergarten in eleven states: NCEDL's multi-state study of pre-kindergarten and study of state-wide early education programs (SWEEP).* Retrieved from: http://fpg.unc.edu/node/4654

Eccles, J. S. (2007). Families, schools, and developing achievement-related motivations and engagement. In J. E. Grusec & P. D. Hastings (Eds.), *Handbook of socialization* (pp. 665–691). New York, NY: Guilford Press.

Eccles, J.S., Adler, T. F., Futterman, R., Goff, S.B., Kaczala, C. M., Meece, J. L., & Midgley, C. (1983). Expectancies, values and academic behaviors. In J. T. Spence (Ed.), *Achievement and achievement motives: Psychological and sociological approaches* (pp. 75–146). San Francisco, CA: Freeman.

Eccles, J. S., Midgley, C., & Adler, T. F. (1984). Grade-related changes in school environment: Effects on achievement motivation. In J. G. Nicholls (Ed.), *The Development of Achievement Motivation* (pp. 285–331). Greenwich, CT: JAI Press.

Eccles, J., Wigfield, A., Harold, R. D., & Blumenfeld, P. (1993). Age and gender differences in children's self-and task perceptions during elementary school. *Child Development, 64*, 830–847.

Eccles, J. S., & Wigfield, A. (2002). Motivational beliefs, values, and goals. *Annual Review of Psychology, 53*, 109–132. doi:0084-6570/02/0201-0109

Edens, K. M., & Potter, E. F. (2013). An exploratory look at the relationships among math skills, motivational factors and activity choice. *Early Childhood Education Journal, 41*(3), 235–243. doi:10.1007/s10643-012-0540-y

Elliott, L., Braham, E. J., & Libertus, M. E. (2017). Understanding sources of individual variability in parents' number talk with young children. *Journal of Experimental Child Psychology, 159*, 1–15. doi:10.1016/j.jecp.2017.01.011.

Ericsson, K. A., Krampe, R. T., & Tesch-Römer, C. (1993). The role of deliberate practice in the acquisition of expert performance. *Psychological Review, 100*(3), 363–406.

Fisher, P. H., Dobbs-Oates, J., Doctoroff, G. L., & Arnold, D. H. (2012). Early math interest and the development of math skills. *Journal of Educational Psychology, 104*(3), 673. doi:10.1037/a0027756.

Foley, A. E., Herts, J. B., Borgonovi, F., Guerriero, S., Levine, S. C., & Beilock, S. L. (2017). The math anxiety-performance link: A global phenomenon. *Current Directions in Psychological Science, 26*(1), 52–58. doi:10.1177/0963721416672463.

Fredricks, J. A., & Eccles, J. S. (2002). Children's competence and value beliefs from childhood through adolescence: Growth trajectories in two male-sex-typed domains. *Developmental Psychology, 38*, 519–533. doi:10.1037//0012-1649.38.4.519

Frome, P. M., & Eccles, J. S. (1998). Parents' influence on children's achievement-related perceptions. *Journal of Personality and Social Psychology, 74*, 435–452. doi:10.1037/0022-3514.74.2.435

Ganley, C. M., & Lubienski, S. T. (2016). Mathematics confidence, interest, and performance: Examining gender patterns and reciprocal relations. *Learning and Individual Differences, 47*, 182–193. doi:10.1016/j.lindif.2016.01.002

Geary, D. C. (2011). Consequences, characteristics, and causes of mathematical learning disabilities and persistent low achievement in mathematics. *Journal of Developmental Behavioral Pediatrics, 32*(3), 250–263.

Griggs, M. S., Rimm-Kaufman, S. E., Merritt, E. G., & Patton, C. L. (2013). The Responsive Classroom approach and fifth grade students' math and science anxiety and self-efficacy. *School Psychology Quarterly, 28*(4), 360. doi:10.1037/spq0000026.

Gunderson, E. A., & Levine, S. C. (2011). Some types of parent number talk count more than others: relations between parents' input and children's cardinal-number knowledge. *Developmental Science, 14*(5), 1021–1032. doi:10.111/j.1467-7687.2011.01050.x

Haase, V. G., Júlio-Costa, A., Pinheiro-Chagas, P., Oliveira, L. F. S., Micheli, L. R., Wood, G. (2012). Math self-assessment, but not negative feelings, predicts mathematics performance of elementary school children. *Child Development Research*, Volume 2012, Article ID 982672, 1–10. doi:10.1155/2012/982672.

Harari, R. R., Vukovic, R. K., & Bailey, S. P. (2013). Mathematics anxiety in young children: An exploratory study. *The Journal of Experimental Education, 81*(4), 538–555. doi:10.1080/00220973.2012.727888

Hassinger-Das, B., Toub, T. S., Zosh, J. M., Michnick, J., Golinkoff, R., & Hirsh-Pasek, K. (2017). More than just fun: A place for games in playful learning [Más que diversión: el lugar de los juegos reglados en el aprendizaje lúdico]. *Infancia y Aprendizaje, 40*(2), 191–218. doi:10.1080/02103702.2017.1292684

Helwig, R., Anderson, L., & Tindal, G. (2001). Influence of elementary student gender on teachers' perceptions of mathematics achievement. *The Journal of Educational Research, 95*(2), 93–102. doi:10.1080/00220670109596577

Hembree, R. (1990). The nature, effect, and relief of mathematics anxiety. *Journal for Research in Mathematics Education, 21*, 33–46.

Heyman, G. D., Dweck, C. S., & Cain, K. M. (1992). Young children's vulnerability to self-blame and helplessness: Relationship to beliefs about goodness. *Child Development, 63*, 401–415.

Hidi, S. (1990). Interest and its contribution as a mental resource for learning. *Review of Educational research, 60*(4), 549–571. doi:10.1.1.938.8376

Hidi, S., Renninger, K. A., & Krapp, A. (2004). Interest, a motivational variable that combines affective and cognitive functioning. In D. Y. Dai & R. J. Sternberg (Eds.), *Motivation, emotion, and cognition: Integrative perspectives on intellectual functioning and development* (pp. 89–115). Mahwah, NJ: Lawrence Erlbaum Associates.

Hill, F., Mammarella, I. C., Devine, A., Caviola, S., Passolunghi, M. C., & Szűcs, D. (2016). Maths anxiety in primary and secondary school students: gender differences, developmental changes and anxiety specificity. *Learning and Individual Differences, 48*, 45–53. doi:10.1016/j.lindif.2016.02.006

Hinnant, J. B., O'Brien, M., & Ghazarian, S. R. (2009). The longitudinal relations of teacher expectations to achievement in the early school years. *Journal of Educational Psychology, 101*(3), 662–670.

Hofer, K. G., Farran, D. C., & Cummings, T. P. (2013). Preschool children's math-related behaviors mediate curriculum effects on math achievement gains. *Early Childhood Research Quarterly, 28*(3), 487–495. doi:10.1016/j.ecresq.2013.02.002

Hughes, J. N. (2011). Longitudinal effects of teacher and student perceptions of teacher-student relationship qualities on academic adjustment. *The Elementary School Journal, 112*(1), 38–60. doi:10.1086/660686

Jacobs, J. E., & Bleeker, M. M. (2004). Girls' and boys' developing interests in math and science: Do parents matter? *New directions for child and adolescent development, 2004*(106), 5–21. doi:10.1002/cd.113

Jacobs, J. E., Lanza, S., Osgood, D. W., Eccles, J. S., & Wigfield, A. (2002). Changes in children's self-competence and values: Gender and domain differences across grades one through twelve. *Child Development, 73*, 509–527. doi:0009-3920/2002/7302-0012

Jameson, M. M. (2014). Contextual factors related to math anxiety in second-grade children. *The Journal of Experimental Education, 82*(4), 518-536. doi:10.1080/00220973.2013.813367

Jones, S. M., Bub, K. L., & Raver, C. C. (2013). Unpacking the black box of the Chicago School Readiness Project intervention: The mediating roles of teacher–child relationship quality and self-regulation. *Early Education & Development, 24*(7), 1043–1064. doi:10.1080/10409289.2013.825188

Klibanoff, R. S., Levine, S. C., Huttenlocher, J., Vasilyeva, M., & Hedges, L. V. (2006). Preschool children's mathematical knowledge: The effect of teacher math talk. *Developmental Psychology, 42*(1), 59–69. doi:10.1037/0012-1649.42.1.59

Köller, O., Baumert, J., & Schnabel, K. (2001). Does interest matter? The relationship between academic interest and achievement in mathematics. *Journal for Research in Mathematics Education, 32*(5), 448–470. doi:10.2307/749801.

Krinzinger, H., Kaufmann, L., & Willmes, K. (2009). Math anxiety and math ability in early primary school years. *Journal of Psychoeducational Assessment, 27*(3), 206–225. doi:10.1177/0734282908330583

La Paro, K. M., Hamre, B. K., Locasale-Crouch, J., Pianta, R. C., Bryant, D., Early, D., Clifford, R., Barbarin, O., Howes, C., & Burchinal, M. (2008). Quality in kindergarten classrooms: Observational evidence for the need to increase children's learning opportunities in early education classrooms. *Early Education and Development, 20*(4), 657–692. doi:10.1080/10409280802541965

LeFevre, J. A., Polyzoi, E., Skwarchuk, S. L., Fast, L., & Sowinski, C. (2010). Do home numeracy and literacy practices of Greek and Canadian parents predict the numeracy skills of kindergarten children? *International Journal of Early Years Education, 18*(1), 55–70. doi:10.1080/09669761003693926

Lerkkanen, M. K., Kiuru, N., Pakarinen, E., Viljaranta, J., Poikkeus, A. M., Rasku-Puttonen, H., Siekkinen, M., & Nurmi, J. E. (2012). The role of teaching practices in the development of children's interest in reading and mathematics in kindergarten. *Contemporary Educational Psychology, 37*(4), 266–279. doi:10.1016/j.cedpsych.2011.03.004

Levine, S. C., Suriyakham, L. W., Rowe, M. L., Huttenlocher, J., & Gunderson, E. A. (2010). What counts in the development of young children's number knowledge? *Developmental Psychology, 46*(5), 1309–1319. doi:10.1037/a0019671

Ma, X. (1997). Reciprocal relationships between attitude toward mathematics and achievement in mathematics. *The Journal of Educational Research, 90*(4), 221–229. doi:101.1080/00220671.1997.10544576

Ma, X., & Kishor, N. (1997). Assessing the relationship between attitude toward mathematics and achievement in mathematics: A meta-analysis. *Journal for Research in Mathematics Education, 28*(1), 26–47. doi:10.2307/749662

Maloney, E. A., Ramirez, G., Gunderson, E. A., Levine, S. C., & Beilock, S. L. (2015). Intergenerational effects of parents' math anxiety on children's math achievement and anxiety. *Psychological Science, 26*(9) 1480–1488. doi:10.1177/ 0956797615592630

Mazzocco, M. M., Hanich, L. B., & Noeder, M. M. (2012). Primary school age students' spontaneous comments about math reveal emerging dispositions linked to later mathematics achievement. *Child Development Research, Volume 2012,* Article ID 170310. doi:10.1155/2012/170310

McCormick, M. P., O'Connor, E. E., Cappella, E., & McClowry, S. G. (2013). Teacher–child relationships and academic achievement: A multilevel propensity score model approach. *Journal of School Psychology, 51*(5), 611–624. doi:10.1016/j. jsp.2013.05.001

Meece, J. L., Wigfield, A., & Eccles, J. S. (1990). Predictors of math anxiety and its influence on young adolescents' course enrollment intentions and performance in mathematics. *Journal of Educational Psychology, 82*(1), 60–70. doi:10.1037/0022-0663.82.1.60

National Mathematics Advisory Panel. (2008). *Foundations for success: The final report of the National Mathematics Advisory Panel.* Washington, DC: U.S. Department of Education; Retrieved from: http://www2.ed.gov/about/bdscomm/list/ mathpanel/report/final-report.pdf.

Nicholls, J. G. (1978). The development of the concepts of effort and ability, perception of academic attainment, and the understanding that difficult tasks require more ability. *Child Development, 49*(3), 800–814.

National Institute for Early Education Research (NIEER). (2007). *Who goes to preschool and why does it matter?* Retrieved from http://nieer.org/wp-content/ uploads/2016/08/15.pdf

Niklas, F., & Schneider, W. (2014). Casting the die before the die is cast: The importance of the home numeracy environment for preschool children. *European Journal of Psychology of Education, 29*(3), 327–345. doi:10.1007/ s10212-013-0201-6.

Parajes, F. (2005). Gender differences in mathematics self-efficacy beliefs. In A. M. Gallagher & J. C. Kaufman (Eds.), *Gender differences in mathematics: an integrative psychological approach* (pp. 294–315). New York, NY: Cambridge University Press.

Parsons, J. (1984). Sex differences in mathematics participation. In M. Steinkamp & M. Maehr (Eds.), *Women in science* (pp. 93-137). Greenwich, CT: JAI Press.

Pesu, L., Viljaranta, J., & Aunola, K. (2016). The role of parents' and teachers' beliefs in children's self-concept development. *Journal of Applied Developmental Psychology, 44*, 63–71. doi:10.1016/j.appdev.2016.03.001

Punaro, L., & Reeve, R. (2012). Relationships between 9-year-olds' math and literacy worries and academic abilities. *Child Development Research, Volume 2012,* Article ID 359089. doi:10.1155/2012/359089

Ramani, G. B., Jaeggi, S. M., Daubert, E. N., & Buschkuehl, M. (2017). Domain-specific and domain-general training to improve kindergarten children's mathematics. *Journal of Numerical Cognition. 3*(2). doi:10.5964/jnc.v3i2.31

Ramani, G. B., Rowe, M. L., Eason, S. H., & Leech, K. A. (2015). Math talk during informal learning activities in Head Start families. *Cognitive Development, 35,* 15–33. doi:10.1016/j.cogdev.2014.11.002

Ramani, G. B., & Siegler, R. S. (2008). Promoting broad and stable improvements in low-income children's numerical knowledge through playing number board games. *Child Development, 79*(2), 375–394. doi:10.1111/j.1467-8624.2007.01131.x

Ramirez, G., Gunderson, E. A., Levine, S. C., & Beilock, S. L. (2013). Math anxiety, working memory, and math achievement in early elementary school. *Journal of Cognition and Development, 14*(2), 187–202.

Ritchie, S. J., & Bates, T. C. (2013). Enduring links from childhood mathematics and reading achievement to adult socioeconomic status. *Psychological Science, 24*(7), 1301-1308. doi:0956797612466268.

Rosenthal, R., & Jacobson, L. (1968). Pygmalion in the classroom. *The Urban Review, 3*(1), 16–20.

Rosenzweig, E. Q., & Wigfield, A. (2016). STEM motivation interventions for adolescents: A promising start, but further to go. *Educational Psychologist, 51*(2), 146–163.

Rowe, M. L., Ramani, G. B., & Pomerantz, E. M. (2016). Parental involvement and children's motivation and achievement. In K. R. Wentzel & D. B. Miele (Eds.), *Handbook of motivation at school* (pp. 459–476). New York, NY: Routledge/Taylor & Francis.

Scalise, N. R., Daubert, E. N., & Ramani, G. B. (2017). Narrowing the early mathematics gap: A play-based intervention to promote low-income preschoolers' number skills. *Journal of Numerical Cognition, 3*(3), doi:10.5964/jnc.v3i3.72

Schiefele, U. (2009). Situational and individual interest. In A. Wigfield (Ed.), *Handbook of Motivation at School* (pp. 197–222). New York, NY: Routledge/Taylor & Francis.

Silinskas, G., Leppänen, U., Aunola, K., Parrila, R., & Nurmi, J. E. (2010). Predictors of mothers' and fathers' teaching of reading and mathematics during kindergarten and Grade 1. *Learning and Instruction, 20*(1), 61–71. doi:10.1016/j.learninstruc.2009.01.002

Skwarchuk, S. L., Sowinski, C., & LeFevre, J. A. (2014). Formal and informal home learning activities in relation to children's early numeracy and literacy skills: The development of a home numeracy model. *Journal of Experimental Child Psychology, 121*, 63–84. doi:10.1016/j.jecp.2013.11.006

Sorhagen, N. S. (2013). Early teacher expectations disproportionately affect poor children's high school performance. *Journal of Educational Psychology, 105*(2), 465–477.

Stephanou, G. (2014). Feelings towards child–teacher relationships, and emotions about the teacher in kindergarten: effects on learning motivation, competence beliefs and performance in mathematics and literacy. *European Early Childhood Education Research Journal, 22*(4), 457–477. doi:10.1080/1350293X.2014.947830

Stipek, D., Feiler, R., Daniels, D., & Milburn, S. (1995). Effects of different instructional approaches on young children's achievement and motivation. *Child Development, 66*(1), 209–223. doi:10.111/j.1467-8624.1995.tb00866.x

Stipek, D., Recchia, S., McClintic, S., & Lewis, M. (1992). Self-evaluation in young children. *Monographs of the Society for Research in Child Development, 57*, 1–95.

Stipek, D., Salmon, J. M., Givvin, K. B., Kazemi, E., Saxe, G., & MacGyvers, V. L. (1998). The value (and convergence) of practices suggested by motivation research and promoted by mathematics education reformers. *Journal for Research in Mathematics Education, 29*(4), 465–488. doi:10.2307/749862

Supekar, K., Iuculano, T., Chen, L., & Menon, V. (2015). Remediation of childhood math anxiety and associated neural circuits through cognitive tutoring. *Journal of Neuroscience, 35*(36), 12574–12583. doi:10.1523/JNEUROSCI.0786-15.2015

Thompson, R. J., Napoli, A. R., & Purpura, D. J. (2017). Age-related differences in the relation between the home numeracy environment and numeracy skills. *Infant and Child Development, 26*(5), e2019. doi:10.1002/icd.2019.

Upadyaya, K., & Eccles, J. S. (2014). How do teachers' beliefs predict children's interest in math from kindergarten to sixth grade? *Merrill-Palmer Quarterly, 60*(4), 403–430.

Upadyaya, K., & Eccles, J. (2015). Do teachers' perceptions of children's math and reading related ability and effort predict children's self-concept of ability in math and reading? *Educational Psychology, 35*(1), 110–127. doi:10.1080/01443410.2014.915927

Vandermaas-Peeler, M. Nelson, J., & Bumpass, C. (2007). "Quarters are what you put into the bubble gum machine": Numeracy interactions during parent-child play. *Early Childhood Research and Practice, 9*(1).

Vukovic, R. K., Kieffer, M. J., Bailey, S. P., & Harari, R. R. (2013). Mathematics anxiety in young children: Concurrent and longitudinal associations with mathematical performance. *Contemporary educational psychology, 38*(1), 1–10. doi:10.1016/j.cedpsych.2012.09.001

Vygotsky, L. S. (1978). Interaction between learning and development. In M. Cole, V. John-Steiner, S. Scribner, & E. Souberman (Eds.), *Mind in society. The development of higher psychological processes* (pp. 79–91). Cambridge, MA: Harvard University Press.

Wang, M. T., & Degol, J. (2013). Motivational pathways to STEM career choices: Using expectancy–value perspective to understand individual and gender differences in STEM fields. *Developmental Review, 33*(4), 304–340. doi:10.1016/j.dr.2013.08.001

Wentzel, K. (2015). Competence within context: Implications for the development of positive student identities and motivation at school. In F. Guay, D. M. McInerney, R. Craven, & H. Marsh (Eds.), *Self-concept, motivation, and identity: Underpinning success with research and practice* (Vol. 5, pp. 299–336). Charlotte, NC: Information Age Publishing.

Weinstein, R. S., Marshall, H. H., Sharp, L., & Botkin, M. (1987). Pygmalion and the student: Age and classroom differences in children's awareness of teacher expectations. *Child Development, 58*(4), 1079–1093. doi:10.2307/1130548

Wigfield, A, Eccles, J. S., Fredricks, J. A., Simpkins, S., Roeser, R. W., & Schiefele, U. (2015). Development of achievement motivation and engagement. In R. Lerner (Series ed.) and M. Lamb (Vol. Ed.), *Handbook of child psychology and developmental science* (7th ed., Vol. 3, pp. 657–700). New York, NY: Wiley.

Wigfield, A., Eccles, J. S., Yoon, K. S., Harold, R. D., Arbreton, A. J., Freedman-Doan, C., & Blumenfeld, P. C. (1997). Change in children's competence beliefs and subjective task values across the elementary school years: A 3-year study. *Journal of Educational Psychology*, *89*, 451–469. doi:10.1037/0022-0663.89.3.451

Wu, S., Amin, H., Barth, M., Malcarne, V., & Menon, V. (2012). Math anxiety in second and third graders and its relation to mathematics achievement. *Frontiers in Psychology*, *3*, 162. doi:10.3389/fpsyg.2012.00162 eCollection 2012

Young, C. B., Wu, S. S., & Menon, V. (2012). The neurodevelopmental basis of math anxiety. *Psychological Science*, *23*(5), 492–501. doi:10.1177/0956797611429134

Yüksel-Şahin, F. (2008). Mathematics anxiety among 4th and 5th grade Turkish elementary school students. *International Electronic Journal of Mathematics Education*, *3*(3), 179–192.

Zippert, E. L., & Ramani, G. B. (2017). Parents' estimations of preschoolers' number skills relate to at-home number-related activity engagement. *Infant and Child Development*, *26*(2), 1–24. doi:10.1002/icd.1968

PART III

MASTERY MOTIVATION

CHAPTER 6

DRAGONFLIES, FIREFLIES, AND DINOSAURS

Harnessing Motivation Through Student-Based Inquiry

Alison K. Billman and Bryce L. C. Becker

"How was your first week of kindergarten, Sam?"[1]
"You don't get to choose what you want to learn, the teacher chooses."

This interaction between the first author and a kindergartner is striking. For one thing, it shows that Sam understands that schools are places of learning, and for another, he has ideas about what he would like to learn and do at school. Sam is motivated to learn, and, in fact, he is likely very curious about the world. However, as early childhood researchers and educators, we are concerned that in his first experiences with schooling, Sam has concluded that school is not a place where he can choose what he wants to learn about—at least in this classroom, he does not have the opportunity to pursue his own interests.

Most children come to school with some motivation to figure out the world around them. Whether you are reading about early childhood development or having conversations with early childhood experts and teachers,

Contemporary Perspectives on Research on
Motivation in Early Childhood Education, pp. 133–154
Copyright © 2019 by Information Age Publishing
All rights of reproduction in any form reserved.

you will likely encounter assertions such as the following: "Young children are naturally curious" or "Young children are naturally motivated to learn" (e.g., Bransford, Brown, & Cockling, 2000; Carlton & Winsler, 1998; Conezio & French, 2002; Dewey, 1910; Gallenstein, 2005; Neuman & Roskos, 2005; Patrick & Mantzicopoulos, 2015; Phillips & Shonkoff, 2000). The commonness of such assertions in conversations about children, education, and schooling might result in a certain level of ennui when considering what really needs to be said in a chapter on motivation and young children.

However, while motivated behaviors may appear to be a natural phenomenon or characteristic of young children interacting with the world, we know through a long history of educational research that students' motivation to learn tends to decline over time (Eccles, Wigfield, Harold, & Blumenfield, 1993; Gottfried, Fleming, & Gottfried, 2001; Guthrie, 2015; Lepper, Corpus, & Iyengar, 2005). In addition, we know that teachers strive to support and motivate children's learning in engaging ways, and they frequently encounter many challenges in creating the contexts that they know will nurture such learning. It is incumbent upon us then to examine this phenomenon to understand how to foster and sustain children's motivation beginning in—or perhaps even before—kindergarten and to support the important work of teachers.

In this chapter, we first establish what we mean by *motivation*. Next, we describe its link to interest, and then consider curricular contexts and pedagogical moves that have been shown to support children's interests and motivation to learn. Finally, we conclude with a set of recommendations for creating communities of motivated learners in early childhood classrooms.

WHAT IS MOTIVATION

When we say children have innate *motivation*, what exactly do we mean? Motivation is a theoretical construct that describes a human state of being within a social context. It is a complex internal process that undergirds focused and sustained engagement in goal-directed activities, and is thus considered integral to learning (Schunk & Mullen, 2012; Schunk, Pintrich, & Meece, 2008; Skinner, Kindermann, Connell, & Wellborn, 2009). It resides internally, yet is influenced by both internal and external factors (e.g., Guthrie & Wigfield, 2005; Katz & Chard, 2000; Turner, 1995; Walker, Pressick-Kilborn, Arnold, & Sainsbury, 2004), and in this way, can be considered a sociocognitive process.

In line with sociocognitive perspectives of learning, motivation involves highly situated interactions amongst individuals' cognitions, behaviors, and surrounding environmental factors (Bandura, 1986, 1997, 2001; Perry,

Turner, & Meyer, 2006; Schunk et al., 2008). Internal factors include a person's thoughts, beliefs, and emotions, while external factors include contextual qualities and experiences such as classrooms, peers, and home and community practices (Schunk & Mullen, 2012). Both internal and external factors affect a person's sense of agency or feeling of control over actions and their consequences (Bandura, 2001, 2006). A person's sense of agency develops through interactions with people and the environment and is rooted in the earliest experiences of a person's life (Bandura, 2006). Human agency includes forethought and intentionality, as well as self-reactiveness and self-reflectiveness. Agency is thus linked to motivation as individuals invest in learning and adapt to their changing environments by setting and adjusting goals (e.g., Locke & Latham, 2002). That is, motivation is a self-regulatory factor as individuals identify and set goals, project future outcomes, evaluate progress, competence and satisfaction, and monitor how these align with their personal standards (Bandura, 2001; Locke, 2000). As such, motivation is a process in contrast to a product because it is ongoing and interactional, and is not itself directly observable. Rather, its existence is inferred through certain behaviors or actions, such as positive talk, engagement, and sustained effort (Schunk et al., 2008). For example, our inferences about Sam's motivation to learn are in part rooted in his statement: "You don't get to choose what you want to learn, the teacher chooses." We infer that his desire to choose means he is motivated to learn about some specific thing or idea.

When educators and academics speak of motivation, they speak not only of an internal state, but also of external behaviors, often described as engagement, self-efficacy, achievement goals, and self-determination (Schunk & Mullen, 2012; Skinner et al., 2009). But even external, observable constructs like engagement can be difficult to define. What does motivated behavior actually look like? Motivated students are often described as taking initiative, paying attention, and persisting (Skinner et al., 2009). They apply learning processes, use active problem-solving strategies, and persist in the face of difficulty, with an overarching focus on developing understanding (Csikszentmihalyi, 1990; Fink, 1998; Perry et al., 2006; Stipek, 1996; Turner, 1995). These behaviors arguably become more crucial over time as children's learning becomes more independent, underscoring the importance of fostering them early in children's school experiences. Yet, these motivated behaviors or engagement also need to be considered in the broader context. "No single individual characteristic or classroom feature is sufficient for explaining motivation" (Perry et al., 2006, p. 328); it is instead their interaction that describes and sustains motivation, and notably, the interaction itself is dynamically situated.

Which contexts, then, influence motivation? Depending on your perspective, you might say that all contexts can be placed on a continuum

of motivating to demotivating. Contexts can include types of social interactions with teachers, parents, siblings, friends, and other community
members (Skinner et al., 2009), and can include characteristics of physical
space and materials or tools (e.g., Engeström, 1987). These contextual features can work synergistically or independently to foster different aspects
of motivation around different activities. Importantly, each context also
has the potential to work cumulatively against motivation. Further, when
the context changes, it is likely that motivation also changes (Nolen, 2007;
Turner, 1995; Turner & Patrick, 2008). In the case of Sam, we do not have
a description of his kindergarten classroom, nor did we meet or talk with
his teacher, so we are missing a description of some important contextual
factors. We wonder, though, what Sam would have said if the teacher had
asked the children to share what they were interested in learning, or if the
teacher had read books or set up a science or some other activity center
that aligned with Sam's interest.

Given these interwoven factors, in the following sections, we describe
knowledge about best practices to sustain intrinsic motivation, both via
internal factors like high interest, and external factors like classroom
pedagogy.

INTEREST AND MOTIVATION

"What would you like to learn about, Sam?"
"Dragonflies, fireflies, and dinosaurs."

Sam's immediate response suggests that he is not only motivated to learn
(e.g., Brophy, 1986, 2010), but he also has been exposed to the topics of
dragonflies, fireflies, and dinosaurs in ways that have initiated specific and
genuine interests. These interests are propelling his desire to learn (e.g.,
Renninger & Su, 2012) and possibly his expectations for what happens in
school classrooms. Interest is important to our discussion because personal
interests prompt—or motivate—meaningful engagement (e.g., Brophy,
2010; Guthrie, Wigfield, & You, 2012). When children—or learners—are
interested in a particular topic, they are more likely to set personal learning
goals and seek out the means to meet those goals (e.g., Brophy, 2010; Hidi
& Renninger, 2006). Interest not only initiates engagement, but learning
often feels less effortful if the learner is interested in the topic (e.g., Dewey,
1913; Hidi & Renninger, 2006). In this sense, interest produces internal or
intrinsic motivation.

Like motivation, the study of interest and its relationship to learning
is not new; in fact, John Dewey might say that Sam's attention has been

caught and that he is poised to act on his interests (Dewey, 1913; Mitchell, 1993). Through decades of research, we know that personal interests can not only initiate engagement, but they also can sustain cognitive engagement even when the learners are very young children, and result in the use of more deep-processing strategies that support knowledge development (e.g., DeLoache, Simcock, & Macari, 2007; Hidi, 2001; Kashdan, Rose, & Fincham, 2004; Krapp, Hidi, & Renninger, 1992; McDaniel, Waddill, Finstad, & Bourg, 2000; Mitchell, 1993; Renninger, 2000; Renninger, Hidi, & Krapp, 1992; Silvia, 2008; Pattison, 2014).

Researchers' definitions of interest are varied and have evolved over time. We define interest as an intrinsic connection to a topic that subsequently motivates attention to that topic. We also subscribe to the theory that interest develops over time through sustained interactions with the environment (Hidi & Renninger, 2006; Renninger, 2000; Renninger & Hidi, 2016). It is the motivational impact of interest on learning that prompts us to include a discussion of its role here.

While some children, like Sam, may come to school with one or more well established interests, it is important to understand that the earlier stages of interest development need to be triggered by something in the environment, such as interactions with people or events that capture attention (e.g., Hidi & Renninger, 2006; Mitchell, 1993). This suggests that teachers and schools are responsible for creating interesting spaces for children to learn. Additionally, interests develop over time and, in order to develop, need to be nurtured and encouraged. If the teacher is the only one choosing what to learn, as Sam perceives, what will happen to his interests and motivation to learn? Thus, in the next section, we discuss what we know as a field about the characteristics of early childhood learning spaces, learning tasks, and interactions that ignite children's interests and foster motivation.

MOTIVATIONAL CONTEXTS

We consider both motivation and interest to be socioculturally situated, so it is important to consider what is unique about classrooms that create motivating contexts—contexts that are also likely to foster and sustain children's interests. The classroom context can be seen as a combination of characteristics, including task and pedagogy, and their interactions with children's interest; indeed, any significant attempt to understand motivation must deal in these interactions (e.g., Perry et al., 2006; Stipek, 2001; see also Salili, Chiu, & Hong, 2001).

The Six Cs of Motivational Contexts

Building on their own and decades of research, Turner and Paris (1995) describe six characteristics (6-Cs) of motivating contexts, namely, *choice, challenge, control, collaboration, constructive meaning,* and *consequences.* Although Turner and Paris focused particularly on describing the motivating characteristics of literacy-based instructional contexts, these 6-Cs are constructs that appear and reappear throughout the literature on maintaining children's motivation to learn (e.g., Deci, 1992; Gallas, 1995; Katz & McClellan 1997; Renninger et al., 1992; Schunk et al., 2008; Turner & Paris, 1995). For this reason, we believe they are applicable to many if not all early childhood learning contexts.

The first C, *choice,* is really what 5-year-old Sam desired, and indeed research suggests that when children are given more choice in the classroom and the tasks they engage in, they are more motivated to learn (Deci, 1992; Mitchell, 1993; Renninger et al., 1992; Schunk et al., 2008; Stipek, 2002; Turner & Paris, 1995). Classroom materials and opportunities to learn must reflect or trigger children's interests and thereby engagement if they are going to foster motivation. Opportunities to choose should be coupled with the right amount of *challenge* for young learners (i.e., a Goldilocks scenario of not too easy and not too hard). Children are more likely to persist with a task in spaces where they are given opportunities to problem solve and can see a purpose for their learning while maintaining a sense of self-efficacy as they do so (Deci, 1992; Renninger et al., 1992; Stipek, 2002; Turner & Paris, 1995). Self-efficacy is also integral to the importance of *control* in any learning environment; when children feel that they share control over their learning, they feel more competent (Schunk et al., 2008; Stipek, 2002; Turner & Paris, 1995); indeed, as Bandura (1997, 2001) argues, self-efficacy is foundational to personal agency and to the human experience (see above). Additionally, because learning is a social endeavor, *collaboration* also serves to maintain motivation and interest (Stipek, 2002; Turner & Paris, 1995; Wharton-McDonald, 2001). Knowledge is coconstructed, and collaboration with peers can foster engagement, persistence, and curiosity. When children see that they are constructing meaning, they see a purpose for engaging in learning activities which in turn, tends to motivate them to be strategic, persistent, and evaluative (Gallas, 1995; Katz & McClellan 1997; Turner & Paris, 1995). Children's engagement increases when learning activities are authentic, meaningful and relevant, as well as aligned with their interests (Mitchell, 1993; Nolen, 2007). Finally, the *consequences* of engaging in a given activity should not be merely evaluative, but rather allow children to have "positive feelings about effort, ownership, achievement, and responsibility" (Turner & Paris, 1995, p. 671; see also Bandura, 2006), and should center on the process of learning itself (Carlton & Winsler, 1998). With the complex mix of interactions between individual and contextual factors, it is impossible to pull out any given task as motivational, although open-ended tasks with authentic learning purposes more readily include the 6-Cs (Turner & Paris, 1995). In describing these six motivating characteristics of classrooms, the greater focus is on the whole of an environment that allows groups of children opportunities to collaborate in purposeful activities with the right amount of challenge, as well as one that triggers their interests.

Teachers' Roles in Fostering Motivation

What then can teachers do to foster and sustain children's motivation to learn? Notably, the characteristics of motivating classroom contexts ultimately rely on teachers knowing their students well, and being willing to take risks to learn new processes and possibly new disciplinary content. The 6-Cs are contextual factors that can be initiated by teachers in their classrooms, but they are also factors that are complemented by teacher moves that support student autonomy, motivation, and engagement. For example, when teachers communicate clear expectations and learning goals from the beginning, children have a better understanding of the goals they are working to accomplish. This helps them to make *choices* and to feel a sense of *control* as they work to *construct meaning* in ways that move them closer to accomplishing the goal. Designing for and allowing *collaboration* in the classroom also fosters motivation because it sets the expectation that constructing knowledge is a collaborative effort and that all children have valuable contributions to make (Wharton-McDonald, 2001). This expectation and opportunity fuels the sense of self-efficacy that is important to a virtuous cycle of motivation and learning (e.g., Bandura, 1977, 1997, 2001; Brophy, 2010). Teachers can also model how to use effective strategies, which help children to approach *challenge* positively and persistently. Additionally, teachers should continuously and formatively assess individuals' skills and use that information to consider how appropriate a task is for a particular child in order to assure the right amount of *challenge* (Pressley, Allington, Wharton-McDonald, Block, & Morrow, 2001; Schunk et al., 2008).

Providing motivational messages and positive feedback, focused on children's learning strategies and processes rather than on evaluation or mastery, not only assists them in feeling capable and thereby supports an appropriate level of *challenge*, but it also models how to develop their own set of personal *consequences*. That is, they learn to evaluate their efforts and self-regulate, rather than taking an extrinsic rubric approach that categorizes the products of their efforts as right or wrong. A focus on the learning process rather than the product fosters future motivation for learning (Schunk et al., 2008; Wharton-McDonald, 2001). Teachers can also support a learning stance by emphasizing that mistakes are part of the learning process and are valuable to *constructing meaning* (Stipek, 2002). When teachers communicate and model this stance, while participating as enthusiastic learners themselves, they can foster the overarching supportive and respectful classroom climate that is foundational to any attempt to sustain and foster motivation in young learners. Notably, teachers' ability to do all of this well relies, in part, on their own motivation and workplace environment, highlighting the complexity of students' learning contexts; (for research on teacher and workplace motivation, see e.g., Claudia, 2015; Han & Yin, 2016; Herzberg, 2003; Kitching, Morgan, & O'Leary, 2009). Considering these contextual factors and teacher moves, we now turn to the area of science as an exemplar of a discipline that is a rich resource for fostering motivation and interest in young learners.

SCIENCE AS A VEHICLE FOR MOTIVATION IN EARLY CHILDHOOD CLASSROOMS

Like Sam, most children come to school with questions about or an avid interest in understanding aspects of the natural world (Duschl, Schweingruber, & Shouse, 2007; Gallenstein, 2005; Lindfors, 1999; Patrick & Mantzicopoulos, 2015; Pattison, 2014; Wells, 1986). Before they enter school, young children are curious about science, and this shapes their learning and learning goals early on (DeLoache, Simcock, & Macari, 2007; Renninger, 1989, 2007). It stands to reason then that opportunities to learn science—the study of the natural world—are appropriate in early childhood classrooms because the goals of science mirror children's natural propensity to make sense of the world around them. From a sociocultural perspective, engaging children in science is not merely supporting their acquisition of facts, but also engaging them in the culture of science with all of its ways of talking and constructing knowledge.

MOTIVATING CHARACTERISTICS OF THE PURSUIT OF SCIENCE KNOWLEDGE

Importantly, many of the characteristics of motivating contexts that Turner and Paris describe are inherent in the cultural practice of science. For example, scientists begin by making *choices* regarding the questions they are asking and, as such, have *control* over what they study and the ways they pursue the answers to their questions. The study of science involves a community of scientists and is thus social and *collaborative*. In addition, the study of science aims to *construct* knowledge of the natural world and of the inquiry methods associated with constructing knowledge. Through a systematic process, scientists ask questions, make observations and interpretations, and use patterns in the data to construct answers to their questions. As such, designing the classroom to include authentic experiences with science—that is, experiences that mirror the goals of the discipline—has the potential to motivate children.

Children Can and Do Learn Science

Studies of young children's science learning show that young children are not only capable of advanced scientific thinking and inquiry, but that opportunities to learn science promote outcomes, such as facility with the practices of scientific inquiry, the ability to use language to explain complex scientific ideas, and the use of strategic reading behaviors that influence comprehension (Duschl, Schweingruber, & Shouse, 2007; French, 2004; Metz, 2008; Peterson & French, 2008; Samarapungavan, Mantzicopoulos, & Patrick, 2008). In an extended science curriculum, Metz (2008) demonstrated that first graders can develop the ability to practice science in authentic ways by framing questions for investigation and then continuing "with elaboration of research design, data collection, and analysis" (p. 158). Samarapungavan and colleagues (2008) examined kindergartners' science learning in a unit designed to engage children in the practices of science and give them opportunities to develop and revise concepts based on evidence. Children in the experimental group made greater gains in both science knowledge and knowledge of inquiry processes.

Unfortunately, many school districts devote less time to teaching science in early childhood and primary classrooms (e.g., Dorph et al., 2007; Fulp, 2000; Saul, 2004). This is a missed opportunity to not only take advantage of young children's intrinsic motivations to learn, but also to begin building perceptions of school contexts as places for pursuing knowledge. Perhaps even more importantly, it is a missed opportunity to nurture and sustain children's personal interests—the pursuit of which may result in sustaining the motivation to learn in later grades. Thus, in the remaining sections, we describe pedagogical models and curricular exemplars that lend themselves particularly well to scientific exploration with young children and that are designed to trigger and build on children's natural interests as a vehicle for sustaining long-term motivation as learners.

Pedagogical Approaches That Promote Motivation

Project-based learning. *Project-based learning* is a term used to label a variety of pedagogical approaches that emerged in the early 20th century and have had a varying degree of popularity and a number of iterations over time (Clark, 2006; Dewey, 1990; DuCharme, 1993; Edwards, 2002; Halvorsen et al., 2012; Katz & Chard, 2000; Kilpatrick, 1918). A primary pillar of this pedagogy is the claim that engagement in a purposeful project or authentic problem-solving activity not only makes educational endeavors more meaningful, but also more efficacious for children's eventual participation in life pursuits outside of school. As such, problems or projects are authentic, more likely to be relevant to children's lives, and more likely to trigger their interests, or in the case of Sam, build on existing interests. In that sense, engaging in real-world problems and projects is the best crucible for learning about the world and how to be in the world. Projects, regardless of topic, also require that children draw on a wide variety of literacy and mathematical skills in order to accomplish the goals of the project. Project-based approaches are characterized by allowing more student *choice* and *control* in identifying the object or topic of study. Project-based learning is also more likely to be a *collaborative* endeavor, with children working in groups to solve problems. Although studies of the project approach in classrooms confirm its impact on children's motivation as well as learning (e.g., Halvorsen et al., 2012; Hertzog, 2007; Kaldi, Filippatou, & Govaris, 2011), we acknowledge that including projects in classrooms is not without its challenges for teachers (e.g., Hertzog, 2007). A hallmark of project-based learning is curriculum that emerges from student interest and is guided by their choice, yet this approach to teaching places a great deal of responsibility on the teacher for having a keen understanding of child development and orchestrating environments that allow children to learn the appropriate knowledge and skills. Considering these challenges, resources such as the work of Helm and Katz (2011) provide scaffolds for designing and implementing projects that motivate and engage children.

Inquiry as a framework for project-based learning. *Inquiry*, although more often associated with the processes of science, refers to endeavors or processes that are used to answer questions across disciplines. Inquiry is considered a skill that is essential for lifelong learning. By nature, inquiry has a focused purpose—a question to be answered. But where do the questions come from? Research shows that children as young as infants and toddlers actively inquire to *construct meaning* (e.g., Lindfors, 1999; Wells, 1986, 2001). Most children arrive at school with questions, but traditional pedagogies place teachers at the helm, and, as Sam said, making the choices. We might infer then that they also ask the questions. However, a classroom environment that prompts curiosity or wonder allows shared questions to naturally emerge from the children, and initiates motivation by triggering interest (e.g., de Boo, 1999; Gallas, 1995; Hill, Stremmel, & Fu, 2005). Common questions build opportunities for *collaboration*.

As an example, Phylis Whitin (2007), a kindergarten teacher, carefully placed a birdfeeder at her classroom window, surrounded with observation tools and informational resources, such as books and posters of birds; this prompted curiosity, questions, and *collaborative* conversations that extended across a school year. As children observed birds coming and going, their observations prompted questions that motivated them to use the resources to identify the birds and to have conversations to learn more about how they were alike and different. *Consequences* were remarkable. Children were engaged and persisted in the challenging tasks of reading and writing to *construct meaning* and adjust their thinking as they encountered new ideas. They *collaborated* and took the lead as experts in sharing knowledge about birds through conversation and writing. What began as simply placing a bird feeder at a window became a year-long inquiry.

Reggio Emelia approach to project-based learning. The Reggio Emelia approach to preschool education is known for its founder's desires to prepare and educate children for a better world. Rooted in Deweyan and Vygotskian theories, children are seen as the protagonists in learning situations that are monitored and facilitated by teachers (e.g., Clyde et al., 2006; Edwards, 2002). *Collaboration* and relationships among learners and teachers are central to this approach. As in other project-based learning approaches, in the Reggio Emelia approach, the curriculum emerges from the children's interests. It is incumbent upon the teacher to know the children and to create environments that allow not only for their interests to emerge, but also for the social construction of knowledge to occur and thrive. In this approach, teachers are rarely if ever responsible for directly teaching skills such as reading, writing or math; rather, the teacher supports children in using these skills in the context of projects designed around children's interests. The role of the teacher is observer and facilitator. Through careful observation, teachers are responsible for recognizing children's interests, envisioning potential inquiries, and then providing resources that align with those interests and facilitating paths for children's inquiries. An important feature of this approach is the documentation or representation of the learning experiences and the knowledge that children are constructing across the duration of the project.

Because expectations outlined in standards policies sometimes extend to as early as preschool, it may seem risky to allow curriculum to be determined by the emerging interests of children. Although project-based pedagogies are known to result in motivated and engaged learners, questions arise as to whether the children in those settings are meeting the learning expectations outlined in documents such as the Next Generation Science Standards and the Common Core State Standards for English Language Arts and Mathematics. Some researchers have thoughtfully constructed frameworks that teachers can use as guidelines for creating units of study that capitalize on the motivational features that are common to project-based approaches. Others have designed and studied the impacts of integrated science-literacy approaches that mirror features of project-based approaches. In the next section, we describe some of these approaches.

Integrated Science and Literacy Curriculum

There are many conceptualizations of integrated curriculum. Some approaches are thematic—the units of study are designed to draw on the skills and knowledge bases of many disciplines as a way to teach for deep understanding of a topic or idea. Some approaches are interdisciplinary—instruction is designed to meet learning goals for two or more disciplines within one unit of study. These approaches draw on the understanding that learning the skills and knowledge in one domain is enhanced or supported with skills and knowledge from another. In addition, knowledge and the disciplines are intertwined; concepts and processes cross disciplinary lines. Although curricula designed for disciplinary integration are informed by varying theories, many, such as those described below, are informed by theories of motivation and intentionally designed to foster motivated and engaged learning.

Concept-Oriented Reading Instruction. Concept-Oriented Reading Instruction (CORI) is designed to integrate reading strategy instruction within units focused on reading to find out more about science with the intent of promoting reading engagement (e.g., Guthrie, Van Meter, McCann, & Wigfield, 1996). Rather than the teacher observing children to identify their interests, the teacher chooses conceptual themes and provides experiences designed to trigger children's interest in the theme. An underlying assumption is that engaged children are motivated to learn and are more social and strategic in their learning. The instructional framework intentionally supports children's engagement and motivation by including opportunities for them to explore materials (e.g., owl pellets), to wonder and pose their own questions, to choose the direction of their inquiry within the topic of the study, and to collaborate with their classmates throughout the unit of study. The goals of this approach are to foster reading engagement and an intrinsic motivation to read. Although researchers have found this framework for organizing units to be efficacious for third, fourth, and fifth graders, it is also an approach that has been applied to but not tested in early primary classroom contexts (Guthrie, 2004, 2015; Guthrie, Van Meter, McCann, & Wigfield, 1996; Swan, 2003).

Preschool Pathways to Science. Preschool Pathways to Science (PrePS) is similar to the CORI approach (Gelman, Brenneman, MacDonald, & Roman, 2010), but rather than a suite of curriculum guides, PrePS provides a framework that guides teachers in a systematic approach for designing science curriculum. The framework focuses on engaging children in learning science processes while providing them with opportunities to develop the language and vocabulary for talking about the science content they are learning. Similar to project-based approaches, Gelman and her colleagues were committed to creating experiences that ignited children's curiosity and interest in science. Rather than describing content, this approach is designed to develop a culture of inquiry that allows *choice* and *collaboration* to promote children's natural knowledge-seeking activities through explorations of the natural world. The framework guides teachers to choose a big idea or central concept (e.g., change or inside/outside). Although some big ideas may be divided into smaller subtopics, the idea is that learning goals are defined in relationship to the central concept. For example, the learning goals around the big idea of change might be related to understanding how living things change or what living things need to grow and change. Children are guided to use processes of science inquiry to investigate and are supported in developing and using language, literacy, and numeracy skills as they make sense of their encounters with various materials and experiences. Over time, children have many experiences and conduct many observations and investigations related to one big idea, resulting in numerous opportunities to deepen their understanding of the concept. Importantly, this approach has been supported through research efforts to study children's science learning and thinking before and after units designed with the PrePS framework. Findings show that many students made measurable gains in understanding science concepts.

Seeds of Science Roots of Reading. Seeds of Science Roots of Reading (SOS/ROR) is an example of an integrated science-literacy curriculum intentionally designed to meet science content learning goals and literacy strategy learning goals in each unit of study (Cervetti, Pearson, Barber, & Bravo, 2007). One of the underlying fundamental principles guiding the design of this second–fifth grade curriculum is the fact that reading and doing science are both acts of inquiry. As such, they both require children to develop sense-making strategies to construct or retrieve information. A second principle is the fact that reading, writing, and talking are essential tools for learning about and communicating science ideas within a science community. Children are guided to *collaborate* in a combination of firsthand and secondhand investigations to do science and to also read, write, and talk about science ideas. With the support of federal grant funds, we and our colleagues at Lawrence Hall of Science have been able to build on the SOS/ROR integrated science-literacy model to develop a model of science-literacy integration for kindergarten and first grade classrooms and test that model in two first grade units (Billman, Pearson, & Rowe, 2016). Although the first edition of SOS/ROR considered authentic tasks essential characteristics of investigation and literacy instruction, the newly redesigned program, including the added kindergarten and first grade units, takes authenticity further by situating each unit within a real-world problem. The real-world problem, also called the problem context, is selected to trigger children's interest; prompt questions; and motivate the engagement that is needed to learn and find out the science information that will in turn allow them to solve or explain the problem. For example, children use their own box model pinball machines to learn about touching forces and to explain how a pinball machine works. They then design a class pinball machine based on what they now know about forces. Although our first-grade pilot was small, not only did students learn science and vocabulary, but teachers also reported that students were highly engaged and motivated to read to find the answers to their questions (Billman et al., 2016).

RECOMMENDATIONS

As we have examined the literature and reflected on our experiences with children, teaching, and curriculum, we are once again in awe of the dedication, expertise, and work of many of the teachers we know in early childhood classrooms. Creating motivating classrooms and engaged learners is hard work. With this in mind, we provide a few recommendations for teachers who want to provide motivating spaces where children get to choose what they want to learn about—at least some of the time.

Identify and capitalize on children's interests. Take time to engage in conversations with children. Children's interests are insights into their prior experiences and may help you gather a set of materials that extend those experiences. Work to make sense of and clarify children's naive ideas as a way of understanding what new experiences will help them build on the knowledge they have.

Provide experiences and materials that trigger children's interests. Consider providing a wide variety of experiences and some that are even new to you. Open-ended explorations better meet the needs of diverse learners.

Provide experiences that challenge children. Experiences that include problem-solving are challenging, contribute to building persistence, and offer opportunities for collaboration.

Surround every inquiry, project, and experience with language. Language is a way of organizing and communicating knowledge. It is essential for participating in a community of learners and constructing knowledge.

Be a learner—take risks. When children encounter new experiences and also see learning in action, they have models that inform their own approaches to learning and engagement with ideas.

CONCLUDING THOUGHTS

"Sam, I heard you have an insect collection."[2]

"It's a bug collection. Guess what … I caught a darner dragonfly. Darners are some of the largest dragonflies in North America. My dragonfly is a darner, I think 'cause my dragonfly is pretty big. Dragonflies were alive when dinosaurs were alive. They were about the size of a robin … I am going to be a dragonfly for Halloween. I get to wear my costume to school."

"Will you tell your friends about dragonflies?"
"Probably not."
"Who do you get to talk to about dragonflies at school?"
"Nobody, 'cause every day is a busy day."

It is universally accepted that all young learners, like Sam, begin school with intrinsic motivation to find out about their world. Sam is clearly motivated to learn about bugs. Yet there are situations or ways of organizing learning experiences that children may encounter that can energize this motivation or not. Importantly, we know these early interactions with school may shape their experiences and careers as learners in later grades. As such, it is critical that young learners' interests and wonder are not only listened to, but also used as the driving forces behind pedagogical decisions and when possible, units of study. Across the literature, scholars overwhelmingly agree that educators' commitment to uplifting and providing the 6-Cs—*choice, challenge, control, collaboration, constructive meaning,* and *consequences* (Turner & Paris, 1995)—is integral to supporting motivation to learn. The overarching message is that, in order to do so, teachers need to know their students, and their students' interests, skills, and abilities, well. Amongst the many models for early childhood pedagogy and curricula, project-based learning and inquiry lend themselves particularly well to maintaining young learners' motivation because they provide authentic learning goals grounded in students' interests. In addition, teachers can draw on multiple pedagogical models and frameworks for designing integrated units of study or even examine the curriculum marketplace for units of study designed to foster engagement and motivation.

We know that the more a person knows about a domain, the more interesting it gets and the more intrinsically motivated the person is to keep learning (e.g., Hidi & Renninger, 2006; Renninger & Hidi, 2016). In this chapter, we have focused on how teachers can capitalize on young children's interest, particularly their interest in the natural world, as a way to jumpstart children's general intrigue with learning. Although a child's interests can change over time in response to experiences and encounters with people and the world, it is not unusual for an interest to endure and have its roots in the early years of a child's life (Renninger, 1992). The question we are left asking ourselves is: How do we help sustain and nurture children's interests from grade to grade and classroom to classroom? We do not know of any research that studies young children's interest and motivation over time—a potentially productive line of research. In the meantime, perhaps returning to Sam's story provides us with some of the best insights.

EPILOGUE: SAM, 11 YEARS OLD

Over the years, there have been many conversations with Sam. With a dad who is a biologist, his scientific interest has been sustained despite not having any science instruction at all in third or fourth grade—something which Sam complained about. In the most recent conversation just as we began preparing this chapter, Sam confirmed that he is still interested in bugs. He went into great detail to provide an overview of his fifth grade project that he and a friend collaborated on during "Genius Hour," a one-hour block each week that his teacher scheduled for children to explore their own interests. With the help of his dad, he and his friend spent time on weekends gathering aquatic insects from two freshwater creeks. They sorted, counted, and identified the order, family, and common names for each type; then they compared the two ecosystems and proposed explanations for the differences in the variety and number of insects. The project took about 6 months and ended with a presentation to his class. And, this project has spawned new ideas and questions. Sam already has plans for his next investigation—collecting land bugs following similar procedures in order to find out about insects in a new set of ecosystems.

At the end of the conversation, Sam was asked what recommendations he would give to teachers of young children. Here they are, in order:

- Once or twice a week have a free time for kids to learn about anything they want so kids can have a choice.
- Have lots of books so kids can find out the things they want to find out about.
- If kids don't have scientist dads, find scientists to come help.

NOTES

1. Sam's words are used throughout this chapter with his permission.
2. This is an excerpt from a 48-minute conversation during the fall of Sam's first grade year in which he shared many more pieces of information about dragonflies and how he was observing and collecting information about them.

REFERENCES

Bandura, A. (1977). Self-efficacy: Toward a unifying theory of behavioral change. *Psychological Review, 34*(2), 191–215.

Bandura, A. (1986). The explanatory and predictive scope of self-efficacy theory. *Journal of Social and Clinical Psychology, 4*(3), 359–373.

Bandura, A. (1997). *Self-efficacy: The exercise of control.* New York, NY: Macmillan.

Bandura, A. (2001). Social cognitive theory: An agentic perspective. *Annual Review of Psychology, 52,* 1–26.

Bandura, A. (2006). Toward a psychology of human agency. *Perspectives on Psychological Science, 1(2),* 164–180.

Billman, A. K., Pearson, P. D., & Rowe, M. (2016, December). *Uniting science knowledge and literacy development: Reading to learn in first grade.* Paper presented at the annual meeting of the *Literacy Research Association,* Nashville, TN.

Bransford, J. D., Brown, A. L., & Cocking, R. R. (Eds.) (2000). *How people learn: Brain, mind, experience, and school.* Washington, DC: National Academy Press. Retrieved from https://pdfs.semanticscholar.org/518f/7866ffb58c0b8d06b5e 970d2a0f32a0e03c3.pdf

Brophy, J. (1986). On motivation students (Occasional Paper No. 101). Institute for Research on Teaching, East Lansing, Michigan State University.

Brophy, J. E. (2010). *Motivating students to learn* (3rd ed.). New York, NY: Routledge.

Carlton, M. P., & Winsler, A. (1998). Fostering intrinsic motivation in early childhood classrooms. *Early Childhood Education Journal, 25*(3), 159–166.

Cervetti, G. N., Pearson, P. D., Barber, J., Hiebert, E. H., & Bravo, M. A. (2007). Integrating literacy and science: The research we have, the research we need. In M. P. Pressley, A. K. Billman, K. H. Perry, K. E. Reffitt, & J. M. Reynolds (Eds.), *Shaping literacy achievement: Research we have, research we need* (pp. 157–174). New York, NY: Guilford Press.

Clark, A. (2006). Changing classroom practice to include the project approach. *Early Childhood Research & Practice, 8*(2), 1–10.

Claudia, V. (2015). The role of motivation in the development of school teachers' career. *Procedia—Social and Behavioral Sciences, 180*(2015), 1109–1115.

Clyde, J. A., Miller, C., Sauer, S., Liebert, K., Parker, S., & Runyon, S. (2006). Teachers and children inquire into Reggio Emilia. *Language Arts, 83*(3), 215–226.

Conezio, K., & French, L. (2002). Science in the preschool classroom: Capitalizing on children's fascination with the everyday world to foster language. *Young Children, 57*(5), 12–18.

Csikszentmihalyi, M. (1990). *Flow: The psychology of optimal experience*. New York, NY: Harper and Row.

de Boo, M. (1999). *Enquiring children, challenging teaching*. Philadelphia, PA: Open University Press.

Deci, E. L. (1992). The relation of interest to the motivation of behavior: A self-determination theory perspective. In K. A. Renninger, S. Hidi, & A. Krapp (Eds.), *The role of interest in learning and development* (pp. 43–70). Hillsdale, NJ: Erlbaum.

DeLoache, J. S., Simcock, G., & Macari, S. (2007). Planes, trains, automobiles-and tea sets: Extremely intense interests in very young children. *Developmental Psychology, 43*(6), 1579–1586.

Dewey, J. (1910). *How we think*. Lexington, MA: Heath.

Dewey, J. (1913). *Interest and effort in education*. Cambridge, MA: Riverside Press.

Dewey, J. (1990). *The child and the curriculum*. Chicago, IL: University of Chicago Press.

Dorph, R., Goldstein, D., Lee, S., Lepori, K., Schneider, S., & Venkatesan, S. (2007). *The status of science education in the Bay Area* (Research brief). Retrieved from the Lawrence Hall of Science, University of California Berkeley website: http://static.lawrencehallofscience.org/rea/bayareastudy/pdf/final_to_print_research_brief.pdf

DuCharme, C. C. (1993). *Historical roots of the project approach in the United States: 1850–1930*. Paper presented at the Annual Convention of the National Association for the Education of Young Children, Anaheim, CA.

Duschl, R. A., Schweingruber, H. A., & Shouse, A. W. (2007). *Taking science to school: Learning and teaching science in grades K–8*. Washington, DC: National Academies Press.

Eccles, J., Wigfield, A., Harold, R. D., & Blumenfeld, P. (1993). Age and gender differences in children's self- and task perceptions during elementary school. *Child Development, 64*, 830–847.

Edwards, C. P. (2002). Three approaches from Europe: Waldorf, Montessori, and Reggio Emilia. *Early Childhood Research & Practice, 4*(1), 2–14.

Engeström, Y. (1987). *Learning by expanding: An activity-theoretical approach to developmental research*. Helsinki, Finland: Orienta-Konsultit.

Fink, R. (1998). Interest, gender, and literacy development in successful dyslexics. In L. Hoffmann, A. Krapp, L. A. Renninger, & J. Baumert (Eds.), *Interest and learning: Proceedings of the Seeon Conference on interest and gender* (pp. 402–408). Kiel, Germany: IPN.

French, L. A. (2004). Science as the center of a coherent, integrated early childhood curriculum. *Early Childhood Research Quarterly, 19*, 138–149.

Fulp, S. L. (2000). *National survey of science and mathematics education: Status of elementary school science teaching*. Retrieved from http://2000survey.horizon-research.com/reports/elem_science.php

Gallas, K. (1995). *Talking their way into science: Hearing children's questions and theories, and responding with curricula*. New York, NY: Teachers College Press.

Gallenstein, N. L. (2005). Engaging young children in science and mathematics. *Journal of Elementary Science Education, 17*(2), 27–41.

Gelman, R., Brenneman, K., MacDonald, G., & Roman, M. (2010). *Preschool pathways to science: Facilitating scientific ways of thinking, talking, doing, and understanding.* Baltimore, MD: Paul H. Brookes.

Gottfried, A. E., Fleming, J. S., & Gottfried, A. W. (2001). Continuity of academic intrinsic motivation from childhood through late adolescence: A longitudinal study. *Journal of Educational Psychology, 93*(1), 3–13.

Guthrie, J. T. (2004). Teaching for literacy engagement. *Journal of Literacy Research, 36*(1), 1–30.

Guthrie, J. T. (2015). Growth of motivations for cognitive processes of reading. In P. D. Pearson & E. H. Hiebert (Eds.), *Research-based practices for teaching Common Core literacy* (pp. 107–122). New York, NY: Teachers College Press.

Guthrie, J. T., Van Meter, P., McCann, A. D., & Wigfield, A. (1996). Growth of literacy engagement: Changes in motivations and strategies during concept-oriented reading instruction. *Reading Research Quarterly, 31,* 306–332.

Guthrie, J. T., & Wigfield, A. (2005). The role of motivation and engagement in reading comprehension assessment. In S. G. Paris & S. A. Stahl (Eds.), *Children's reading comprehension and assessment* (pp. 187–214). Mahway, NJ: Lawrence Erlbaum.

Guthrie, J. T., Wigfield, A., & You, W. (2012). Instructional contexts for engagement and achievement in reading. In S. L. Chirstenson, A. L. Reschly, & C. Wylie (Eds.), *Handbook of Research on Student Engagement* (pp. 601–634). New York, NY: Springer.

Halvorsen, A. L., Duke, N. K., Brugar, K. A., Block, M. K., Strachan, S. L., Berka, M. B., & Brown, J. M. (2012). Narrowing the achievement gap in second-grade social studies and content area literacy: The promise of a project-based approach. *Theory & Research in Social Education, 40*(3), 198–229.

Han, J., & Yin, H. (2016). Teacher motivation: Definition, research development and implications for teachers. *Cogent Education, 2016*(3), 1–18.

Helm, J. H., & Katz, L. G. (2011). *Young investigators: The project approach in the early years* (2nd ed.). New York, NY: Teachers College Press.

Hertzog, N. B. (2007). Transporting pedagogy: Implementing the project approach in two first-grade classrooms. *Journal of Advanced Academics, 18,* 530–564.

Herzberg, F. (2003, January). One more time: How do you motivate employees? *Harvard Business Review, January 2003,* 87–96.

Hidi, S. (2001). Interest, reading, and learning: Theoretical and practical considerations. *Educational Psychology Review, 13*(3), 191–209.

Hidi, S., & Renninger, K. A. (2006). The four-phase model of interest development. *Educational Psychologist, 41*(2), 111–127.

Hill, L. T., Stremmel, A. J., & Fu, V. R. (2005). *Teaching as inquiry: Rethinking curriculum in early childhood education.* New York, NY: Pearson Education.

Kaldi, S., Filippatou, D., & Govaris, C. (2011). Project-based learning in primary schools: Effects on pupils' learning and attitudes. *Education 3–13, 39*(1), 35–47.

Kashdan, T. B., Rose, P., & Fincham, F. D. (2004). Curiosity and exploration: Facilitating positive subjective experiences and personal growth opportunities. *Journal of Personality Assessment, 82*(3), 291–305.

Katz, L., & Chard, S. C. (2000). *Engaging children's minds: The project approach* (2nd ed.). Stamford, CT: Ablex.

Katz, L. G., & McClellan, D. E. (1997). *Fostering children's social competence: The teacher's role. Volume 8 of the NAEYC Research into Practice Series*. Washington, DC: National Association for the Education of Young Children.

Kilpatrick, W. H. (1918). *The project method: The use of the purposeful act in the educative process*. New York, NY: Teachers College.

Kirschner, P. A., Sweller, J., & Clark, R. E. (2006). Why minimal guidance during instruction does not work: An analysis of the failure of constructivist, discovery, problem-based, experiential, and inquiry-based teaching. *Educational Psychologist, 41*(2), 75–86.

Kitching, K., Morgan, M., & O'Leary, M. (2009). It's the little things: Exploring the importance of commonplace events for early-career teachers' motivation. *Teachers and Teaching, 15*(1), 43–58.

Krapp, A., Hidi, S., & Renninger, K. A. (1992). Interest, learning and development. In K. A. Renninger, S. Hidi, & A. Krapp (Eds.), *The role of interest in learning and development* (pp. 3–25). Hillsdale, NJ: Lawrence Erlbaum.

Lepper, M. R., Corpus, J. H., & Iyengar, S. S. (2005). Intrinsic and extrinsic motivational orientations in the classroom: Age differences and academic correlates. *Journal of Educational Psychology, 97*(2), 184–196.

Lindfors, J. W. (1999). *Children's inquiry: Using language to make sense of the world*. New York, NY: Teachers College Press.

Locke, E. A. (2002. Motivation, cognition, and action: An analysis of studies of task goals and knowledge. *Applied Psychology: An International Review, 49*(3), 408–429.

Locke, E. A., & Latham, G. P. (2002). Building a practically useful theory of goal setting and task motivation: A 35-year odyssey. *American Psychology, 75*, 705–717.

McDaniel, M. A., Waddill, P. J., Finstad, K., & Bourg, T. (2000). The effects of text-based interest on attention and recall. *Journal of Educational Psychology, 92*(3), 492–502.

Metz, K. E. (2008). Narrowing the gulf between the practices of science and the elementary school science classroom. *Elementary School Journal, 109*(2), 138–161.

Mitchell, M. (1993). Situational interest: Its multifaceted structure in the secondary school mathematics classroom. *Journal of Educational Psychology, 85*, 424–436.

Neuman, S. B., & Roskos, K. (2005). Whatever happened to developmentally appropriate practice in early literacy. *Young Children, 60*, 1–6.

Nolen, S. B. (2007). Young children's motivation to read and write: Development in social contexts. *Cognition and Instruction, 25*, 219–270.

Patrick, H., & Mantzicopoulos, P. (2015). Young children's motivation for learning science. In K. Cabe Trundle & M. Saçkes (Eds.), *Research in early childhood science education* (pp. 7–34). New York, NY: Springer.

Pattison, S. (2014). *Exploring the foundations of science interest development in early childhood* (Doctoral dissertation). Retrieved from https://ir.library.oregonstate.edu/xmlui/handle/1957/54783

Perry, N., Turner, J. C., & Meyer, D. K. (2006). Student Engagement in the classroom. In P. Alexander & P. Winne (Eds.), *Handbook of Educational Psychology* (pp. 327–348). Mahwah, NJ: Erlbaum.

Peterson, S. M., & French, L. (2008). Supporting young children's explanations through inquiry science in preschool. *Early Childhood Research Quarterly, 23*, 395–408.

Phillips, D. A., & Shonkoff, J. P. (Eds.). (2000). *From neurons to neighborhoods: The science of early childhood development.* Washington, DC: National Academies Press.

Pressley, M., Allington, R. L., Wharton-McDonald, R., Block, C. C., & Morrow, L. M. (Eds.). (2001). *Learning to read: Lessons from exemplary first-grade classrooms.* New York, NY: The Guilford Press.

Renninger, K. A. (1989). Individual patterns in children's play interests. In L. T. Winegar (Ed.), *Social interaction and the development of children's understanding* (pp. 147–172). Norwood, NJ: Ablex.

Renninger, K. A. (1992). Individual interest and development: Implications for theory and practice. In K. A. Renninger, S. Hidi, & A. Krapp (Eds.), *The role of interest in learning and development* (pp. 361–376). Hillsdale, NJ: Lawrence Erlbaum Associates.

Renninger, K. A. (2000). Individual interest and its implication for understanding intrinsic motivation. In C. Sansone & J. M. Harackiewicz (Eds.), *Intrinsic and extrinsic motivation: The search for optimal motivation and performance* (pp. 373–404). San Diego, CA: Academic Press.

Renninger, K. A. (2007). *Interest and motivation in informal science learning* (Learning Science in Informal Environments Commissioned Paper). Board on Science Education, The National Academies.

Renninger, K. A., & Hidi, S. (2016). *The power of interest for motivation and engagement.* New York, NY: Routledge.

Renninger, K.A., Hidi, S., & Krapp, A. (Eds.). (1992). *The role of interest in learning and development.* Hillsdale, NJ: Erlbaum.

Renninger, K. A., & Su, S. (2012). Interest and its development. In R. M. Ryan (Ed.), *The Oxford handbook of human motivation* (pp. 167–187). Oxford, England: Oxford University Press.

Salili, F., Chiu, C., & Hong, Y. (Eds.) (2001). *Student motivation: The culture and context of learning.* New York, NY: Kluwer Academic/Plenum.

Samarapungavan, A., Mantzicopoulos, P., & Patrick, H. (2008). Learning science through inquiry in kindergarten. *Science Education, 92*(5), 868–908.

Saul, W. (Ed.). (2004). *Crossing borders in literacy and science instruction.* Newark, DE: International Reading Association.

Schunk, D. H., & Mullen, C. A. (2012). Self-efficacy as an engaged learner. In S. L. Christenson, A. L. Reschly, & C. Wylie (Eds.), *Handbook of research on student engagement* (pp. 219–235). New York, NY: Springer.

Schunk, D. H., Pintrich, P. R., & Meece, J. L. (2008). *Motivation in education: Theory, research, and applications.* Upper Saddle River, NJ: Pearson/Merrill Prentice Hall.

Silvia, P. J. (2008). Interest: The curious emotion. *Current Directions in Psychological Science, 17*(1), 57–60.

Skinner, E. A., Kindermann, T. A., Connell, J. P., & Wellborn, J. G. (2009). Engagement and disaffection as organizational constructs in the dynamics of motivational development. In K. R. Wentzel & A. Wigfield (Eds.), *Handbook of motivation at school* (pp. 223–245). New York, NY: Routledge.

Stipek, D. J. (1996). Motivation and instruction. In D. C. Berliner & R. C. Calfee (Eds.), *Handbook of educational psychology* (pp. 85–113). New York, NY: Routledge.

Stipek, D. J. (2001). Classroom context effects on young children's motivation. In F. Salili, C. Chiu, & Y. Hong (Eds.) *Student motivation: The culture and context of learning* (pp. 273–292). New York, NY: Kluwer Academic/Plenum.

Stipek, D. (2002). *Motivation to learn: Integrating theory and practice* (4th ed.). Boston, MA: Allyn & Bacon.

Swan, E. A. (2003). *Concept-oriented reading instruction: Engaging classrooms, lifelong learners.* New York, NY: Guilford Press.

Turner, J. C. (1995). The influence of classroom contexts on young children's motivation for literacy. *Reading Research Quarterly, 30*(3), 410–441.

Turner, J., & Paris, S. G. (1995). How literacy tasks influence children's motivation for literacy. *The Reading Teacher, 48*(8), 662–673.

Turner, J. C., & Patrick, H. (2008). How does motivation develop and why does it change? Reframing motivation research. *Educational Psychologist, 43*(3), 119–131.

Walker, R. A., Pressick-Kilborn, K., Arnold, L. S., & Sainsbury, E. J. (2004). Investigating motivation in context: Developing Sociocultural Perspectives. *European Psychologist, 9*(4), 245–256.

Wells, G. (1986). *The meaning makers: Children learning language and using language to learn.* Portsmouth, NH: Heinemann Educational Books.

Wells, G. (Ed.). (2001). *Action, talk, and text: Learning and teaching through inquiry* (Vol. 16). New York, NY: Teachers College Press.

Wharton-McDonald, R. (2001). Andy Schultheis. In M. Pressley, R. L. Allington, R. Wharton-McDonald, C. Collins Block, & L. Mandel Morrow (Eds.), *Learning to read: Lessons from exemplary first-grade classrooms* (pp. 115–137). New York, NY: Guilford Press.

Whitin, P. (2007). The ties that bind: Emergent literacy and scientific inquiry. *Language Arts, 85*(1), 20–30.

Wigfield, A., & Eccles, J. S. (2002). The development of competence beliefs, expectancies for success, and achievement values from childhood through adolescence. In A. Wigfield & J. S. Eccles (Eds.), *Development of achievement motivation* (pp. 91–120). New York, NY: Academic Press.

CHAPTER 7

FOSTERING CHILDREN'S INTRINSIC MOTIVATION IN PRESCHOOL

Wilfried Smidt and Stefanie Kraft

INTRODUCTION

This review focuses on an important issue in the field of early childhood education, as it refers to aspects of fostering the intrinsic motivation of children in preschool. Since birth, children's interactions in their environment play a crucial role as they lead to learning and related acquisition of knowledge. Children's intrinsic motivation for learning can be characterized in such a way that it does not require external inducements (e.g., rewards and praise, as would be the case for extrinsic motivation) but rather is inherent within the child—that is, it becomes apparent from a strong curiosity for learning. In contrast to extrinsic motivation, intrinsic motivation has been considered as more desirable and shown to be associated with better learning results (Deci, Koestner, & Ryan, 1999). Intrinsically motivated children are more likely to perceive greater pleasure of learning, they tend to utilize strategies that enable a deeper appreciation and application of what has been learned, they acquire greater knowledge, they feel more comfortable about themselves and they are more likely to persist in goal-directed tasks (Carlton & Winsler, 1998).

Contemporary Perspectives on Research on
Motivation in Early Childhood Education, pp. 155–175
Copyright © 2019 by Information Age Publishing
All rights of reproduction in any form reserved.

However, somewhat in contrast to the well-documented relevance of children's intrinsic motivation in learning, there are hints which indicate that children's intrinsic motivation is likely to decrease during school time (Stipek, 1996). Previous work suggests that, although there are individual differences already in preschool, children's intrinsic motivation is relatively high at the beginning of school and subsequently declines, particularly when children have finished elementary school (Broussard & Garrison, 2004) (see Lai, 2011, for a brief overview). Consequently, the first years of a child's life—until they enter school—have been considered as particularly important to boost children's intrinsic motivation in order to prepare them for successful learning in school and later life: "The early childhood years are crucial for establishing robust intrinsic motivational orientations which will last a lifetime" (Carlton & Winsler, 1998, p. 159). More generally speaking, the maintenance and strengthening of children's intrinsic motivation claims supportive educational environments.

Recognizing this crucial significance, empirical studies and theoretical work focus on children's intrinsic motivation in the early years in order to investigate potentials and obstacles for successful fostering of children's intrinsic learning motivation (Stipek, Feiler, Daniels, & Milburn, 1995; Carlton & Winsler, 1998; Nolen, 2001; Wu, 2003; Natale, Viljaranta, Lerkkanen, Poikkeus, & Nurmi, 2009; Patrick, Mantzicopoulos, & Samarapungavan, 2009). The present contribution points in this direction and aims to recapitulate and critically discuss previous research findings on the possibilities and barriers related to the promotion of children's intrinsic motivation in preschool. Since the contribution is conceptualized as a review, and restricted space is available, we decided to limit our focus on the fostering of children's intrinsic motivation in *preschools* and comparable institutions (e.g., day care centers) that are typically attended by children aged between 3 to 5 or 6 years. This prioritization can also be supported by the fact that in many (industrial) states, non-familial institutions such as preschools have been considered as a regular part of children's educational biography; that is, most children of preschool-age attend a non-familial institution. For instance, in Austria, more than 90% of the 3- to 5-year-old children join a preschool or a comparable institution.

For the purpose of structuring and condensing the multiplicity of characteristics, which may be conducive or rather hindering with regard to the fostering of children's intrinsic motivation in preschool, we refer to a framework utilized by the German educational researcher Andreas Helmke (2007). This framework—which might not be known to many international readers interested in preschool education—was initially developed due to the explanation of differences in teaching quality in schools (Prenzel, 2007). Recently, the framework has also been adapted to the preschool sector (e.g., Smidt, 2015). Although focusing on the quality of educational processes in the first place, a central component of this framework, which makes it particularly valuable for the purpose of this contribution, refers to student's intrinsic learning motivation and its dependency from several personal and contextual variables. The framework may help to outline four broader sets of characteristics, which are assumed to be directly or indirectly related to children's intrinsic motivation: didactical characteristics, pre-school teacher's personal characteristics, children's personal characteristics and contextual characteristics of the preschool class. The structure of the review is as follows: Section 2 introduces children's intrinsic motivation as a relevant attribute associated with the number of child-related outcomes. Section 3 constitutes the core element of this review—that is, concerning the promotion of children's intrinsic motivation in preschool—are illus-trated. To conclude, in Section 4, we will critically discuss the considered research findings with respect to implications for further research and—if possible—educational practice.

INTRINSIC MOTIVATION

If the objective is to specify intrinsic motivation, it is sensible to initially refer to broader definitions of motivation. Motivation can be considered as multifaceted and quite complex construct (Mata, 2011) that comprises a constellation of several interrelated components, such as interests, beliefs, values, perceptions, and actions (Lai, 2011). From a comprehensive under-standing, motivation refers to underlying reasons for behavior (Guay et al., 2010) and people's motivation may be heterogeneous in terms of these underlying reasons (Mata, 2011). Similarly, Broussard and Garrison (2004, p. 106) stated that motivation refers to "the attribute that moves us to do or not to do something." In order to specify the underlying reasons for behavior and activities, a distinction between extrinsic and intrinsic motivation is often made. In the case of extrinsic motivation, which is not in the focus of the present contribution, the reasons for activities refer to a variety of external reinforcements that can be material (e.g., money, marks, privileges) or immaterial (e.g., praise, respect, trust) (Carlton & Winsler, 1998; Lai, 2011). In contrast, relying on the self-determination theory of Deci and Ryan (Deci & Ryan, 1985; Deci et al., 1999), intrinsic motivation can be described as the motivation that boosts, sustains and guides activities through personal curiosity, interest, satisfaction and joy, which stem from the innate need of the experience of competence and self-determination. Importantly, with regard to intrinsic motivation in early childhood, secure relationships with caregivers are considered to be crucial, since they encourage and motivate children to autonomously explore their environments. With increasing age and developmental status (for instance, in terms of the development of verbal communication skills), children's striving for autonomy increases as they seek to further regulate the initiation and direction of their actions (Carlton & Winsler, 1998). As an activity is motivated by internal inducements, intrinsic motivation is related to a higher level of self-determination compared with extrinsic motivation (Lai, 2011). A substantial body of research exists that points to positive relations with a number child-related outcomes and serves to substantiate its importance (Lai, 2011). For example, research conducted in schools indicates that academic intrinsic motivation is relatively stable from childhood to high school years and that the extent of intrinsic motivation is positively related to subsequent intrinsic motivation (Gottfried, Fleming, & Gottfried, 2001). Furthermore, intrinsic motivation has been shown to be positively associated with school achievement in reading and math (Broussard & Garrison, 2004). In addition, study findings reveal positive relations between a student's intrinsic motivation to learn and their well-being at school as well as a decreased likelihood of dropping out when their intrinsic motivation was higher (see Froiland, Oros, Smith, & Hirchert, 2012, for an overview). Because of the empirically observable significance of the intrinsic motivation described above, we would like to shed light on conditional factors of intrinsic motivation.

FOSTERING CHILDREN'S INTRINSIC MOTIVATION

The main question of this section is: Which factors have to be present to enhance intrinsic motivation? Following a pertinent framework considered by Helmke (2007), we will refer to four broader sets of variables that, directly or indirectly, may influence children's intrinsic motivation in preschool. One of these sets incorporates didactical characteristics of the educational practices provided in the preschool classroom (e.g., instructional approach, granting of autonomy and freedom, working with peers, task characteristics, forms of evaluation). Thus, we provide an overview of empirical evidences related to relations between didactical characteristics and children's intrinsic motivation (Section 3.1). However, the effects of didactical aspects should not be examined in isolation, since educational practices are embedded in educational institutions in which caregivers and children with individual personal attributes are involved. Furthermore, preschools may be characterized by varying contextual factors. Therefore, when thinking about the prospects of fostering preschool children's intrinsic motivation, factors regarding preschool teacher's personal characteristics (Section 3.2), children's personal characteristics (Section 3.3) and contextual characteristics of the preschool classes (Section 3.4) must also be taken into account. Consequently, we will focus on the three latter sets of variables that may have an indirect influence on children's intrinsic motivation as well.

Didactical Characteristics

A couple of studies investigate the direct influences of didactical characteristics on children's intrinsic motivation. While referring to these characteristics, these studies utilize different methodologies: some of them deal with didactic concepts in a broader way (different instructional approaches), and others emphasize particular aspects of such didactical concepts (granting of autonomy and freedom, cooperation and collaboration with peers, characteristics of tasks, forms of evaluation). In this section we want to give an overview of studies focusing on the impact of didactic concepts on intrinsic motivation. Subsequently, we focus on studies that investigated particular aspects of these didactic concepts and their significance for intrinsic motivation. Studies focusing on didactic concepts in a broad way pay attention to *instructional approaches* in preschools. They deal with specific preschool teaching practices and the (implicit or explicit) caregiver's attitude behind these practices. Didactical concepts in which these practices and attitudes are embedded can be located on a continuum ranging from direct instruction focusing on basic skills to approaches, such as independent studying, that is, "instructions that involve children in more open-ended, child-initiated activities" (Chiatovich & Stipek, 2016, p. 1). Siraj-Blatchford (2007) claimed that, regardless of the applied didactical concept, each concept is aimed at achieving a high level of intrinsic motivation and participation in learning processes.

The effects of different instructional approaches in preschools on achievement outcomes having been sufficiently investigated so far, yet the relations between instructional approaches and factors regarding motivation have not been assessed nearly as frequently. Stipek and colleagues (1995) investigated effects of different instructional approaches in preschools on basic skill achievements and motivation-related measures. The findings demonstrate that "children in child-centered programs were favored on most of the motivation related measures" (p. 220). Namely, children in child-centered programs rated their abilities on number and letter/reading skills higher, had higher expectations for success, chose tasks with a higher level of difficulty, showed less dependency on adults for permission and approval, evidenced more pride in their accomplishment and claimed to worry less about school.

Moreover, didactical orientation regarding the degree of direct instruction abounds in the implementation and use of specific curricula that aim to support aspects of development. Tzurial, Kaniel, and Kanner (1999) examined positive effects of the "Bright Start" program on the development of task-intrinsic motivation. The Bright Start Curriculum is "designed to increase learning effectiveness and prepare children with the cognitive tools for school learning" (p. 111). Among other goals, Bright Start aims to develop and increase task-intrinsic motivation. The core of the program forms seven cognitive instructional units that focus on preschool children's cognitive functioning (e.g., number concepts, comparison, classification). Children who participated in the Bright Start program showed higher task-intrinsic motivation than children in the comparison group. These results show that, in contrast to findings from Stipek et al. (1995), positive effects of more instructive learning settings can be found.

Patrick and colleagues (2009) investigated whether inquiry-based science instruction influences children's motivation for learning science in a positive way. Inquiry-based learning implicates a "process of constructing, evaluating, and sharing knowledge" (p. 182) in which children are given the opportunity to be active learners. The authors "investigate children's motivation for science by examining reports of their beliefs or perceptions of themselves (i.e., their competence and liking)" (p. 167). Children who participated in a program focusing on inquiry-based learning perceived their science competence as being higher/greater than children who attended regular preschool classrooms where science lessons were not inquiry-based. Moreover, children who experienced science in an inquiry-based way liked science more than children who received regular science instruction. Pakarinen et al. (2008) investigated the effects of instructional approaches on intrinsic learning motivation in preschool children by analyzing classroom quality. Three domains of classroom interaction were examined: emotional support, classroom organization and instructional support. The results show that the quality of classroom organization predicted children's learning motivation. Children's learning motivation was higher if the quality of classroom organization increased. Indicators of high quality *classroom organization* include the following: *behavior management* (i.e., proactive rather than reactive management, including rules and expectations that were clearly communicated and consistent praise for meeting expectations); *productivity* (i.e., a classroom in which everyone is involved in learning activities and everyone knows what is expected of them), and *instructional learning formats* (i.e., formats that provide interesting and stimulating materials by using different modalities and by actively engaging students) (Center for Early Education and Development, n.d.).

The studies introduced so far investigated didactic concepts in a broad way and in terms of diverse instructional approaches. The following studies take a closer look at specific facets of didactic concepts and their impacts on children's intrinsic motivation. For instance, the degree to which *autonomy and freedom in choosing learning content, methods, and goals* is granted was investigated by Wu (2003). The study examined whether preschool children were more intrinsically motivated to learn a second language (L2) if they were exposed to an innovative teaching method, which is based on instructional strategies that have been developed in line with an extension of the framework of L2 intrinsic motivation based on self determination theory (SDT) (Deci & Ryan, 1985). This teaching method is characterized by a predictive learning environment that provides necessary instructional support, open-ended activity types that encourage learners' creativity and opportunities for practicing individual learning strategies by autonomous choosing a preferred physical and social learning environment. It is also characterized by providing learning material that meets learners' interests and daily lives and an evaluation form that is informative, emphasizes self-improvement and attributes success or failure to controllable variables (e.g., effort and learning strategies) rather than on uncontrollable variables (e.g., luck or task difficulty) (see Wu, 2003, pp. 508–509). Freedom in choosing learning content, methods and outcomes had positive effects on children's perceived autonomy, which, in turn, predicted children's intrinsic motivation.

Gutman and Sulzby (1999) examined low-income African American preschool children's intrinsic motivation in autonomy-supportive versus controlling interactions during an emergent writing task. In the autonomy-supportive context, the child is allowed to make his or her own choices. The teacher indicates that he or she listens to and understands the child. His guidance is more informational than controlling. Results suggest that children in the autonomy-supportive context, where they are allowed to make choices, showed more interest in writing than children in the controlling interaction context. Moreover, they showed more independent mastery in an autonomy-supportive context after initially being in a controlling context. Both interest and mastery as well as children's statements regarding their competence were considered as operationalization of motivation. Carlton and Winsler (1998) attempt to explain positive effects of autonomy-supportive environments by referring to Deci and Ryan (1987). The latter indicate that autonomy is associated with a feeling of control about own actions and that autonomy-supportive tasks and environments therefore enhance a feeling of self-determination.

Furthermore, *cooperation and collaboration with peers* is an aspect of didactic concepts that may influence children's intrinsic motivation. Nolen (2001) made an ethnographic study in preschool that focused on the interdependency between children's literacy motivation and classroom literacy culture. Results show that if reading and writing activities varied and were meaningful (in terms of being connected to real life) and supported by student assistance and collaboration, children's interest in reading and writing were not diminished. With peers helping or tutoring them, most children stuck to their tasks and progressed. A study by Mata (2011) showed that preschool children are highly motivated to learn how to read and write. In discussing these results, she stated the fact that children in preschools are lacking the experience of comparison and competition with other children may explain the high levels of intrinsic motivation. Stipek (1996), after reviewing some findings regarding the negative effects of competition on motivation, argued that it was, in particular, the long-term application of competition that might focus students' attention on external reasons for engaging in a task and away from intrinsic interest. Thus, they may be less likely to voluntarily return to the activity after engaging in competition.

The characteristics of tasks constitute another crucial point that may exert influence on children's intrinsic motivation. Stipek (1996) describes four qualities of tasks that are required for children's intrinsically motivated engagement in tasks. Tasks should have a *moderate level of difficulty* and should vary (in terms of *novelty and complexity*). Moreover, tasks should be adapted to the personal interests of children (in terms of *personal meaningfulness*), and the form of *instruction of a task* should be encouraging rather than fraught with negative comments. Wu (2003) described above indicates a moderately challenging task as well as necessary instructional support to be predictive for children's perceived competence. Perceived competence, in turn, has been identified as a moderating variable that correlates with intrinsic motivation. Qu and Ong (2016) also focus on a task-related topic. They examined whether reminders to think about alternatives during tasks have an influence on preschool children's cognitive flexibility, intrinsic motivation and mood. Results show that the source of the reminder, being either a tester who has introduced the task to the child or a partner who participated together with the child in the task, moderates the impact of the reminders on intrinsic motivation. Children who were reminded of alternatives during a task by a partner were significantly more intrinsically motivated than children who were either reminded by the tester or were not reminded at all.

There is another aspect regarding didactic concepts we would like to mention, that is, the *forms of evaluation*. Here, we subsume different forms of evaluation with regards to attribution as well as rewards. Stipek (1996) indicates that external evaluations can diminish children's intrinsic interest because they shift their attention toward external expectations. Nevertheless, the nature of evaluation plays an important role. If the evaluation contains information about competencies or steps needed for improvement, it is less likely that it will decrease intrinsic motivation. Evaluation that rates individual mastery is also more likely to maintain intrinsic motivation than competitive or normative evaluation. Wu (2003) found that an evaluation that emphasizes self-improvement influences children's perceived competence positively, which, in turn, effects children's intrinsic motivation.

Natale et al. (2009) investigated the relationship and interdependency between teachers' causal attributions and children's reading-related task motivation and performance. They assume two possible effective directions. On the one hand, children's task motivation may influence teachers' causal attributions. On the other hand, teachers' attributions, which may be expressed in their emotional responses towards the child and in their classroom practices and instruction, may be associated with children's motivation. The authors found that a high level of children's task motivations at the beginning of the preschool year predicted the teacher's attribution of success to ability and effort (both internal causes) later on during the preschool year. In turn, this ability and effort attribution predicted children's task motivation at the end of the preschool year. In contrast, teachers' attributions of the child's success to task easiness or to teachers' help (both external causes) decreased children's motivation later on. If children failed tasks, and the teacher attributes failure to a lack of effort, children's task motivation was diminished. Furthermore, higher levels of task motivation at the beginning of the preschool year corresponded to teachers attributing failures to task difficulty less. If teachers attributed children's failure to lacking teachers' or parental help, task motivation decreased later on.

The effects of rewards on intrinsic motivation has been studied extensively. Stipek (1996) claims that rewards are the most thoroughly researched factor believed to influence intrinsic motivation. Indeed, there does exist a large body of research on rewards, and most of the studies have shown that external rewards decrease intrinsic motivation (see Deci et al., 1999, for a review). However, effects or rewards may differ depending on the specific application of rewards. Deci and Ryan (1985) distinguish between the controlling and the information function of rewards. Rewards employed to control behavior can undermine personal autonomy and, therefore, undermine intrinsic motivation. Rewards in which the information value is salient may have more positive effects on motivation. "The competence feedback implicit in praise is presumably why, in most studies, praise, although external, does not reduce intrinsic motivation" (Stipek, 1996, p. 97).

Studies in the 1970s (Anderson, Manoogian, & Reznick, 1976; Dollinger & Thelen, 1978; Lepper, Greene, & Nisbett, 1973) tested a so-called "overjustification" hypothesis, which proposes that children who are initial intrinsically motivated shed these motivations if an extrinsic reward is added. This hypothesis has been largely confirmed. Thus, children that expected a reward for engaging in an activity showed less subsequent intrinsic motivation than children who received a reward unexpectedly or did not get a reward at all (Lepper et al., 1973). Anderson et al. (1976) confirmed the overjustification hypothesis for tangible rewards (e.g., money, awards). However, verbal reinforcement did not have an overjustification effect and even enhanced intrinsic motivation. Dollinger and Thelen (1978), in turn, found negative effects of tangible and of self-administered rewards but not of verbal or of symbolic rewards.

A recent study (Alvarez & Booth, 2014) shows that preschool children are more motivated to engage in a task if they received knowledge-infused rewards. Children who completed a motor task and afterwards received rewards in the form of causally rich explanations of novel pictures were engaged in the tasks longer (more trials) than children who were provided with a causally weak explanation, no explanation or tangible rewards. The authors explained the positive effect of knowledge-infused rewards by stressing that these rewards redirect attention in a meaningful way back to the task and are in line with the pleasure of learning. A study that focuses on effects of rewards on intrinsic motivation of prosociality was conducted by Ulber, Hamann, and Tomasello (2016). They found negative effects of material rewards on motivation to act prosocial, namely, to regularize unfair resource allocations in different types of sharing situations. If the children received praise for sharing something with others or received no reaction, children's intrinsic motivations to share were maintained. Summarizing this section, we can conclude that there is a body of research, which highlights the importance of didactical characteristics to foster preschool children's motivation. However, regarding Helmke's framework (2007), there are other sets of variables that should be taken into account as well when looking for strategies to foster intrinsic motivation. We are going to take a closer look at these variables in the following sections.

Preschool Teacher's Personal Characteristics

In contrast to the importance of didactical characteristics for the fostering of children's intrinsic motivation in preschool, which is documented by several studies that directly focus on intrinsic motivation, far less is known about the role of diverse personal characteristics of preschool teachers, which may be related to didactical aspects (and in a broader sense, to educational practices) in preschool. In addition, this is rather indirectly associated with the development of children's intrinsic motivation. Due to the lack of research findings that directly refer to intrinsic motivation in preschool, we exemplify some more broadly scoped studies, which nonetheless may substantiate the general significance of preschool teacher's personal characteristics. In this regard, vocational qualification, professional experience as well as competencies in terms of knowledge, beliefs, motivational orientations and self-regulating-skills will be considered.

The importance of *vocational qualification* of preschool teachers for the quality of educational practices is widely debated. For instance, a review of studies conducted by Whitebook (2003) suggests that a preschool teacher's education at a college degree level seems a quite good condition to achieve a high educational quality in preschools in terms of developmental appropriate practices, as it has been captured with well-proven standardized observation instruments. Whitebook argued, at that time, that putting preschool education at the bachelor's level remains an academic question as long as in-depth questions about optimal characteristics of preschool teacher training lying behind formal requirements have not been clarified. Findings of Early et al. (2007) point in the same direction. Focusing on the relation between an academic degree (bachelor's or higher) and the quality of educational practices in preschool classes, the authors reanalyzed seven large-scale studies conducted in the United States. The results implicated no substantial associations between preschool teachers' academic qualifications and educational quality, and the authors suggest,

> that policies focused solely on increasing teachers' education will not suffice for improving classroom quality or maximizing children's academic gains. Instead, raising the effectiveness of early childhood education likely will require a broad range of professional development activities and supports targeted toward teachers' interactions with children. (p. 558)

Another characteristic of preschool teachers that has been considered in the context of discussions about the improvement of educational practices refers to *professional experience*. Study findings on this topic are inconsistent, and different explanations have been provided so far. Some research findings of the National Institute of Child Health and Human Development and Early Child Care Research Network indicates that more experienced preschool teachers receive a better classroom quality. This suggests that professionally experienced pedagogues tend to better adjust their educational practices according to standards of developmentally appropriate practices than their less experiences counterparts. In contrast, some research indicates negative relations between preschool teachers' professional experience and educational quality. An explanation refers to the high workload of preschool teachers and a corresponding decline of work motivation (e.g., Smidt, 2012, for an overview).

Another broad component of preschool teacher's personal characteristics that has been also discussed with regard to relations with educational practices in preschools refers to *competencies* in terms of knowledge, beliefs, motivational orientations, and self-regulating-skills. However, the state of research is particularly scarce. This is particularly true with regard to knowledge, which is often operationalized in terms of general pedagogical knowledge (i.e., knowledge about the basics of education, such as children's learning processes, early childhood development and diagnostic or philosophy of education), subject-matter content knowledge (i.e., knowledge about a specific subject matter, such as the history or theories) and pedagogical content knowledge (i.e., knowledge about didactical principles of the pedagogical work, such as developmentally appropriate practices, pedagogical concepts in early childhood education and learning opportunities in preschool). The research base is small; there have been only a few studies, which partly indicate rather large knowledge deficits of preschool teachers (Anders, 2012). Reliable findings on relations between knowledge and educational practices in preschool are still greatly lacking to date.

Turning to beliefs, pedagogues working in preschools hold multifaceted beliefs about issues in children's education, which are supposed to serve as filters, frameworks and guides for their educational practices (Fives & Buehl, 2012). Research has revealed relations between educational beliefs and educational practices and can support these assumptions. Relevant components of preschool teachers' educational beliefs include general educational approaches, tasks of preschools, personal professional roles, the importance of subject matters and children's learning processes (Anders, 2012). In addition, motivational orientations and self-regulating skills such as emotional attitudes, locus of control and self-efficacy have also been considered to be related to educational practices (e.g., Kunter, Kleickmann, Klusmann, & Richter, 2013). For instance, in a Turkish study, preschool teachers reported having low self-efficacy expectations for teaching math. In close relation to this, a majority of preschool teachers were believed to ineffectively teach math in preschool (Takunyaci & Takunyaci, 2014). Also, explicitly referring to motivation, Pakarinen et al. (2010) reported that preschool teachers' stress levels negatively predicted intrinsic learning motivation in preschool children.

Finally, *personality traits* such as the Big Five (i.e., agreeableness, conscientiousness, extraversion, neuroticism, openness) have been considered to manifest themselves in "characteristic adaptations" (McCrae & Costa, 1996, p. 69), such as educational activities. Relations to educational practices have been particularly stressed in research that focus on school teachers (Kunter et al., 2013), but far less is known with regard to preschool teachers. Few studies generally found differences between the personality traits of preschool teachers and normative samples in terms of higher openness and agreeableness in the preschool teacher sample. In addition, initial findings may provide first hints on the predictive importance of preschool teachers' personality traits in their educational practices, although the pattern of results is fairly blurred (Smidt, 2016).

Children's Personal Characteristics

Somewhat similar to the importance of preschool teachers' personal characteristics, the research base on relations of children's personal characteristics and their intrinsic motivation seems also relatively scarce. Focusing on children's personal characteristics seems to be important, because intrinsic motivation is assumed to be interrelated with other personal variables such as—for instance—beliefs, expectancies, goal orientations, interests, beliefs and self-efficacy (Lai, 2011; Mata, 2011) which themselves may correspond with experiences related to characteristics such as children's gender or family background. We can refer to a few studies that relate to children's intrinsic motivation or closely related concepts. In this regard, we will report findings on the importance of the following child-related characteristics: gender, family background, emotions and feelings and personality. Regarding conceivable *gender* differences in intrinsic motivation, the findings are inconsistent. Focusing on preschool children, Mata (2011) found no noticeable differences in intrinsic motivation in reading and writing between boys and girls. However, a differing pattern of results has been reported by Guay et al. (2010), who investigated young elementary school students and found that girls had higher intrinsic motivation in writing and reading, whereas boys were shown to have higher intrinsic motivation in mathematics.

Some other studies refer to the importance of *family background* in terms of home children's learning experiences, which have been considered as particularly important. A study focusing on Chinese preschoolers indicates that parental modelling on reading, the number of books available in the family and the number of years parents spent to teach their children Chinese characters was positively related to children's intrinsic motivation in reading (Zhou & Salili, 2008). Findings from a Germany study also point to the significance of the home learning environment: Richter, Lehrl, and Weinert (2016) longitudinally investigated relations between the observed quality of parent-child-interactions that preschool-aged children received at home and their subsequent enjoyment of learning in elementary school. Their findings indicate that the interaction quality that children experienced positively correlated with enjoyment in the second grade. These findings gain additional importance against the background that a lower socioeconomic status and the language background (at least one parent was a native speaker of a language other than German) corresponded with a lower interaction quality between parents and children.

A Greek study conducted by Stephanou (2014) focuses on children's *emotions and feelings* and possible relations to preschool children's intrinsic learning motivation. Children's feelings were captured in terms of feelings about the recognized quality of their relationship with the preschool teacher, whereas children's emotions referred to questions about how happy and satisfied children were with their preschool teacher. The study findings indicate that children's feelings and emotions were positively related to their intrinsic learning motivation in both literacy and mathematics.

A final characteristic that has also been discussed with regard to the importance to children's intrinsic motivation mentions *personality traits*, which have been often assessed in terms of the Big Five (i.e., agreeableness, conscientiousness, extraversion, neuroticism, and openness) (McCrae & Costa, 1996). Zupančič (2008) examined different personality profiles of preschool-aged children, which were related to their social skills as well as internalizing and externalizing behavior. It has been mentioned that the "early child individual differences [in personality, W.S. and S.K.] foreshadow many positive and negative developmental outcomes" (p. 21). We would like to point out that, although not all of the abovementioned children's characteristics are directly relying on intrinsic motivation, the findings regarding children's gender, family background, emotions, feelings and personality traits can provide additional hints related to children's intrinsic motivation. These aspects should be examined in future studies.

Contextual Characteristics of Preschool Groups

As with preschool teacher's personal characteristics, it is obvious that research focusing on possibilities and barriers of the promotion of children's intrinsic motivation in preschool rarely considers contextual characteristics of the preschool classes, which may frame the educational practices and which may indirectly influence the development of children's intrinsic motivation. We will consider the following contextual characteristics: preschool group size, caregiver-child-ratio and socioeconomic preschool group composition. These variables have been considered as particularly important predictors of educational practices in preschool, and they have also been discussed in terms of "structural quality" (Kuger & Kluczniok, 2008).

The importance of *preschool group size* (i.e., number of children per group) has been discussed over the past several decades (Vandell & Wolfe, 2000). Although legal requirements often define some standards with regard to the group size, preschool group sizes may vary substantially in practice. Summarizing the research findings on the importance of preschool group size for the quality of educational practices, there is evidence that a lower group size (fewer children per group) corresponds with better educational quality in terms of developmental appropriate practices (e.g., Huntsman, 2008; Vandell & Wolfe, 2000). Although it is difficult to separate distinct effects of preschool group size due to associations with other variables (e.g., caregiver-child-ratio), some studies indicate that relations between group size and the quality of educational hold even after controlling for other variables (Vandell & Wolfe, 2000).

Another significant contextual characteristic that is closely related to preschool group size refers to the *caregiver-child-ratio*. As mentioned by Huntsman (2008), there are various ways to calculate the ratio of children to caregiver in child care settings; one of the most common ways is to calculate the number of children per caregiver (or preschool teacher). Summarizing the large body of previous research on relations between caregiver-child-ratio and the quality of education practices in preschool (with very few exceptions), the findings clearly indicate that lower ratios (a smaller number of children per caregiver) is positively associated with the quality of educational practices (e.g., Huntsman, 2008)—that is, "caregivers offer more stimulating, responsive, warm, and supportive care" (Vandell & Wolfe, 2000, p. 14).

We now turn to the final contextual variable—*socioeconomic preschool group composition*—which has been considered as an increasingly important structural characteristic; research findings substantiate its predictive importance for educational practices in preschool classes and as well as preschool children's learning outcomes. A review of U.S.-American research conducted by Reid and Kagan (2015) suggests that the preschool group composition in terms of high proportions of minorities and children from families with low socioeconomic background will likely negatively correspond with children's learning and achievement. Additional research has linked socioeconomic preschool group composition to the quality of educational practices, which, for their part, are associated with the development of children's competencies. For instance, in a German study, Kuger and Kluczniok (2008) found that a higher proportion of children with an immigration background in the preschool group corresponded with lower educational quality; this effect remained apparent after controlling for several other variables. To summarize the previous section: By addressing preschool group size, caregiver-child-ratio and socioeconomic preschool group composition, we aimed to emphasize the significance of contextual characteristics that may have indirect influence on intrinsic motivation of preschool children.

DISCUSSION AND CONCLUSION

There is no dispute that the early childhood years are crucial with regard to the children's intrinsic motivation, which has been shown to be related to a number of important child-related outcomes, such as performance and well-being in school. Bearing this in mind, it is suitable to take a closer look at the possibilities and barriers associated with the promotion of children's intrinsic motivation. We accomplished this by investigating children's intrinsic motivation in preschools, which are a regular part of children's educational biography in many states. After introducing an understanding of intrinsic motivation, we referred to four broader sets of characteristics, which were assumed to provide answers on the issue in question. Subsequently, we will discuss some implications and future research avenues.

With regard to didactical characteristics, we could identify some aspects that have been examined and found to be influential towards children's intrinsic motivation. Studies have focused on autonomy-supportive interaction (Wu, 2003), cooperation and collaboration with peers (Nolen, 2001), specific tasks characteristics (Wu, 2003; Qu & Ong, 2016) and different forms of evaluation (Alvarez & Booth, 2014; Deci et al., 1999; Natale et al., 2009; Ulber et al., 2016; Wu, 2003) with regard to their effects on children's intrinsic motivation. However, the results are fragmentary, and didactical aspects—with regards to their possible effects on children's intrinsic motivation—are not sufficiently examined. Most of the introduced studies focus on very specific didactical characteristics, and very little is known about didactical concepts in a broader sense as well as their influences on intrinsic motivation of children (an exception is Stipek et al., 1995). The ongoing debate about different didactical concepts (ranging from direct instructions to child-directed approaches) and their pros and cons seems to be as yet more rhetorical than empirical. Some authors suggest that the debate about differing instructional concepts "should be framed in less black-and white terms" (Stipek et al., 1995, p. 220) (see also Chiatovich & Stipek, 2006). Carlton and Winsler (1998, p. 164f) highlight that "teachers need to provide structure and assistance, without completely controlling every learning activity. Neither extreme of the totally teacher-directed or the completely child-centered classroom seen in many early childhood programs is optimal for promoting motivation and self-regulation." In any case, more studies that focus on the correlation between didactical concepts and children's intrinsic motivation are desirable.

Regardless of the chosen didactical concepts, it must be kept in mind that didactical approaches or, more particularly, specific tasks or inputs must be developmentally appropriate. Different didactical approaches may vary pertaining to their developmental appropriateness. Burts, Hart, Charlesworth and Kirk (1990) have shown that children in developmentally inappropriate preschools show more stress than children in appropriate preschools. Presumably, stress has a negative impact on intrinsic motivation. Therefore, it is reasoned that didactical approaches must be developmentally appropriate when they should foster children's intrinsic motivation.

As reported, factors regarding classroom quality have effects on children's intrinsic motivation (Pakarinen et al., 2008). Additional research in this field seems necessary. For instance, specific forms of interaction (e.g., sustained-shared thinking, scaffolding, metacognition) may influence the quality of interaction and, therefore, may influence intrinsic motivation. Another research gap we could identify refers to specific developmental areas in which intrinsic motivation has not been investigated so far. Specifically, most of the present studies have focused on motivation for reading, writing or learning a second language. Motivation in other domains of development (e.g., the motivation for mathematical or natural science issues or the motivation for social behavior) has been less examined (notable exceptions are Patrick et al., 2009, and Ulber et al., 2016, respectively).

The same conclusion—that is, a call for further research—can be made with regard to research on the role of children's personal characteristics for their intrinsic motivation. Although the studies considered in Section 3.3. may generally sensitize for the importance of children's characteristics in terms of gender, family background, emotions and feelings, and personality, the findings still suggest an incomplete picture that must be amended by future studies. Bearing in mind the well documented standards on developmentally appropriate practices in preschool, it is crucial that preschool teachers tune their interactions and educational activities to children's individual needs in order to foster them in an adequate way so that they are not completely overtaxed nor underchallenged. Against this background, future studies should further investigate the genuine role of children's individual characteristics; this is particularly true with regard to their personality traits, where the state of research seems to be particularly scarce.

Whereas our review of research on the relevance of didactical characteristics and children's personal characteristics revealed some noticeable findings with respect to preschool-aged children's intrinsic motivation, a quite different picture emerged with regard to preschool teacher's personal characteristics and contextual characteristics of the preschool group. Due to the insufficient number of studies that focus on the importance of preschool teacher's personal skills as well as contextual preschool group characteristics for the fostering of children's intrinsic motivation, we have mainly relied on research that refer to the quality of educational practices in preschool in terms of developmentally appropriate practices (i.e., a stimulating, responsive, warm and supportive care provided by the preschool teacher). This understanding of educational quality has been shown to predict children's subsequent socioemotional and cognitive competencies and comprises many of the didactical aspects considered in Section 3.1. Taken together, the presented research findings provide more or less strong hints for links between vocational qualification, professional experience, competencies (i.e., knowledge, beliefs, motivational orientations and self-regulating-skills) and personality traits to the quality of educational practices.

The same is true with regard to the considered contextual variables group size, caregiver-child-ratio, and socioeconomic preschool group composition. The reservation must be made, however, that the pattern of research findings are partly inconsistent and controversial as is the case with formal vocational education (Whitebook, 2003; Early et al., 2007) and professional experience (Smidt, 2012) or rather preliminary and unclear as it is the case with preschool teachers' competencies in terms of knowledge, beliefs, motivational orientations, and self-regulating-skills (e.g, Anders, 2012; Fives & Buehl, 2012) and personality traits (Smidt, 2016). In a diluted form, this is also true for contextual variables, where it is sometimes difficult to disentangle the genuine predictive role of preschool group size and caregiver-child-ratio, and where additional research on the predictively of socioeconomic preschool group composition is still required (Reid & Kagan, 2015).

However, despite these limitations, the aforementioned findings should have the potential to encourage researchers to further investigate the role of preschool teacher's personal characteristics as well as contextual preschool class characteristics in order to shed more light on possibilities and barriers that relate to the promotion of children's intrinsic motivation in preschool.

REFERENCES

Alvarez, A. L., & Booth, A. E. (2014). Motivated by meaning: Testing the effect of knowledge-infused rewards on preschoolers' persistence. *Child Development, 85*(2), 783–791.

Anders, Y. (2012). *Modelle professioneller Kompetenzen für frühpädagogische Fachkräfte* [Professional competences of early childhood teachers]. München, Germany: Aktionsrat Bildung/VBW.

Anderson, R., Manoogian, S. T., & Reznick, J. S. (1976). The undermining and enhancing of intrinsic motivation in preschool children. *Journal of Personality and Social Psychology, 34*(5), 915–922.

Broussard, S. C., & Garrison, M. E. (2004). The relationship between classroom motivation and academic achievement in elementary school-aged children. *Family and Consumer Sciences Research Journal, 33*(2), 106–120.

Burts, D.C., Hart, C. H., Charlesworth, R., & Kirk, L. (1990). A comparison of frequencies of stress behaviors observed in kindergarten children in classrooms with developmentally appropriate vs. developmentally inappropriate practices. *Early Childhood Research Quarterly, 5*, 407–423.

Carlton, M. P., & Winsler, A. (1998). Fostering intrinsic motivation in early childhood classrooms. *Early Childhood Education Journal, 25*(3), 159–166.

Center for Early Education and Development (n.d.). *Overview of the CLASS.* Retrieved from http://www.cehd.umn.edu/CEED/projects/-atc/resources/CLASSOverview.pdf

Chiatovich, T., & Stipek, D. (2016). Instructional approaches in kindergarten: What works for whom? *The Elementary School Journal, 117*(1), 1–29.

Deci, E. L., & Ryan, R. M. (1985). *Intrinsic motivation and self-determination in human behavior.* New York, NY: Plenum.

Deci, E. L., & Ryan, R. M. (1987). The support of autonomy and the control of behavior. *Journal of Personality and Social Psychology, 53*, 1024–1037.

Deci, E. L., Koestner, R., & Ryan, R. M. (1999). A meta-analytic review of experiments examining the effects of extrinsic rewards on intrinsic motivation. *Psychological Bulletin, 125*(6), 627–668.

Dollinger, S. J., & Thelen, M. H. (1978). Overjustification and children's intrinsic motivation: Comparative effects of four rewards. *Journal of Personality and Social Psychology, 36*(11), 1259–1269.

Early, D. M., Maxwell, K. L., Burchinal, M., Bender, R. H., Ebanks, C., Henry, G. T., ... Zill, N. (2007). Teachers' education, classroom quality, and young children's academic skills: results from seven studies of preschool programs. *Child Development, 78*(2), 558–580.

Fives, H., & Buehl, M. M. (2012). Spring cleaning for the "messy" construct of teachers' beliefs: What are they? Which have been examined? What can they tell us? In K. R. Harris, S. Graham, & T. Urdan (Eds.), *APA educational psychology handbook: Individual differences and cultural and contextual factors* (pp. 471–499). Washington, DC: American Psychological Association

Froiland, J. M., Oros, E., Smith, & Hirchert, T. (2012). Intrinsic motivation to learn: The nexus between psychological health and academic success. *Contemporary School Psychology, 16*(1), 91–100.

Gottfried, A. E., Fleming, J. S., & Gottfried, A. W. (2001). Continuity of academic intrinsic motivation from childhood through late adolescence: A longitudinal study. *Journal of Educational Psychology, 93*(1), 3–13.

Guay, F., Chanal, J., Ratelle, C. F., Marsh, H. W., Larose, S., & Boivin, M. (2010). Intrinsic, identified, and controlled types of motivation for school subjects in young elementary school children. *British Journal of Educational Psychology, 80*(4), 711–735.

Gutman, L. M., & Sulzby, E. (1999). The role of autonomy support versus control in the emergent writing behaviors of African-American kindergarten children. *Reading Research and Instruction, 39*(2), 170–184.

Helmke, A. (2007). *Unterrichtsqualität erfassen, bewerten, verbessern.*[Capturing, evaluating, and improving classroom quality]. Seelze-Velber, Germany: Kallmeyer.

Huntsman, L. (2008). *Determinants of quality in child care: A review of the research evidence.* Ashfield, England: NSW Department of Community Services.

Kuger, S., & Kluczniok, K. (2008). Process quality in preschools—Concepts, implementation, and findings. *Zeitschrift für Erziehungswissenschaft, 10*(11, special issue), 159–177.

Kunter, M., Kleickmann, T., Klusmann, U., & Richter, D. (2013). The development of teachers' professional competence. In M. Kunter, J. Baumert, W. Blum, U. Klusmann, S. Krauss, & M. Neubrand (Eds.), *Cognitive activation in the mathematics classroom and professional competence of teachers* (pp. 63–88). New York, NY: Springer.

Lai, E. (2011). *Motivation: A literature review* (Research Report). Pearson Research Report.

Lepper, M. R., Greene, D., & Nisbett, R. E. (1973). Undermining Children's Intrinsic Interest with Extrinsic Reward: A test of the "overjustification" hypothesis. *Journal of Personality and Social Psychology, 28*(1), 129–137.

Mata, L. (2011). Motivation for reading and writing in kindergarten children. *Reading Psychology, 31*(3), 272–299.

McCrae, R. R., & Costa, P. T., Jr. (1996). Toward a new generation of personality theories: Theoretical contexts for the five-factor model. In J. S. Wiggins (Ed.), *The five-factor model of personality: Theoretical perspectives* (pp. 51–87). New York, NY: Guilford Press

Natale, K., Viljranta, J., Lerkkanen, M. K., Poikkeus, A. M., & Nurmi, J. E. (2009). Cross-lagged association between kindergarten teachers'causal attributions and children's task motivation and performance in reading. *Educational Psychology, 29*(5), 603–619.

Nolen, S. B. (2001). Constructing literacy in the kindergarten: Task structure, collaboration, and motivation. *Cognition and Instruction, 19*(1), 95–142.

Pakarinen, E., Kiuru, N., Lerkkanen, M. K., Poikkeus, A. M., Siekkinen, M., & Nurmi, J. E. (2008). Classroom organization and teacher stress predict learning motivation in kindergarten children. *European Journal of Psychology of Education, 25*(3), 281–300.

Patrick, H., Mantzicopoulos, P., & Samarapungavan, A. (2009). Motivation for Learning Science in Kindergarten: Is there a Gender Gap and Does Integrated Inquiry and Literacy Make a Difference. *Journal of Research in Science Teaching, 46*(2), 166–191.

Prenzel, M. (Ed.) (2007). *Studies on the educational quality of schools. The final report of the DFG Priority Programme.* Münster, Germany: Waxmann.

Qu, L., & Ong, J. Y. (2016). Impact of reminders on children's cognitive flexibility, intrinsic motivation, and mood depends on who provides the reminder. *Frontiers in Psychology, 6*(1904), 1–14.

Reid, J. L. & Kagan, S. L. (2015). *A better star: Why classroom diversity matters in early education.* Retrieved from http://www.prrac.org/pdf/A_Better_Start.pdf

Richter, D., Lehrl, S., & Weinert, S. (2016). Enjoyment of learning and learning effort in primary school: The significance of child individual characteristics and stimulation at home and at preschool. *Early Child Development and Care, 186*(1), 96–116.

Siraj-Blatchford, I. (2007). Effektive Bildungsprozesse: Lehren in der frühen Kindheit [Effective educational processes: Teaching in early childhood]. In F. Becker-Stoll & M. R. Textor (Eds.), *Die Erzieherin-Kind-Beziehung* [The caregiver-child-relationship] (pp. 97–114). Berlin, Germany: Cornelsen Scriptor.

Smidt, W. (2012). *Zielkindbezogene pädagogische Qualität im Kindergarten. Eine empirisch-quantitative Studie* [Target child related educational quality in preschools. A quantitative study]. Münster, Germany: Waxmann.

Smidt, W. (2015). Educational processes in early childhood education: activities of target children in preschools. In W. Schnotz, A. Kauertz, H. Ludwig, A.

Müller, & J. Pretsch (Eds.), *Multidisciplinary research on teaching and learning* (pp. 3–18). Basingstoke, England: Palgrave Macmillan.

Smidt, W. (2016). Occupational activities of nonacademic and academic pedagogues working in the field of childhood education - an Investigation of differences and predictor variables. *Early Child Development and Care, 186*(1), 2–22.

Stephanou, G. (2014). Feelings towards child–teacher relationships, and emotions about the teacher in kindergarten: effects on learning motivation, competence beliefs and performance in mathematics and literacy, *European Early Childhood Education Research Journal, 22*(4), 457–477.

Stipek, D. (1996). Motivation and instruction. In D. C. Berliner & R. C. Calfee (Eds.), *Handbook of educational psychology* (pp. 85–113). New York, NY: Macmillan.

Stipek, D., Feiler, R., Daniels, D., & Milburn. S. (1995). Effects of different instructional approaches on young children's achievement and motivation. *Child Development, 66*(1), 209–223.

Takunyaci, M., & Takunyaci, M. (2014). Preschool teachers' mathematics teaching efficacy belief. *Procedia - Social and Behavioral Sciences, 152*, 673–678.

Tzurial, D., Kaniel, S., & Kanner, E. (1999). Effects of the "Bright Start" Program in kindergarten on transfer and academic achievement. *Early Childhood Research Quarterly, 14*(1), 111–141.

Ulber, J., Hamann, K., & Tomasello, M. (2016). Extrinsic rewards diminish costly sharing in 3-year-olds. *Child Development, 87*(4), 1192–1203.

Vandell, D. L., & Wolfe, B. (2000). *Child care quality: Does it matter and does it need to be improved?* Retrieved from http://www.irp.wisc.edu/publications/sr/pdfs/sr78.pdf

Whitebook, M. (2003). *Early education quality: higher teacher qualifications for better learning environments—a review of the literature.* Retrieved from http://cscce.berkeley.edu/files/2003/Early_Ed_Quality.pdf

Wu, X. (2003). Intrinsic motivation and young language learners: the impact of the classroom environment. *System, 31*, 501–517.

Zhou, H., & Salili, F. (2008). Intrinsic reading motivation of Chinese preschoolers and its relationships with home literacy. *International Journal of Psychology, 43*(5), 912–916.

Zupančič, M. (2008). The Big Five: Recent developments in Slovene child personality research. *Horizons of Psychology, 17*(4), 7–32.

CHAPTER 8

DEVELOPMENTAL DIFFERENCES IN YOUNG CHILDREN'S MASTERY MOTIVATION

Olivia N. Saracho

Motivation is the compelling reason behind all activities and is the fore-runner and foundation to learning. Early motivation anticipates young children's later academic success (Turner & Johnson, 2003). Young children possess an immeasurable energy for surviving and learning. Behaviors that are essential for survival (such as eating or drinking water) should be satisfying. Young children *survive* through exploration of their world. The instant fulfilment of achievement contributes to their cognitive development. To motivate children and make them aware of their utmost conceivable learning, it is essential to know how their motivation to learn develops (Ostroff, 2012). When children are motivated, they participate in learning activities, continue with challenging tasks, consider themselves to be proficient, perceive success to be within their control, and enjoy their success (Turner & Johnson, 2003).

All children are born with inquisitiveness and a desire to learn about their world. Developmental theorists (e.g., Hunt, 1965; Piaget, 1952; White 1959) stated that children are motivated to discover the world around them, which is their learning source. This type of motivation is thought to

Contemporary Perspectives on Research on
Motivation in Early Childhood Education, pp. 177–190
Copyright © 2019 by Information Age Publishing
All rights of reproduction in any form reserved.

be intrinsic, universal, and essential to the children's development. White (1959) maintained that children can control their situation through discovery and play. He indicated that children have "the urge that makes for competence" (p. 305) and he proposed that this impulse be labeled *effectance* or the *motivational aspect of competence*. Additionally, Harter (1975) described effectance motivation as a "desire to solve cognitively challenging problems for gratification inherent in discovering the solution" (p. 370). She emphasized some important elements which include curiosity, preference for challenge, internal criteria of success, and working for personal gratification.

Young children are usually motivated learners. They are engrossed in their environment, are confident that they are able to learn more, and improve their skill but challenging experiences discourage them. When individuals become proficient in their environment, it is referred to as motivation. Although experiences create mastery motivation, the individuals' purpose to be proficient and to pursue ongoing learning has a vital effect on most of them. Researchers who study school-aged children find that such yearning is usually studied within academic conditions and define it as intrinsic achievement orientation or task motivation. Several children react to external motives when they engage in learning. They want to *show* competence by performing better than others or to gain praise which is defined as extrinsic motivation (Senko, Durik, & Harackiewicz, 2008).

INTRINSIC MOTIVATION VERSUS EXTRINSIC MOTIVATION

For more than 4 decades, motivation studies have multiplied with information on the theory of young children's motivation, the way it develops in relation to the children's functioning, and how it is formed by their environment. Several elements have an impact on motivation including "situation (environment and external stimulus), temperament (state and organism internal state), goal (purpose of behavior and attitude) and tools (tools to reach the target" (Pakdel, 2013, p. 240).

Starting at birth and during their life span, young children are motivated by novelty, adaptation, and enjoyment (Ostroff, 2012). After children are born, they have an innate necessity to interact with their environment, which facilitates their learning and acquisition of knowledge. In daily practices, motivation frequently indicates the reasons for the individuals' behaviors. Psychologists suggest several methods of reasoning about motivation, such as determining if motivation surfaces from outside (extrinsic) or inside (intrinsic) the individual. "Motivation is an intrinsic phenomenon" (Pakdel, 2013, p. 240). Actually, there are two forms of motivation: intrinsic (internal) motivation vs extrinsic (external) motivation. To focus on this inquiry, it is important to distinguish between intrinsic and extrinsic motivation. Cherry (2017) makes a distinction between these two types of motivation (see Table 8.1). They have distinct causes of stress and enjoyment that independently influence the individuals' motivation. When children achieve a task for pleasure, it is referred to as *intrinsic motivation*. On the other hand, when children achieve a task to receive external rewards or to prevent negative penalties, it is referred to as *extrinsic motivation*. Intrinsic motivation is when children want to engage in an experience just for the pleasure that results from that experience. In contrast, extrinsic motivation is when children want to engage in an experience for an expected result such as praise or a reward (Carlton & Winsler, 1998).

Table 8.1.
Intrinsic Versus Extrinsic Motivation

Extrinsic refers to any motivation that emerges from outside of the individual and frequently includes rewards such as trophies, money, social recognition, or praise. For example:

- Studying to get a good grade
- Cleaning the room to prevent ones parents' discipline.
- Joining a sports team to triumph and get awards
- Entering a contest to win a scholarship

All of the above instances indicate that the behavior is motivated by an aspiration to receive a reward or evade an unfavorable consequence.

Intrinsic refers to any motivation that emerges from the individual, such as completing a difficult task only for the individual satisfaction of finding a solution. For example:

- Participating in a sport because the activity provides pleasure
- Working out a word puzzle because the challenge is enjoyable and exhilarating
- Joining a game because it is fun.

In each of these instances, the individual's behavior is motivated by an internal aspiration to engage in an activity because it is worthwhile.

The motivation that drives their learning is based exclusively within them and does not demand any outer rewards for its continuance. Individuals are motivated to meet their goals, needs, and instincts (Pakdel, 2013). Motivation with young children is the process by which children's goal-directed action is initiated and continued (Pintrich & Schunk, 1996). Goal-directed behavior may be intrinsic, extrinsic, or a mixture of both. Intrinsic motivation is composed of three fundamental psychological needs that are assumed to be: *the needs for competence, relatedness, and autonomy (self-determination)*. *Competence* refers to understanding how to accomplish several external and internal outcomes and being effective in achieving the necessary actions. *Relatedness* refers to being able to develop secure and firm associations with others in a social environment. *Autonomy* refers to having the ability to self-initiate and self-regulate one's own actions. Young children develop these three psychological needs (Carlton & Winsler, 1998, Deci, Vallerand, Pelletier, & Ryan, 1991).

Development of Intrinsic Motivation

Children develop motivation patterns that begin at an early age. The early childhood years are critical for establishing a strong intrinsic motivational sense of direction which will continue throughout a lifetime. Children explore their environment to learn. When children are born, they have an inherent inquisitiveness to learn about their world. Such intrinsically initiated learning is frequently called *mastery motivation* (Carlton & Winsler, 1998). Children learn when they explore their world around them. For example, children work very hard when they are trying to build a block structure. Or they might be curious to find out how "gadgets" work. They are motivated to solve problems, discover in what way objects work, and finish tasks they had initiated. Theorists refer to these behaviors as intrinsic motivation (Hauser-Cram, 1998) because children respond to a condition.

Russian developmental psychologist, Alexander Zaporozhets[1] (1965), found that children spontaneously expose themselves to the essential attributes of a condition. They test everything in their environment to prepare for difficult conflicts. In various experiments in his laboratory, children were trained to press buttons in a particular sequence (matching lights that are being flashed) or to push a toy car through a maze. Zaporozhets describes the following scenario:

A child sat at the switchboard and could, by pushing buttons, make, for example, a doll move in different directions (Plate 4B). The subject was given the task of leading the doll around an obstacle and bringing it to a certain point. The experimenter first demonstrated the work of the mechanism, but the children could not understand immediately the principle of its operation. That is why, when they started to solve the problem, they usually began by pushing different buttons chaotically, trying to achieve the desired goal at once. But with such methods, the doll rushed about chaotically, and the necessary result could not be achieved. The difficulties in the practical solution of the problem made the child study the situation and it was here that a characteristic change in behavior took place. When the buttons were pushed, quick energetic movements of the hand became slow, careful, and probing, the movements accompanied by glances toward the moving doll. In other words, just at the moment that the executive actions were becoming orienting-exploratory, an elementary method was being created to test any system of button control. (p. 97)

Zaporozhets states that the children's development is planned and it requires practice and learning. Adults provide children with learning methods in their environment and familiarize them with the systems. They also teach them to select the specifics of their environment. As a result, the children incorporate a particular system of commonly recognized stimuli. The young children's exploration facilitate their learning. In the experiment by Zaporozhets children spontaneously subjected themselves to the influential properties of a situation. They experimented to prepare themselves for future difficult situations (Ostroff, 2012). Young children initiate their learning, which is part of their mastery motivation.

MASTERY MOTIVATION

Researchers differ in their definition of mastery motivation, although it is a steady premise that concentrates on the individuals' intrinsic need to search, comprehend, and manipulate their surroundings. For example, Busch-Rossnagel (1997) defined it as "the impetus to achieve and improve one's skills in the absence of any physical reward" (p. 1), whereas Cain and Dweck (1995) described it as when children "persist at challenging tasks and are slow to interpret poor performance as failure" (p. 26). Other researchers (e.g., Messer, McCarthy, McQuiston, MacTurk, Yarrow, & Vietze, 1986) believe that "mastery behavior can be considered to represent infants' persistence and investigation of problems and objects" (p. 366). Mastery motivation is a multidimensional, intrinsic psychological influence that motivates individuals to make an effort to overcome their tendency to quit before completing a task (Morgan, Józsa, & Liao, 2017). It is a "psychological force that stimulates an individual to attempt independently, in a focused and persistent manner, to solve a problem or master a skill or task which is at least moderately challenging for him or her" (Morgan, Harmon, & Maslin-Cole, 1990, p. 319). It refers to an ability or task that is marginally difficult for them (Morgan et al., 1990). Fundamental elements of mastery motivation consist of (1) efforts to independently master a task without any guidance; (2) persistence in mastering a task and overcoming any complications that might surface; and (3) choosing an appropriate task that is neither very easy nor very hard. It is important to separately establish a moderate challenge when children spend less time with tasks that they believe that they are either very easy or very hard (Redding, Morgan, & Harmon 1988). Selecting the appropriate tasks will offer young children with optimum challenges (Hauser-Cram, 1998).

A number of researchers specify that mastery motivation is displayed in behaviors such as (a) task exploration and persistence (e.g., Barrett, Morgan, & Maslin-Cole, 1993; Busch-Rossnagel, 1997), (b) satisfaction from exploration and achievements (e.g., Barrett et al., 1993; Busch-

Rossnagel, 1997), and (c) flexible reactions to failure (Cain & Dweck, 1995). Mastery motivation stimulates young children's independent efforts to master tasks that are relatively demanding for them (Morgan et al., 1990). It emphasizes the children's persistence and the process to master the tasks instead of focusing on their capability to resolve a problem (Busch-Rossnagel & Morgan, 2013). There are three domains of the mastery motivation construct: *cognitive/object*, *social*, and *gross motor*. The *cognitive/object domain* refers to the children's attempts to master toys and solve cognitive problems; the *social domain* refers to the children's attempts to interact effectively with others, and the *gross motor domain* focuses on the children's attempts to master physical skills (Morgan, MacTurk, & Hrncir, 1995). Within each domain, there are two main components: *instrumental* and *expressive* (Barrett & Morgan, 1995). The *instrumental* component is defined by persistence and the duration of task-directed behavior. It motivates an individual to make an effort, in an absorbed and determined way, to resolve a problem or master an ability or task which is at first rather challenging (Morgan et al., 1990). The *expressive* component of mastery motivation creates emotional responses where the individuals are working on a task or just finished it. This impact may possibly be obviously communicated, detected, and assume various configurations as the children mature. This definition of mastery motivation evolved over the last 30 years from Morgan's and his colleagues' (e.g., Morgan et al., 1990; Morgan et al., 1995; Morgan et al., 2017) research and is more restricted than those of earlier investigators (e.g., White, 1959). Apparently, mastery motivation is an essential motivational paradigm that surfaces early in the young children's development and affects behaviors that assist in their future learning and development (Turner & Johnson, 2003). Preschool children's normal inquisitiveness is the leading factor in their early motivation. During kindergarten and elementary school, children's natural curiosity is still the most important motivating factor. However, during the early years, children begin to recognize mastery over their environment or that their skills can be used not merely for their own sake but in other ways that serve and meet other motives and needs.

Researchers have investigated the infants, toddlers, and preschool children's mastery motivation, which is supposed to be a forerunner to future academic motivational development. According to Yarrow, Klein, Lomonaco, and Morgan (1975), motivated infants reach for and manipulate novel items, which are their cognitive-motivational behaviors. Yarrow and associates (1975) found that the infants' mastery motivation predicted the preschool children's intelligence quotient (IQ) based on the Stanford-Binet Intelligence Scales. Likewise, Józsa and Molnár (2013) showed that mastery motivation is an established predictor of kindergarten and later school success and that it was more predictive of school achievement than

IQ measures and tests of basic skills. Lately, Józsa and Barrett (2016) revealed that preschool children's mastery motivation predicts their school performance in first and second grades. Wang (2016) indicated that perseverance at mastery tasks after 6 months predicted the preschool children's cognitive and fine motor aptitude including the preschool age children with global developmental delays. Young children need to be assessed for their mastery motivation because it has an impact on education and early intervention.

Mastery behaviors develop in three stages from birth to approximately 3 years of age (Barrett & Morgan, 1995). Such mastery behaviors first surface in efforts to manage occurrences (or toys), then it attempts to terminate a task that meets the required task-related mastery standards, and lastly, it assesses personal performance based on the required standards. At the final stage, satisfaction is frequently observed in response to the achievement of challenging tasks, whereas embarrassment is seen as a response to failure on simple tasks (Stipek, Recchia, & McClintic, 1992). During this process, individual changes in mastery behaviors may be affected by evaluative responses (Busch-Rossnagel, 1997; Busch-Rossnagel, Knauf-Jensen, & DesRosiers, 1995; Kelley, Brownell, & Campbell, 2000; Lewis, 1992).

A DEVELOPMENTAL SEQUENCE OF MOTIVATION

For more than 4 decades, motivation has attracted substantial interest in early childhood research and has become an important developmental concept (Shonkoff & Phillips, 2000). It has been found that an inherent principle for patterns of motivation emerge early in life (Carlton & Winsler, 1998). Marx and Tombaugh (1967) discuss the children's developmental changes based on age. Table 8.2 provides young children's developmental sequence for motivation.

Most developmental psychologists maintain that children start life as motivated individuals. Developmentally, children advance through numerous changes in motivation. They struggle to understand their world and to contribute to it. Children's motivation progresses and displays different behaviors through each phase of their life. Motivated children behave themselves in a different way at various stages of life. Newborns have restricted voluntary motor movements. They attempt to dominate their surroundings. Once they realize the outcomes of their actions, they become motivated to carry on the same actions. The motivated infants, who are under the age of 6 months, study objects through stretching, mouthing, and visual exploration.

Psychologists study the infants' normal sucking behavior in the laboratory. They wire pressure-sensitive pacifiers to computers which control the

Table 8.2.
Developmental Sequence for Motivation

Age	Behaviors
Infants (Birth to 9 Months)	• During their initial weeks of life, infants dominate the speed of their sucking (e.g., increase or decrease) to be able to consider or recurrently experience enjoyable visual stimuli. This inquiry implies that infants are greatly more refined than had been formerly assumed and that infants' motivation and goals can be measured by cautiously interpreting infant behavior from the standpoint of their individual behavioral repertoire (Carlton & Winsler, 1998). • Six-month-old motivated infants study items through reaching, mouthing, and visual search (Jennings, 1993).
Infant/toddler (9 to 24 months)	• Nine-month-old motivated infants start to recognize basic concepts of cause-and-effect. They initiate and participate in goal-directed activities with unknown tasks (Jennings, 1993). • Between nine and 24 months, infants continue to control incidents and plan their actions to achieve their aims. They start to assess themselves and become motivated to achieve on their own. Their capability to achieve their goals determines their success (Barrett & Morgan, 1995).
Toddlers/Preschoolers (24-36 Months)	• Between 24 and 36 months, children understand the standards. They are able to evaluate themselves, perform a series of behaviors to accomplish a purpose, and react properly to successes and failures. Children can determine which activities are difficult for them and become proud when completing challenging tasks. When they fail to achieve simple tasks, they become embarrassed and are less proud about their successes (Barrett & Morgan, 1995, Lewis, Alessandri, & Sullivan, 1992).
Preschoolers (3-5 Years)	• Three-year-old children want to do well instead of only completing socially worthwhile tasks (Barrett & Morgan, 1995). They use self-talk to initiate social interactions (Vygotsky, 1934/1986) and use their verbal abilities to solve problems such as talking to themselves while solving a problem (Sawyer, 2017). • Rewards are extremely important to them (Carlton & Winsler, 1998). • Children will become motivated when they receive praise on their efforts, which will increase their self-esteem (Deci et al., 1991). • Preschool children's normal curiosity is the most important component in their early motivation. • Preschool motivated children start to self-select difficult tasks and select challenging tasks rather than simple ones (Hauser-Cram, 1998, Stipek, 1996).

(Table continues on next page)

Table 8.2.
(Continued)

Age	Behaviors
Kindergarten children	• Kindergarten children's natural curiosity continues to be the best fundamental motivating influence. • Children start to understand that their abilities can assist them to accomplish their purposes and needs. Success and praise motivate young children. Competition, achievement, and support are essential (Ray, 1992). • Kindergarten children's normal curiosity has the foremost influence in their initial motivation. However, they begin to focus on mastery throughout their environment. They discover that their abilities can be used for their personal well-being and can help them to undertake additional motives and needs.
School-age children	• School-age children are "mastery-oriented" who search for challenges and have great, successful endurance when they encounter difficulties in trying to solve challenging problems (Dweck, 1986). • School-age children's natural curiosity continues to be the best fundamental motivating influence. • School-age children start to understand that their abilities can assist them to accomplish their purposes and needs. Success and praise motivate young children. Competition, achievement, and support are essential (Ray, 1992). • School-age children start to focus on mastery throughout their environment.They discover that their abilities can be used for their personal well-being and can help them to undertake additional motives and needs.

display of various stimuli. During their initial weeks of life, infants dominate the speed of their sucking (e.g., increase or decrease) to determine or persistently experience enjoyable visual stimuli. That is, infants will methodically suck on the pacifier at the speed that gives them their preferred (face-like) stimuli instead of the speed that provides them with either less attractive stimuli or no stimuli. Infants beforehand select to practice with the pacifier which dominates the demonstration of stimuli instead of one that does not (Rovee-Collier, 1987). In addition, infants learn to replicate and increase their sucking speeds when they are able to control the stimuli (DeCasper & Carstens, 1981). This inquiry implies that infants are greatly more refined than had been formerly assumed and that the infants' motivation and goals can be measured by cautiously interpreting infant behavior from the standpoint of their individual behavioral repertoire (Carlton & Winsler, 1998).

Developmental Changes

Six-month-old motivated infants study items through reaching, mouthing, and visual search. Nine-month-old motivated infants start to recognize basic concepts of cause-and-effect. They initiate and participate in goal-directed activities with unknown tasks. Motivated infants who are 18 months-old start to analyze their behaviors with standard ones (Jennings, 1993). Motivated toddlers make an effort to reach the standard. Motivated preschool children start to choose demanding tasks and favor tasks that "make them think" rather than easy ones (Stipek, 1996).

Preschool children's normal curiosity is the most important component in their early motivation. Preschool motivated children start to self-select difficult tasks and select challenging tasks rather than simple ones (Hauser-Cram, 1998; Stipek, 1996). Kindergarten and elementary school children's natural curiosity continues to be the best fundamental motivating influence. During this period, children start to understand that their abilities can assist them to accomplish their purposes and needs. Success and praise motivate young children. Competition, achievement, and support are essential (Ray, 1992). Preschool, kindergarten, and elementary school children's normal curiosity has the foremost influence in their initial motivation. However, kindergarten and elementary school children start to focus on mastery throughout their environment. They discover that their abilities can be used for their personal well-being and can help them to undertake additional motives and needs.

School-age children are "mastery-oriented" who search for challenge and have great, successful persistence when they encounter difficulties in trying to solve difficult problems. In comparison, those children with the maladaptive ("helpless") patterns avoid challenge and have low persistence when they encounter challenging problems. These children exhibit negative "affect" (such as anxiety) and negative self-cognitions because they credit the results of their previous experiences where they had minimal control over the incidents that had an impact on them (Dweck, 1986). Children who become familiar with vulnerability credit their successes to external causes such as luck and their disappointments to internal factors such as ability (Dweck & Elliott 1983).

CONCLUSION

Children are born with an instinctive yearning to learn about their world. Their motivation depends on their experiences. Support methods can be used to improve their motivation development, self-regulation, and learning abilities. Rewards need to be carefully selected and appropriately used to emphasize the learning process instead of the product, which will also develop their motivation abilities. Children can achieve their maximum ability when they are permitted to maintain their motivation and enthusiasm in learning through the years (Carlton & Winsler, 1998).

Most children enter school with some motivation to figure out the world around them. Whether you are reading about early childhood development or having conversations with early childhood experts and teachers, you will likely encounter assertions such as the following: "Young children are naturally curious" or "Young children are naturally motivated to learn" (e.g., Bransford, Brown, & Cockling, 2000; Carlton & Winsler, 1998; Conezio & French, 2002; Dewey, 1910; Gallenstein, 2005; Neuman & Roskos, 2005; Patrick & Mantzicopoulos, 2015; Shonkoff & Phillips, 2000). The commonness of such assertions in conversations about children, education, and schooling might result in a certain level of ennui when considering what really needs to be said in a chapter on motivation and young children.

Presently, research with mastery motivation have been progressing. Since play is critical in early childhood education and its programs are social establishments where children learn through play, it is important that future research on mastery motivation incorporate the impact of the social context in which children learn. In a play setting, it is important to consider the effects peers have on each other, and how the social dynamics of a classroom affect the children. Similar issues will certainly appear as the paradigm of mastery motivation integrate the shared complexities of the social situations in which children learn. These and similar issues on children's motivation can be examined in future research to understand how the play environment can optimize mastery-oriented behavior in young children (Hauser-Cram, 1998).

NOTE

1. Alexander Vladimirovich Zaporozhets (Russian: александр владимирович запорожец; 1905–1981) was a Soviet developmental psychologist and Lev Vygotsky's (1934/1986) student.

REFERENCES

Barrett, K. C., & Morgan, G. A. (1995). Continuities and discontinuities in mastery motivation during infancy and toddlerhood: A conceptualization and review. In R. H. MacTurk & G. A. Morgan (Eds.), *Mastery motivation: Origins, conceptualizations, and applications* (pp. 57–93). Norwood, NJ: Ablex.

Barrett, K. C., Morgan, G. A., & Maslin-Cole, C. (1993). Three studies on the development of mastery motivation in infancy and toddlerhood. In D. Messer (Ed.), *Mastery motivation in early childhood: Development, measurement and social processes* (pp. 83–108). New York, NY: Routledge.

Bransford, J. D., Brown, A. L., & Cocking, R. R. (2000). How children learn. In D. Bransford, A. L. Brown, & R. R. Cocking (Eds.), *How people learn: Brain, mind, experience and school* (pp. 79–113). Washington, DC: National Academy Press.

Busch-Rossnagel, N. A. (1997). Mastery motivation in toddlers. *Infants and Young Children, 9,* 1–11.

Busch-Rossnagel, N. A., Knauf-Jensen, D. E., & DesRosiers, F. S. (1995). Mothers and others: The role of the socializing environment in the development of mastery motivation. In R. H. MacTurk, & G. A. Morgan (Eds.), *Mastery motivation: Origins, conceptualizations, and applications* (pp. 117–145). Norwood, NJ: Ablex.

Busch-Rossnagel, N. A., & Morgan, G. A. (2013). Introduction to the mastery motivation and self-regulation section. In K. C. Barrett, N. A. Fox, G. A. Morgan, D. J. Fidler, & L. A. Daunhauer (Eds.), *Handbook of self-regulatory processes in development: New directions and international perspectives* (pp. 247–264). New York, NY: Psychology Press.

Cain, K. M., & Dweck, C. S. (1995). The relation between motivational patterns and achievement cognitions through the elementary school years. *Merrill-Palmer Quarterly, 41,* 25–52.

Carlton, M. P., & Winsler, A. (1998). Fostering intrinsic motivation in early childhood classrooms. *Early Childhood Education Journal, 25,* 159–166.

Conezio, K., & French, L. (2002). Science in the preschool classroom: Capitalizing on children's fascination with the everyday world to foster language and literacy development. *Young Children, 57*(5), 12–18.

Cherry, K. (2017). *Motivation: Psychological factors that guide behavior.* Retrieved from https://www.verywell.com/what-is-motivation-2795378

DeCasper, A. J., & Carstens, A. A. (1981). Contingencies of stimulation: Effects on learning and emotion in neonates. *Infant Behavior and Development, 4,* 19–35. doi:10.1016/S0163-6383(81)80004-5

Deci, E. L., Vallerand, R. J., Pelletier, L. G., & Ryan, R. M. (1991). Motivation and education: The self-determination perspective. *Educational Psychologist, 26*(3–4), 325–346.

Dewey, J. (1910). *How we think.* New York, NY: D.C. Heath.

Dweck, C. S. (1986). Motivational processes affecting learning. *American Psychologist, 41*(10), 1040–1048. doi:10.1037/0003-066X.41.10.1040

Dweck, C. S., & Elliott, E. S. (1983). Achievement motivation. In P. H. Mussen (Gen. Ed.) & E. M. Hetherington (Vol. Ed.), *Handbook of child psychology: Social and personality development* (Vol. IV, pp. 643–691). New York, NY: Wiley.

Gallenstein, N. (2005). Engaging young children in science and mathematics. *Journal of Elementary Science Education, 17,* 27–41.

Harter, S. (1975). Developmental differences in the manifestation of mastery motivation on problem-solving tasks. *Child Development, 46*(2), 370–378.

Hauser-Cram, P. (1998). I think I can, I think I can: Understanding and encouraging mastery motivation in young children. *Young Children, 53*(4), 67–71.

Hunt, J. McV. (1965). Intrinsic motivation and its role in psychological development. In Nebraska symposium on motivation. In D. Levine (Ed), *Nebraska symposium on motivation* (pp. 189–282). Lincoln, NE: University of Nebraska Press.

Jennings, K. D. (1993). Mastery motivation and the formation of self-concept from infancy through early childhood. In D. J. Messer (Ed.), *Mastery motivation in early childhood: Development, measurement, and social processes* (pp. 36–54). New York, NY: Routledge.

Józsa, K., & Barrett, K. C. (2016). *Predicting school related skills and early school achievement in Hungarian school-age children from mastery motivation, IQ, and parental education: A longitudinal study.* Unpublished manuscript

Józsa, K., & Molnár, É. D. (2013). The relationship between mastery motivation, self-regulated learning and school success: A Hungarian and wider European perspective. In K. C. Barrett, N. A. Fox, G. A. Morgan, D. J. Fidler, & L. A. Daunhauer (Eds.), *Handbook of self-regulatory processes in development: New directions and international perspectives* (pp. 265–304). New York, NY: Psychology Press. doi:10.4324/9780203080719.ch13

Kelley, S. A., Brownell, C. A., & Campbell, S. B. (2000). Mastery motivation and self-evaluative affect in toddlers: Longitudinal relations with maternal behavior. *Child Development, 71*(4), 1061–1071. doi:10.1111/1467-8624.00209

Lewis, M. (1992). The self in self-conscious emotions. In D. Stipek, S. Recchia, & S. McClintic (Eds.), *Self-regulation in young children: Monographs of the Society for Research in Child Development*, 57(1, Serial No. 226).

Lewis, M., Alessandri, S. M., & Sullivan, M. W. (1992). Differences in shame and pride as a function of children's gender and task difficulty. *Child Development, 63*(3), 630–638. doi:10.1111/j.1467-8624.1992.tb01651.x

Marx, M. H., & Tombaugh, T. N. (1967). *Motivation*. San Francisco, CA: Chandler.

Messer, D. J., McCarthy, M. E., McQuiston, S., MacTurk, R. H., Yarrow, L. J., & Vietze, P. M. (1986). Relation between mastery behavior in infancy and competence in early childhood. *Developmental Psychology, 22*(3), 366–372. doi:10.1037/0012-1649.22.3.366

Morgan, G. A., MacTurk, R. H., & Hrncir, E. J. (1995). Mastery motivation: Overview, definitions, and conceptual issues. In R. H. MacTurk, & G. A. Morgan (Eds.), *Mastery motivation: Origins, conceptualizations, and applications* (pp. 1–18). Norwood, NJ: Ablex.

Morgan, G. A., Józsa, K., & Liao, H.-F. (2017). Introduction to the special issue on mastery motivation: Measures and results across cultures and ages. *Hungarian Educational Research Journal, 7*(2), 5–14. doi:10.14413/HERJ/7/2/1

Morgan, G., Harmon, R., & Maslin-Cole, C. (1990). Mastery motivation: Definition and measurement. *Early Education & Development, 1*(5), 318–339. doi:10.1207/s15566935eed0105_1

Neuman, S. B., & Roskos, K. (2005). The state of state pre-kindergarten standards. *Early Childhood Research Quarterly, 20*, 125–145. doi:10.1016/j.ecresq.2005.04.010

Ostroff, W. L. (2012). *Understanding how young children learn: Bringing the science of child development to the classroom*. Alexandria, VA: Association for Supervision and Curriculum Development.

Pakdel, B. (2013). The historical context of motivation and analysis theories individual motivation. *International Journal of Humanities and Social Science, 3*(18). Retrieved from http://www.ijhssnet.com/journals/Vol_3_No_18_October_2013/23.pdf

Patrick, H., & Mantzicopoulos, P. (2015). The role of meaning systems in the development of motivation. In C. M. Rubie-Davies, J. M. Stephens, & P. Watson (Eds.), *The Routledge international handbook of social psychology of the classroom* (pp. 67–79). New York, NY: Routledge.

Piaget, J. (1952). *The origins of intelligence in children.* New York, NY: International Universities Press.

Pintrich, P. R., & Schunk, D. H., (1996). *Motivation in education: Theory, research, and applications.* Englewood Cliffs, NJ: Prentice-Hall.

Ray, N. L. (1992). Motivation in education (ED 349 298). Retrieved from https://files.eric.ed.gov/fulltext/ED298349.pdf

Redding, R. E., Morgan, G. A., & Harmon, R. J. (1988). Mastery motivation in infants and toddlers: Is it greatest when tasks are moderately challenging? *Infant Behavior and Development, 11*(4), 419–430. doi:10.1016/0163-6383(88)90003-3

Rovee-Collier, C. K. (1987). Learning and memory. In J. D. Osofsky (Ed.), *Handbook of infant development* (2nd ed., pp. 98–148). New York, NY: Wiley.

Senko, C., Durik, A., & Harackiewicz, J. (2008). Historical perspectives and new directions in achievement goal theory. In J. Shah & W. Gardner (Eds.), *Handbook of motivation science* (pp. 100–113). New York, NY: Guilford Press.

Shonkoff, J. P., & Phillips, D. A. (Eds.). (2000). *From neurons to neighborhoods: The science of early childhood development.* Washington, DC: National Academy Press.

Stipek, D. J. (1996). Motivation and instruction. In D. Berliner & R. Calfee (Eds.), *Handbook of educational psychology* (pp. 85–113). New York, NY: Macmillan.

Stipek, D., Recchia, S., & McClintic, S. (1992). Self-evaluation in young children. *Monographs of the Society for Research in Child Development, 57*(1, Serial No. 226).

Turner, L. A., & Johnson, B. (2003). A model of mastery motivation in at-risk preschoolers. *Journal of Educational Psychology, 95,* 495–505. doi:10.1037/0022-0663.95.3.495

Vygotsky, Lev S. (1986). *Thought and language.* Cambridge MA: The MIT Press. (Original work published 1934)

Wang, P. J. (2016). *Bidirectional relations among maternal interactive behavior, mastery motivation, anddevelopmental ability in children with global developmental delay* (Unpublished doctoral dissertation). School and Graduate Institute of Physical Therapy, National Taiwan University

White, R. W. (1959). Motivation reconsidered: The concept of competence. *Psychological Review 66*(5), 297–333. doi:10.1037/h0040934

Yarrow, L. J., Klein, R., Lomonaco, S., & Morgan, G. (1975). Cognitive and motivational development in early childhood. In B. Z. Friedlander, G. M. Sterritt, & G. E. Kirk, (Eds.), *Exceptional infant: Assessment and intervention* (pp. 491–502). New York, NY: Bruner/Mazel.

Zaporozhets, A. V. (1965). The development of perception in the preschool child. In P. H. Mussen (Ed.), *European research in cognitive development.* Monographs of the Society for Research in Child Development, *30*(2), 82–101 (Serial no. 100) 0037-976X.

PART IV

SOCIAL MOTIVATION

CHAPTER 9

TEACHERS' BELIEFS ABOUT SOCIALLY WITHDRAWN YOUNG CHILDREN

Kristen A. Archbell, Amanda Bullock, and Robert J. Coplan

Teachers play a critical and unique role in children's lives, providing nurturance and robustly impacting a wide range of developmental outcomes (Dobbs & Arnold, 2009). In the educational context, teachers are expected to act as leaders, guiding the classroom through their daily ventures. In doing so, teachers are in the position to facilitate and promote developmentally appropriate social interactions among students. Children are aggregated together in a classroom as a *social unit*, and are expected to follow preestablished expectations and social rules set out by the classroom teacher (Farmer, McAuliffe Lines, & Hamm, 2011). In this context, teachers play a pivotal part in providing opportunities for children to develop age appropriate social skills, which can, in turn, contribute to a positive classroom atmosphere.

Teachers view socioemotional skills as essential for young children's healthy development (Lee, 2006), and often hold these skills in higher regard compared to some academic skills, such as early literacy and mathematic ability (Hollingsworth & Winters, 2013). Moreover, teachers believe they should place emphasis on pedagogical strategies to optimize the development of social competence among children (Lee, 2006). Therefore,

*Contemporary Perspectives on Research on
Motivation in Early Childhood Education*, pp. 193–207
Copyright © 2019 by Information Age Publishing
All rights of reproduction in any form reserved.

teachers' beliefs about children's social skills and behavioral characteristics have been of particular interest among researchers.

Teachers' beliefs can directly and indirectly impact student outcomes. For example, teachers' beliefs about child development have been found to influence teachers' responses to children's classroom behaviors (Cunningham & Sugawara, 1988). Teachers' attitudes and reactions about children's overt displays of behavior may also impact peers' perceptions of children (Chang, 2003), which may alter the classroom ecology. Farmer and colleagues (2011) further suggested that teachers shape peer dynamics by managing student interactions, and provide assistance to students who struggle in the social domain. Teachers also have the ability to assist students in developing social roles that may promote peer acceptance (e.g., Wentzel, 2003). Moreover, teachers' perceptions of classroom behaviors also appear to impact children's learning outcomes. For example, teachers' beliefs about different social behaviors may influence their perceptions of children's intelligence and academic abilities (Coplan, Hughes, Bosaki, & Rose-Krasnor, 2011).

In this essay, we review extant theory and research pertaining to teachers' beliefs about young children's *social withdrawal* in the classroom. In the following pages, we provide an overview of social withdrawal, with a focus on children's different motivations for withdrawing from peer interaction. This is followed by a more in-depth review of empirical research examining teachers' beliefs, reactions, and responses to social withdrawal in early childhood. Strategies that teachers can incorporate into their classrooms to assist socially withdrawn children are then presented, as well as other implications for teachers and educational practitioners. Finally, caveats and some directions for future research are discussed.

OVERVIEW OF SOCIAL WITHDRAWAL
IN EARLY CHILDHOOD

The peer group provides an important and unique context for young children's social, emotional, cognitive, and moral development (Rubin, Bukowski, & Bowker, 2015). Concomitantly, researchers have proposed and widely demonstrated that children who experience a relatively low quantity and/or quality of social interactions are at increased risk for a wide range of maladaptive outcomes (Rubin, Coplan, & Bowker, 2009).

Rubin (1982) originally proposed two distinct causal processes that may account for children's lack of social interaction. *Active isolation* refers to the process whereby some children spend time alone in the presence of available peers because they are rejected, excluded, and/or ostracized. Scholars have suggested various factors that may lead to active isolation, including children's display of socially immature, socially unskilled, and non-normative behaviors such as aggression and impulsivity (Rubin et al., 2015). In contrast, *social withdrawal* denotes the process whereby children remove themselves from the peer group. Social withdrawal is best construed as an umbrella term that encompasses different underlying reasons as to why children choose to remove themselves from opportunities for social interaction (Rubin et al., 2009). In this chapter we focus on two specific subtypes of social withdrawal, shyness and unsociability.

Shyness. *Shyness* is a temperamental trait characterized by wariness and anxiety in the face of social novelty and perceived social evaluation (Rubin et al., 2009). Using different nomenclature, researchers have examined children's wariness and anxiety in the presence of novelty (e.g., behavioral inhibition), social novelty (e.g., fearful shyness) social familiarity (e.g., anxious-solitude), and perceived social evaluation (e.g., self-conscious shyness) (see Rubin et al., 2009 for a detailed review). From a *motivational* perspective, shy children are characterized as withdrawing from social interactions because of conflict between social-approach and -avoidance motivations. That is, shy children desire interaction with their peers (i.e., high approach motivation), but avoid them because of social fear and anxiety (i.e., high avoidance motivation).

Researchers have suggested that this approach-avoidance conflict manifests behaviorally in peer contexts in the form of reticent behaviors (Coplan, Prakash, O'Neil, & Armer, 2004), which include prolonged watching of other children engaged in play without attempting to join in (onlooking) and being unoccupied. Results from a series of studies suggest that shyness is associated with the more frequent display of reticent behaviors during unstructured play activities at preschool and kindergarten (e.g., Coplan, Arbeau, & Armer, 2008; Coplan, Gavinski-Molina, Lagacé-Séguin, & Wichmann, 2001).

Shyness in early childhood is also contemporaneously and prospectively linked to a host of negative socioemotional outcomes (Rubin et al., 2009). For example, in the peer group, young shy children are faced with greater peer exclusion and rejection (e.g., Coplan et al., 2008), are less popular (Eggum-Wilkens, Valiente, Swanson, & Lemery-Chalfant, 2014), and are more likely to be disliked than their non-shy age-mates (e.g., Gazelle & Ladd, 2003). Perhaps as a result, shy young children demonstrate a higher risk for developing internalizing problems such as anxiety and depression, lower self-worth, and loneliness (e.g., Coplan et al., 2004; Eggum-Wilkens et al., 2014; Gazelle & Ladd, 2003).

Shyness is also associated with school difficulties in early childhood. Coplan and Arbeau (2008) suggested that feelings of fear and wariness might be heightened in the early childhood school environment. Upon entering school, shy children are challenged with a large group of unfamiliar peers and experience increased academic demands; particularly verbal participation in the classroom (Coplan & Arbeau, 2008). Even when shy children become familiar with the school environment, they may still experience school adjustment difficulties (e.g., Coplan et al., 2008; Evans, 2001). Indeed, there is evidence to suggest that shy children have lower language and attention skills, cognitive competence, and academic achievement (e.g., Coplan et al., 2008; Evans, 2001; Hughes & Coplan, 2010).

Overall, shy children tend to dislike school and have less close and more dependent teacher-student relationships (e.g., Coplan et al., 2008). However, characteristics of teachers' interactions and relationships with shy children may also serve a *protective* role (Arbeau, Coplan, & Weeks, 2010). For example, Buhs, Rudasill, Kalutskaya, and Griese (2015) reported that in classrooms with high levels of teacher sensitivity, shyness was negatively associated with peer rejection and positively associated with student engagement. In contrast, in classrooms with lower levels of teacher sensitivity, shyness was unrelated to peer rejection and student engagement. These findings suggest that teacher sensitivity has a buffering effect on the school adjustment of shy children.

Unsociability

Unsociability (sometimes also referred to as *social disinterest* or *affinity for aloneness*) refers to a non-fearful preference for solitude (Asendorpf & Meier, 1993). From a motivational perspective, unsociability is conceptualized as reflecting both low social-approach and low social-avoidance motives (Asendorpf, 1990; Coplan, Ooi, Rose-Krasnor, & Nocita (2014). In this regard, unsociable children are thought to be content to play alone, but are also willing to engage with others and are adept at social interactions. For example, unsociable children speak as often as their sociable counterparts when engaged in conversations with peers (Asendorpf & Meier, 1993).

A small number of studies have investigated the adjustment outcomes of unsociable children in early childhood. There is some evidence that unsociability is associated with greater peer exclusion and peer neglect (Coplan et al., 2004; Harrist, Zaia, Bates, Dodge, & Petit, 1997). However, unsociability does not appear to put young children at risk for increased internalizing difficulties. For example, Coplan and colleagues (2004) found that child unsociability (as rated by mothers) was negatively associated with observed initiations of peer interaction, positively associated to teacher-rated behavioral withdrawal, but not significantly related to the display of anxiety or to children's perceived competence. Additionally, unsociable children have not been found to differ in their social-cognitive abilities from their non-withdrawn age-mates (Harrist et al., 1997). Taken together, researchers tend to consider unsociability in early childhood as a benign form of social withdrawal (Asendorpf & Meier, 1993; Coplan et al., 2004; Harrist et al., 1997).

TEACHERS' BELIEFS ABOUT SOCIAL WITHDRAWAL VERSUS OTHER PROBLEM BEHAVIORS

Historically, researchers have suggested that young socially withdrawn children go largely unnoticed in the classroom (Evans, 2001). Moreover, it was argued that teachers may even view withdrawn children favorably because their quiet nature helps maintain order in the classroom and may serve to reduce the demands of the classroom environment (Rubin, 1982). However, more recently, there is emerging evidence to support the notion that teachers recognize socially withdrawn behaviors to be problematic, particularly *shy* behaviors (Arbeau & Coplan, 2007; Coplan, Bullock, Archbell, & Bosaki, 2015).

Early research examining teachers' beliefs about children's social withdrawal did not differentiate between underlying *motivations* to withdraw from social situations. For example, socially withdrawn behavior was broadly conceptualized as delayed age-appropriate social skills, insecurity, and poor expressive abilities (Algozzine, Ysseldyke, Christenson, & Thurlow, 1983), avoidance of social involvement or communication with others (Safran & Safran, 1984), or as a type of socially immature behavior (Cunningham & Sugawara, 1988). Most of these studies sought to compare teachers' beliefs about social withdrawal with other types of problematic classroom behaviors (e.g., aggression or disruptive behaviors).

In one of the first studies to investigate teachers' beliefs about social withdrawal, Brophy and Rohrkemper (1981) asked teachers about their strategies for responding to student problem behaviors in the classroom. Among the results, teachers reported that they would use a combination of restrictive and helping strategies (i.e., rewards and punishments) in response to socially withdrawn behaviors. Algozzine et al. (1983) similarly reported that teachers would utilize a teacher-directed intervention for socially withdrawn children. These findings suggest that teachers believe meaningful change in student behavior is possible, and that they have the ability to affect behavioral change through their own actions. Taken together, results from these early studies provide some initial evidence of teachers' recognition that a general conceptualization of children's social withdrawal (albeit, highlighting anxious underpinnings) might warrant concern and intervention.

In a series of studies, Safran and Safran (1984, 1985) examined teachers' tolerance of different classroom behaviors. They found that teachers had a higher tolerance for socially withdrawn behavior compared to other problematic behaviors (i.e., aggression). The authors emphasized that although teachers viewed social withdrawal to be problematic, immediate attention was not required as these behaviors do not appear to disrupt the classroom environment, nor are they threatening to other students.

Cunningham and Sugawara (1988) examined teachers' beliefs about socially immature and defiant behaviors in a sample of pre-service teachers. Pre-service teachers completed a series of self-report questionnaires including the Teacher Tolerance Scale (i.e., social defiance behaviors, social immaturity behaviors), the Costs Scale (i.e., costs to the teacher, class, and the student), and the Strategies Scale (i.e., choice of helping strategy, restrictive strategy). The authors measured social immaturity using 20 behavior items including social withdrawal, lack of self-confidence, tension and inability to relax, sensitivity, shyness and bashfulness, physical complaints, and anxiety. Many of the behavioral markers defining social immaturity are consistent with social withdrawal, particularly shyness (Coplan et al., 2004)—thus demonstrating the murky conceptualization of social withdrawal in early research on teachers' beliefs.

Not surprisingly, socially defiant behaviors were perceived to have more adverse effects in the classroom (Cunningham & Sugawara, 1988). Teachers indicated more tolerance for socially immature behaviors, and were oriented toward helping socially immature children. Moreover, socially defiant behaviors were viewed as more costly to the teacher and to the class, whereas teachers viewed socially immature behaviors as significantly more costly in terms of the child (i.e., implications for socioemotional development). Even from the pre-service teacher level, teachers seem cognizant of the potentially detrimental outcomes for young socially immature children. Although these results are reported with a sample of pre-service teachers, research has established that teacher beliefs and responses remain relatively stable from pre-service teaching onwards in terms of children's temperament (e.g., Deng et al., 2017).

More recently, teachers' beliefs about socially withdrawn behavior have been examined with the consideration of peer implications. For example, Chang (2003) investigated the impact of teachers' beliefs about socially withdrawn and aggressive students on children's peer preferences. Among the results, teachers expressed more aversion to aggression and more empathy to social withdrawal. In turn, these beliefs were found to impact peer rejection among aggressive students, but not socially withdrawn students. This provides some evidence that teachers' beliefs are influential, impacting peer preferences in the classroom. It remains to be seen how this process may play out for socially withdrawn students.

Taken together, results from these early studies suggest that teachers were aware of the potentially problematic outcomes for children who exhibit socially withdrawn behaviors. However, teachers seemed to be more tolerant of withdrawn behaviors in the classroom as compared to overt misbehaviors. In this regard, these findings appear to foreshadow Evans's (2001) postulation that socially withdrawn children may go unnoticed in the classroom, especially in the presence of disruptive peers.

The majority of the aforementioned studies investigating teachers' beliefs about social withdrawal conceptualize this construct quite broadly. Contemporary theory and research related to social withdrawal now consider this construct to be multidimensional (Coplan, Ooi, & Nocita, 2015). Similarly, more recent studies examining teachers' beliefs about social withdrawal have also conceptualized this construct as stemming from different underlying social motivations, exploring teachers' beliefs about *shyness* and *unsociability* (Arbeau & Coplan, 2007; Coplan et al., 2015). In the subsequent section, we review teachers' beliefs about shyness and unsociability as distinct constructs.

TEACHERS' BELIEFS ABOUT SHYNESS VERSUS UNSOCIABILITY

In the last 10 years, researchers have begun to examine teachers' differential beliefs about subtypes of social withdrawal. These studies typically involved presenting early childhood educators and teachers with hypothetical vignettes depicting boys and/or girls displaying shy and unsociable behaviors (e.g., Arbeau & Coplan, 2007; Coplan et al., 2015; Li, Coplan, Archbell, Bullock, & Chen, 2016). Following each vignette, teachers responded to a series of items assessing their attitudes, beliefs, emotional reactions, and intervention strategies. Overall, results from these studies provide converging evidence that teachers clearly differentiate between hypothetical shy and unsociable children.

For example, Arbeau and Coplan (2007) reported kindergarten teachers attributed greater *intentionality* to unsociable as compared to shy behaviors. The authors posited that this reflects teachers' understanding that shy children desire social interaction, but their anxieties prevent them from comfortably engaging with their peers (Coplan et al., 2004). This may point toward teachers' recognition of the underlying motivations that result in children withdrawing from social situations. Consistent with this notion, kindergarten teachers in this sample reported less tolerance for, and a greater intention to intervene, in response to shy versus unsociable behaviors. Moreover, when intervening with shy children, teachers indicated that they would most likely promote social skill acquisition.

Coplan and colleagues (2011) further examined these issues in a study of elementary school teachers' beliefs about hypothetical shy, talkative, and average students. Similar to previous studies with teachers of younger children, in response to shy behaviors, elementary teachers were more likely to endorse *indirect* strategies (reporting the behavior to parents or principals, seeking additional information, or simply monitoring the situation) and *peer-focused* strategies (involving classmates, seeking to increase social interaction among children). These teacher intervention strategies were notably encouraging, as there is evidence of some success of interventions (outside of the school context) that focus on developing positive relationships with peers (Coplan, Schneider, Matheson, & Graham, 2010).

Taken together, these findings suggest that teachers of young children may indeed pay attention to shy children in the classroom—as they indicate this behavior warrants attention. This could reflect increased awareness of the risk of socio-emotional adjustment difficulties for shy children (e.g., Rubin et al., 2009). Moreover, promoting social skills appears to be a particularly appropriate response to shy behaviors, given that shy children often lack appropriate levels of social competence. In support of this, there is evidence that interventions focusing on the development of social skills are particularly beneficial for young shy children in decreasing socially wary behaviors and increasing children's social competence (e.g., Coplan et al., 2010). In contrast, teachers appear to be more likely to leave unsociable children "alone," perhaps because of their awareness of the relatively benign nature of this form of social withdrawal (Coplan et al., 2004).

Arbeau and Coplan (2007) also asked kindergarten teachers if they believed that shyness and unsociability would interfere with child development. Results indicated that teachers perceived higher *social* and *academic costs* for the depiction of shy children. More recently, Coplan and colleagues (2015) reported similar findings in a sample of early childhood educators (ECEs), who also anticipated more negative outcomes for hypothetical shy compared to unsociable children. For example, as compared to their shy counterparts, unsociable children were rated by ECEs as having greater likeability and were less likely to be excluded or ignored by their peers.

Coplan et al. (2015) also investigated ECEs' *emotional reactions* in response to shy and unsociable behaviors. Depictions of shyness did not elicit a strong response of anger, but ECEs indicated that they would be most worried about shy behavior compared to all other behaviors presented. The authors suggested that this reflects future-oriented concerns, which may therefore demonstrate teachers' awareness of shy children's risk for socioemotional difficulties (Coplan et al., 2015). Teachers may readily pick up on cues that shy children exhibit; *wanting* to play with others, while simultaneously experiencing social fearfulness. Thus, due to the approach-avoidance conflict (Asendorpf, 1990), teachers may worry more about shy children's social adjustment. In comparison, ECEs' reported little worry in response to unsociable behaviors (Coplan et al., 2015), consistent with postulations about the relatively benign nature of this form of social withdrawal.

Across both of these studies, teachers appear to have quite an *accurate* set of beliefs about the implications of shyness versus unsociability for young children's social development and school adjustment. As mentioned previously, shy behaviors in the classroom are associated with internalizing problems, peer difficulties, and a lack of academic success (Rubin et al., 2009). Indeed, shy children's feelings of anxiety may interfere with their ability to demonstrate competence in both the social and academic domains (Coplan & Arbeau, 2008). Teachers appear to also hold more negative perceptions of shy compared to unsociable children's social, emotional, and academic competence.

The link between shyness and academic achievement bears additional scrutiny. Shy children are less likely to verbally participate in class (Coplan & Arbeau, 2008), which in turn, may negatively impact teachers' perceptions of shy children's academic abilities (Coplan et al., 2015). For example, it is possible that extremely shy children may know the answer to questions posed by a classroom teacher, but are simply too nervous to speak in front of the class. Shy students may also experience debilitating anxiety when called upon to speak in front of their classmates, which may result in a temporary mental lapse.

Also similar to previous studies, Coplan et al. (2011) found that teachers perceived shy children as possessing poorer verbal skills and likely to display poorer academic performance as compared to more talkative and average children. These results align with research demonstrating that shy children tend to score lower on standardized tests of language and present other academic difficulties (Evans, 2001). However, results from subsequent analyses further indicated that teachers rated shy children as less *intelligent* than their more talkative counterparts. Coplan et al. (2011) speculated that teachers' negative perceptions of shy children's academic abilities may create a *self-fulfilling prophecy*, whereby shy children may come to "live down" to the low expectations a teacher may have for them. Indeed, there is research to substantiate the idea that students' self-perceptions shift according to teacher expectations (e.g., Rubie-Davies, Hattie, & Hamilton, 2006).

To summarize, the earliest studies of teachers' beliefs about social withdrawal (which construed this construct in broad and undifferentiated terms) suggests that teachers viewed these behaviors as less problematic than more overt problem behaviors, such as aggression. This led to the idea that teachers might ignore socially withdrawn students in their classrooms. However, contemporary studies have examined teachers' beliefs about distinct subtypes of social withdrawal (i.e., shyness vs. unsociability).

Results from these studies demonstrate teachers' growing awareness of the distinction among children's motivations for engaging in socially withdrawn behaviors at school. Moreover, teachers perceive shyness as a notable problem at school, worry about shy children, and anticipate negative social and academic consequences for shy students. In contrast, unsociable behaviors are perceived as largely normative and do not appear to merit intervention or worry.

IMPLICATIONS FOR TEACHERS AND PROFESSIONAL DEVELOPMENT

Shy children are at increased risk for a host of negative socio-emotional and academic difficulties. Research has established that teachers show concern for shy behaviors and believe shyness warrants intervention. With this in mind, what can teachers *do* to create classroom environments that foster healthy social and academic development for shy children?

Drawing upon the extant literature, Kalutskaya, Archbell, Rudasill, and Coplan (2015) suggested several different specific strategies for teachers to promote positive experiences for shy children in the classroom. For example, verbal participation among shy children has been found to increase when teachers ask indirect questions and provide personal comments (Evans, 2001). Teachers can also lessen anxiety among shy children by gradually exposing them to intimidating tasks and providing praise for each successive step (O'Connor, Cappella, McCormick, & McClowry, 2014). Similarly, teachers should engage in discussions with shy children about upcoming changes to routines, allowing children to mentally prepare (Henderson & Fox, 1998). Finally, applying *learner-centered* techniques may assist shy children in gaining confidence, which may subsequently result in higher levels of verbal participation. For example, Evans (2001) found that teachers would ask shy children questions that they knew the answer to, which may result in increased confidence and comfort in the classroom.

Teachers can also adapt recent approaches to early intervention developed for shy children outside of the classroom environment. For example, Coplan and colleagues (2010) developed an intervention program for extremely shy preschoolers comprised of a didactic component (i.e., circle time—where relevant social skills are taught via interactions with puppets and songs/games emphasize appropriate social skills) and adult-facilitated free play (where leaders assist children in initiating appropriate social interactions and model socially competent behaviors). Such programs offer important skills and strategies for children that may foster peer relationships and promote healthy socio-emotional development not only for shy individuals, but also for all children in the classroom (see O'Connor et al.,

2015). Therefore, it would be advantageous for professional development programs to highlight appropriate strategies to help intervene in response to behavior-specific problems. This is particularly critical for teachers of young children, as the transition to formal school presents many challenges to children with different temperamental traits.

Although teachers generally present positive views toward unsociability (Arbeau & Coplan, 2007; Coplan et al., 2015), researchers have suggested that teachers should continue to monitor these children and promote social skills, as positive social interaction imparts copious benefits for children during early education (Coplan & Arbeau, 2008). Indeed, it is argued that too much time alone in childhood may take away from important peer experiences, where children learn to deal with conflict, compromise and negotiate, and develop perspective-taking skills (Rubin et al., 2015). Therefore, young unsociable children may likely benefit from at least *some* amount of regular social interaction.

CONCLUSIONS AND FUTURE DIRECTIONS

This essay presents a review of the literature on children's motivations to withdraw from peer interactions and teachers' beliefs about different forms of social withdrawal. We also highlight how teachers can support the social and academic development of socially withdrawn (especially *shy*) children in early educational settings (Kalutskaya et al., 2015). There is growing evidence to suggest that teachers view shyness as a particularly problematic form of social withdrawal and are aware of the socio-emotional and academic difficulties that shy children experience (Arbeau & Coplan, 2007; Coplan et al., 2015; Coplan et al., 2011). Teachers also appear to display appropriate knowledge regarding intervention strategies, but would likely benefit from further professional development (Coplan et al., 2011). In contrast, teachers seem to view unsociability as a comparatively benign form of social withdrawal in early childhood (Arbeau & Coplan, 2007; Coplan et al., 2015). However, researchers suggest that teachers should still cautiously monitor unsociable children's peer interactions (Arbeau & Coplan, 2007).

In terms of future directions, there are several areas that merit additional research attention. For example, much of the research that we have reviewed herein relied exclusively on teachers' self-reported responses to depictions of hypothetical children (e.g., Arbeau & Coplan, 2007; Coplan et al., 2015). This is a notable shortcoming of this body of research. Teachers' behaviors in the classroom may or may not directly correspond to their responses to hypothetical vignettes. Thus, there is a strong need for future studies to couple self-reports that examine teachers' beliefs about children's behaviors along with direct observations of teachers' classroom actions. For instance, Dobbs and Arnold (2009) examined preschool teachers' perceptions toward children's internalizing and externalizing behaviors, and incorporated the use of classroom observations. They found that teachers gave more commands to children they perceived as having greater behavioral problems.

Deng and colleagues (2017) found that pre-service teachers appear to hold similar beliefs about shy children as previously reported in samples of in-service teachers. However, little is known about how teachers' beliefs about social withdrawal develop initially and—importantly—if they evolve over time as a function of experience and/or additional training. Therefore, future studies may consider examining the impact of teacher characteristics (i.e., educational experience, self-efficacy, and personality traits) on the development of teachers' beliefs about social withdrawal. Results from such studies can provide additional insight to assist in the development of training opportunities for pre-service and in-service teachers.

Also related to teachers training and experience is the notion of *gender* differences. There is growing evidence to suggest that social withdrawal (and particularly shyness) may have more negative implications for boys versus girls, because such behaviors violate gender-stereotypes regarding male dominance and assertion (see Doey, Coplan, & Kingsbury, 2014 for a review). However, as highlighted by Doey et al. (2014), although socially withdrawn boys appear to elicit more negative responses from parents and peers than withdrawn girls, these gender differences have not typically been evidenced in studies of teachers (e.g., Arbeau & Coplan, 2007; Coplan et al., 2015; Coplan et al., 2011). These scholars suggest that teacher training might help to reduce gender biases among kindergarten and elementary school teachers. Nevertheless, these inconsistent findings warrant continued research to determine if teachers hold gender-based beliefs about social withdrawal. Future research may benefit from incorporating Implicit Association Testing (IAT) into research designs, as IAT is less susceptible to response bias (Steffans, 2004).

Finally, almost all of the studies reviewed in this chapter were conducted in the West. As such, the findings presented in this chapter may not be generalizable to different cultures. Indeed, there is evidence to suggest context-specific differences in teachers' perceptions and implications of subtypes of social withdrawal in non-Western cultures (e.g., Li et al., 2016). Future research should continue to explore teachers' beliefs toward subtypes of social withdrawal in early childhood from a wide range of cultural contexts.

Overall, the findings from these studies have important implications on teachers and socially withdrawn children. Teachers' beliefs can have an impact on children's self-perceptions as well as perceptions of their peers.

Moreover, teachers' beliefs toward children's socially withdrawn behaviors can inform appropriate intervention strategies, which, in turn, can positively impact the social and emotional development of young socially withdrawn children. Although teachers may be aware of the distinct motivations underlying unsociable and shy children's behavior and respond accordingly, providing teachers with additional resources and strategies will benefit both teachers and socially withdrawn children alike.

REFERENCES

Algozzine, B., Ysseldyke, J. E., Christenson, S., & Thurlow, M. L. (1983). A factor analysis of teachers' intervention choices for dealing with students' behavior and learning problems. *The Elementary School Journal, 84*, 189–197.

Arbeau, K. A., & Coplan, R. J. (2007). Kindergarten teachers' beliefs and responses to hypothetical prosocial, asocial, and antisocial children. *Merrill-Palmer Quarterly, 53*, 291–318.

Arbeau, K. A., Coplan, R. J., & Weeks, M. (2010). Shyness, teacher-child relationships, and socio-emotional adjustment in grade 1. *International Journal of Behavioral Development, 34*, 259–269.

Asendorpf, J. B. (1990). Beyond social withdrawal: Shyness, unsociability, and peer avoidance. *Human Development, 33*, 250–259.

Asendorpf, J. B., & Meier, G. H. (1993). Personality effects on children's speech in everyday life: Sociability—mediated exposure and shyness—mediated reactivity to social situations. *Journal of Personality and Social Psychology, 65*, 1072–1083.

Brophy, J. E., & Rohrkemper, M. M. (1981). The influence of problem ownership on teachers' perceptions of and strategies for coping with problem students. *Journal of Educational Psychology, 73*, 295–311.

Buhs, E. S., Rudasill, M. K., Kalutskaya, I. N., & Griese, E. R. (2015). Shyness and engagement: Contributions of peer rejection and teacher sensitivity. *Early Childhood Research Quarterly, 30*, 12–19.

Chang, L. (2003). Variable effects of children's aggression, social withdrawal, and prosocial leadership as functions of teacher beliefs and behaviors. *Child Development, 74*, 535–548.

Coplan, R. J., & Arbeau, K. A. (2008). The stresses of a "brave new world": Shyness and school adjustment in kindergarten. *Journal of Research in Childhood Education, 22*, 377–389.

Coplan, R. J., Arbeau, K. A., & Armer, M. (2008). Don't fret, be supportive! Maternal characteristics linking child shyness to psychosocial and school adjustment in kindergarten. *Journal of Abnormal Child Psychology, 36*, 359–371.

Coplan, R. J., Bullock, A., Archbell, K. A., & Bosaki, S. (2015). Preschool teachers' attitudes, beliefs, and emotional reactions to young children's peer group activities. *Early Childhood Research Quarterly, 30*, 117–127.

Coplan, R. J., Gavinski-Molina, M. H., Lagacé-Séguin, D. G., & Wichmann, C. (2001). When girls versus boys play alone: Nonsocial play and adjustment in kindergarten. *Developmental Psychology, 37,* 464–474.

Coplan, R. J., Hughes, K., Bosacki, S., & Rose-Krasnor, L. (2011). Is silence golden? Elementary school teachers' strategies and beliefs regarding hypothetical shy/quiet and exuberant/talkative children. *Journal of Educational Psychology, 103,* 939–951.

Coplan, R. J., Ooi, L. L., Rose-Krasnor, L., & Nocita, G. (2014). "I want to play alone": Assessment and correlates of self-reported preference for solitary play in young children. *Infant and Child Development, 23,* 229–238.

Coplan, R. J., Ooi, L. L., & Nocita, G. (2015). When one is company and two is a crowd: Why some children prefer solitude. *Child Development Perspectives, 9,* 133–137.

Coplan, R. J., Prakash, K., O'Neil, & Armer, M. (2004). Do you "want" to play? Distinguishing between conflicted shyness and social disinterest in early childhood. *Developmental Psychology, 40,* 244–258.

Coplan, R. J., Schneider, B. H., Matheson, A., & Graham, A. (2010). "Play skills" for shy children: Development of a social skills facilitated play early intervention program for extremely inhibited preschoolers. *Infant and Child Development, 19,* 223–237.

Cunningham, B., & Sugawara, A. I. (1988). Preservice teachers' perceptions of children's problem behaviors. *Journal of Educational Research, 82,* 34–39.

Deng, Q., Trainin, G., Rudasill, K., Kalutskaya, I, Wessels, S., Torquati, J., & Coplan, R. J. (2017). Elementary preservice teachers' attitudes and pedagogical strategies toward hypothetical shy, exuberant, and average children. *Learning and Individual Differences, 56,* 85–95.

Dobbs, J., & Arnold, D. H. (2009). Relationship between preschool teachers' reports of children's behavior and their behavior toward those children. *School Psychology Quarterly, 24,* 95–105.

Doey, L., Coplan, R. J., & Kingsbury, M. (2014). Bashful boys and coy girls: A review of gender differences in childhood shyness. *Sex Roles, 70,* 255–266.

Eggum-Wilkens, N. D., Valiente, C., Swanson, J., Lemery-Chalfant, K. (2014). Children's shyness, popularity, school liking, cooperative participation, and internalizing problems in early school years. *Early Childhood Research Quarterly, 29,* 85–94.

Evans, M. A. (2001). Shyness in the classroom and home. In W. R. Crozier & L. E. Alden (Eds.), *International handbook of social anxiety: Concepts, research, and interventions relating to the self and shyness* (pp. 159–183). Westport, CT: Wiley.

Farmer, T. W., McAuliffe Lines, M., & Hamm, J. V. (2011). Revealing the invisible hand: The role of teachers in children's peer experiences. *Journal of Applied Developmental Psychology, 32,* 247–256.

Gazelle, H., & Ladd, G. W. (2003). Anxious solitude and peer exclusion: A diathesis-stress model of internalizing trajectories in childhood. *Child Development, 75,* 829–849.

Harrist, A. W., Zaia, A. F., Bates, J. E., Dodge, K. A., & Petit, G. S. (1997). Subtypes of social withdrawal in early childhood: Sociometric status and social—cognitive differences across four years. *Child Development, 68,* 278–294.

Henderson, H. A., & Fox, N. A. (1998). Inhibited and uninhibited children: Challenges in school settings. *School Psychology Review*, *27*, 492–505.

Hollingsworth, H. L., & Winters, M. K. (2013). Teachers' beliefs and practices relating to development in preschool: Importance placed on social-emotional behaviors and skills. *Early Child Development and Care*, *183*, 1758–1781.

Hughes, K. & Coplan, R. J. (2010). Exploring the processes linking shyness and academic achievement in childhood. *School Psychology Quarterly*, *25*, 213–222.

Kalutskaya, I., Archbell, K. A., Rudasill, K. M., & Coplan, R. J. (2015). Shy children in the classroom: From research to educational practice. *Translational Issues in Psychological Science*, *1*, 149–157.

Lee, J. S. (2006). Preschool teachers' shared beliefs about appropriate pedagogy for 4-year-olds. *Early Childhood Education Journal*, *33*, 433–441.

Li, Y., Coplan, R. J., Archbell, K. A., Bullock, A., & Chen, L. (2016). Chinese kindergarten teachers' beliefs about young children's classroom behavior. *Early Childhood Research Quarterly*, *36*, 122–132.

O'Connor, E. E., Cappella, E., McCormick, M. P., & McClowry, S. G. (2014). Enhancing the academic development of shy children: A test of the efficacy of *INSIGHTS*. *School Psychology Review*, *43*, 239–259.

Rubie-Davies, C., Hattie, J., & Hamilton, R. (2006). Expecting the best for students: Teacher expectations and academic outcomes. *British Journal of Educational Psychology*, *76*, 429–444.

Rubin, K. H. (1982). Non-social play in preschoolers: Necessary evil? *Child Development*, *53*, 651–657.

Rubin, K. H., Bukowski, W. M., & Bowker, J. C. (2015). Children in peer groups. In R. M. Lerner (Series Ed.), M. H. Bornstein & T. Leventhal (Vol. Eds.), *Handbook of child psychology and developmental science: Ecological settings and processes in developmental systems* (Vol. 4, 7th ed., pp. 175–222). New York, NY: Wiley-Blackwell.

Rubin, K. H., Coplan, R. J., & Bowker, J. (2009). Social withdrawal in childhood. *Annual Review of Psychology*, *60*, 141–171.

Safran, S. P., & Safran, J. S. (1984). Elementary teachers' tolerance of problem behaviors. *The Elementary School Journal*, *85*, 237–243.

Safran S. P., & Safran, J. S. (1985). Classroom context and teachers' perceptions of problem behaviors. *Journal of Educational Psychology*, *77*, 20–28.

Steffans, M. C. (2004). Is the implicit association test immune to faking? *Experimental Psychology*, *51*, 165–179.

Wentzel, K. R. (2003). Motivating students to behave in socially competent ways. *Theory into Practice*, *42*, 319–326.

CHAPTER 10

COACHING TO IMPROVE MOTIVATION IN EARLY CHILDHOOD PRACTITIONERS AND PARENTS

Jon Lee, Andy J. Frey, Zachary Warner, and Laura Kelley

COACHING TO IMPROVE ADULT MOTIVATION IN EARLY CHILDHOOD

Motivation is a pervasive and fundamental aspect of our work in early childhood education. It is a powerful force that drives a child's persistence, decision-making, and desire to learn. As educators, we use motivation to help shape futures and draw out potential. However, the role of motivation in the classroom is not only relevant for students; the motivations of teachers and parents are also powerful allies in supporting a student's growth and development. Adult motivation is influenced by two key variables: importance and confidence (Miller & Rollnick, 2012). Teachers and parents reveal what they find important by the methods they choose to influence students, and demonstrate confidence through their willingness to try new practices that represent significant deviations from their current or preferred behavior. Thus, the importance assigned to a perspective new practice and perceived confidence in demonstrating the necessary skills

Contemporary Perspectives on Research on
Motivation in Early Childhood Education, pp. 209–228
Copyright © 2019 by Information Age Publishing
All rights of reproduction in any form reserved.

that accompany it are factors that can drive teachers' and parents' own persistence, decision making, and desire to learn (Miller & Rollnick, 2012). Therefore, if importance is cultivated and confidence is strengthened, teachers and parents may be more likely to accept suggested and, at times, required changes to how they support students.

What motivates the choices teachers and parents make regarding the practices they implement is amplified when considering the ever-growing number of students who face social and behavioral challenges affecting their academic achievement, and the increasing calls for teachers to be held accountable in implementing quality instructional practices that meet these needs (Vidair, Sauro, Blocher, Scudellari, & Hoagwood, 2014). Teachers themselves acknowledge the importance of these challenges in their self-expressed desire for more training in evidence-based practices (EBP) focusing on behavior management (Reinke, Stormont, Herman, Puri, & Goel, 2011), as many do not feel adequately prepared by their teacher education programs in this area (Siebert, 2005). Yet, there remain substantial challenges (e.g., inadequate professional development, poor student–teacher–parent engagement, classroom disorganization, etc.) that arise for teachers in learning, using, and sustaining new skills that affect the implementation of EBPs in educational settings (Becker & Domitrovich, 2011; Hemmeter, Snyder, Kinder, & Artman, 2011).

Parents face their own unique motivational challenges, as aberrant child behavior is decidedly difficult for many parents to manage. Although parent training and education programs have long been a recognized delivery system for facilitating change in parenting practices in support of young children's growth and development, research on these programs does not always bear out their efficacy (see Reyno & McGrath, 2006). For example, a major barrier to positively impacting family dynamics and managing a child's problem behavior has been access to the family by competent professionals (Frey et al., 2013). The access issue may be par-tially motivation-related, as Reyno and McGrath (2006) write that "many parents who stand to benefit the most from this training (i.e., those who are economically disadvantaged or socially isolated) display limited atten-dance with clinic-based programs and are less likely to complete treatment" (p. 100). In response, those advocating EBPs have begun to seek out better methods for communicating that tap teacher and parent motivation.

In schools, coaching has emerged as a vehicle for the ongoing profes-sional development (PD) and educational activities that are necessary for teachers as they work to learn and implement EBPs (Darling-Hammond, 2009). Denton and Hasbrouck (2009) describe coaching as a practice in which a person with specialized knowledge works with a teacher to change their current behavior and practice. An emerging body of research demonstrates coaching-based PD has a positive effect on both teachers' instructional practice (Hsieh, Hemmeter, McCollum, & Ostrosky, 2009) and child outcomes (Powell, Diamond, Burchinal, & Koehler, 2010; Wasik & Hindman, 2011). For example, Driscoll, Wang, Mashburn, and Pianta (2011) found that preschool teachers were 13 times more likely to implement an intervention when they had access to a coach, and multiple studies suggest that access to support such as a coach results in greater self-efficacy and better implementation (Forman, Olin, Hoagwood, Crowe, & Saka, 2009; Ransford, Greenberg, Domitrovich, Small, & Jacobson, 2009; Wenz-Gross & Upshur, 2012). Furthermore, Stormont, Reinke, Newcomer, Marchese, and Lewis (2015) conducted a systematic review of the coaching literature and concluded that 83% of interventions that utilized a coach as a component of the intervention yielded positive results. Despite evidence suggesting a positive association between coaching and implementation, Powell and Diamond (2013) note, "the proliferation of coaching-based PD programs far exceeds available research knowledge on coaching with early childhood teachers" (p. 97). The authors go on to argue that advances in coaching-based PD are hindered by an inattention to the processes and specific uses of coaching within early childhood settings.

In an effort to combat this issue, Powell and Diamond (2013) identified three dimensions to consider when describing and evaluating coaching efforts in early childhood settings. The first, *structure*, pertains to the delivery and receipt of coaching, and includes the number, duration, and frequency of coaching sessions. The second dimension, *process*, involves the coach actions or activities aimed at promoting behavior change. Finally, the third dimension is *content*, which includes the practice coaching is intended to influence. We agree with Powell and Diamond that understanding the ways coaching is implemented is critical for the design and scaling of coaching-based PD, and concur that examining coaching practice based on structure, process, and content provides a much-needed lens for describing and evaluating coaching-based PD. Moreover, we argue that in addition to these dimensions, the integration of a theory of change is crucial to the success of coaching because coaching by definition is designed to help facilitate changes in behavior. More specifically, we contend that by leveraging a theory of change that prioritizes adult motivation, coaching could be a critical, malleable factor when addressing not only challenges in school-based EBP adoption, but adoption among parents as well.

Several pioneers of the coaching literature have eloquently described why motivation is so important to coaching teachers. Lyon, Stirman, Kerns, and Bruns (2011) suggest teachers with the lowest levels of competence are also those who are least likely to engage in or benefit from PD activities, and Guskey (1994) concluded that the magnitude of change a person is asked to make is inversely related to the likelihood they will follow through. These findings are significant given the fact that EBPs are frequently chosen at the building or administrative level, and Erchul (2011) notes teachers are often unable to reject the EBP they are being required to implement even if they view it as "unfamiliar, time consuming, or philosophically unappealing" (p. 200). This creates a unique and challenging situation in which a coach must encourage the adoption of an intervention the teacher may not agree with by providing guidance that was not asked for. Unlike teachers, parents get to choose the practices they implement, seemingly making motivation a non-issue. For example, Dishion et al. (2008) suggests that family-centered intervention programs that work to support parents in changing their own parenting practices (i.e., increased use of positive behavioral supports) benefits children's behavioral outcomes (i.e., lower frequency of problem behaviors). However, the same feelings teachers experience when confronted with a new intervention may too be those of parents when approached by schools about their potential involvement in parent training and educational activities. Shaw, Dishion, Supplee, Gardner, and Arnds (2006) note that "one of the barriers to implementing family interventions within service settings is parent motivation" (p. 2), which has often been hampered by years of acrimonious parent-school interactions and relationships (Dishion et al., 2008). Furthermore, Patterson and Chamberlain (1994) concluded that parental motivation to change is a critical yet often neglected factor in improving parenting practices.

Coaching offers a framework for practitioners to provide positive social influence to parents and teachers as they face new changes. Erchul (2011) suggests "the added value of this social influence lens to change teacher's beliefs, attitudes, and behaviors to enhance EBP implementation is considerable," and that "intervention integrity is fundamentally an exercise in social influence and, once viewed in this way, there are multiple viable frameworks to be applied" (pp. 76–77). We argue that Erchul's statements about teachers ring true for parents as well, and that a particular theory of change, motivational interviewing (MI; Miller & Rollnick, 2012), offers such a framework of influence and is well-aligned with the goal of promoting changes in teacher and parent behavior. The purpose of this chapter is to advocate for the promise of MI as a framework for coaching that both prioritizes adult motivation and provides a blueprint for effectively navigating the complex relationship that develops between a coach and the individuals contemplating change who are so crucial to early childhood education. Herein we (1) describe MI and its application in the context of school-based coaching, (2) analyze the coaching interventions that have cited MI as part of their logic model using Powell and Diamond's (2013) framework, and (3) highlight some of the strengths and potential challenges of MI-based coaching approaches. We conclude with a discussion of some possible areas for future research.

MOTIVATIONAL INTERVIEWING

Miller and Rollnick (2012) define MI as a conversational style "designed to strengthen personal motivation for and commitment to a specific goal by eliciting and exploring the person's own reasons for change within an atmosphere of acceptance and compassion" (p. 29). Motivational interviewing builds on Carl Rogers's (1959) theory involving the critical skills necessary to facilitate change (Frey et al., 2011), and adapts client-centered therapy into four fundamental processes, four core practitioner skills, and a "spirit" used to create an optimal environment for the consideration of change.

Miller and Rollnick (2012) describe the first of these four processes as engagement, during which the coach works to build a collaborative relationship, discover the teacher or parent's values and ideals as related to education and the future, and affirm those values and the teacher or parent's autonomy. Once engaged, the coach begins the process of focusing, which involves exploring the teacher or parent's current condition, benefits of change as opposed to the consequences of the status quo, and possible behavior change goals in relation to the teacher or parent's expressed values and ideals to highlight importance. During the third process, evocation, the coach brings forth the argument for change by supporting the teacher or parent in building a rich and detailed narrative of change, moving the conversation regarding specific behavior change from preparation to mobilization, and affirming expressions of confidence. Once the teacher or parent has begun to spontaneously produce comments suggesting a commitment to change, the last process, planning, is used to review possible roadblocks and create the supports necessary for the change to take place.

Throughout these processes, the coach uses a set of core conversational skills (open-ended questions, affirmations, reflections, and summaries; OARS) to respond differentially to sustain talk (i.e., talk in support of the status quo) and change talk (i.e., talk in support of change). This strategy is based on empirical evidence documenting the relationship between how people talk about change and their actions (Glynn & Moyers, 2010; Moyers & Martin, 2006), and that goal-directed change talk is associated with subsequent behavior change (Sellman, MacEwan, Deering, & Adamson, 2007; Sellman, Sullivan, Dore, Adamson, & MacEwan, 2001). MI helps to facilitate the change process by developing a supportive environment and relationship that evokes change talk, or the person's own words about their personal motivation to change. The use of MI is guided by a specific mindset referred to as the "spirit," which involves four underlying constructs: partnership, compassion, acceptance, and evocation. Partnership is exemplified by the coach resisting the urge to fix the teacher or parent's challenges, and instead allowing the teacher or parent to take a leading role in determining the direction of dialogue. Compassion is expressed through the active promotion of the teacher or parent's well-being and by giving priority to those needs over those of the coach. Acceptance is suffused throughout the MI process and requires that the teacher or parent's values and ideals are affirmed and used to guide interactions. Lastly, evocation embodies the coach's active elicitation of the teacher or parent's personal motivations for change (in MI, arguments for change are often discussed using the categories of desires, abilities, reasons, and needs). In the next section, we describe the process used to identify programs currently leveraging MI as a coaching framework.

LITERATURE REVIEW

The authors of this chapter conducted a thorough search of multiple databases for peer-reviewed journal articles describing programs that utilized MI-inspired coaching to facilitate training and adoption of EBPs. Various combinations of the following descriptors were included in the initial search: social, emotional, behavioral, intervention, treatment, therapy, program, school, education, classroom, parent, home, home visitation, coach, coaching, coaches. Limiting the search to ensure the articles were peer-reviewed and published within the last 15 years resulted in 219 articles. From these, research focusing on sports, medical or physiological needs, special needs populations only, or those of purely mental health or academic foci was excluded. Manualized interventions supported by empirical studies within schools were included, as were programs focused on parents in support of their children's social, behavioral, and academic achievement. Based on the defined criteria, our search resulted in six evidence-based programs that meet our narrow definition of intervention programs using MI-inspired coaching procedures with teachers or parents to address the social competency and problem behavior of young children in preschool and the primary grades. We now describe each of these interventions using the dimensions forwarded by Powell and Diamond (2013), beginning with those focusing on parents.

The Parent Motivation Inventory

Some of the earliest work to utilize MI as a theory of behavior change with parents was completed by Nock and associates (Nock & Ferriter, 2005; Nock & Kazdin, 2005; Nock & Photos, 2006). In a series of articles, Nock and his colleagues developed and tested a conceptual framework to enhance

parental participation in interventions designed for children (the Participation Enhancement Intervention; PEI; see Nock & Kazdin, 2005), which
led to the development of the Parent Motivation Inventory (PMI). Their
premise for the development of the PEI was that treatment attendance and
adherence to treatment plans are the most basic necessities for effective
treatment delivery. In regard to the treatment of youth, this necessarily
concerns the parent's motivation to provide for their child's attendance
and to support adherence to treatment plans (i.e., interventions). Until
the development and subsequent testing of the PMI, no tools existed to
measure a parent's motivation for their child's treatment. *Structurally*, the
PEI provided very brief (5–15 minute) interviews targeting parent motivation at several points during their child's treatment. These authors used
elements of MI as the *processes* to encourage behavior change. Along with
MI elements, the PEI included the distribution of specific *content* about the
importance of attending treatments and staying on track with treatment
plans, and helped parents develop plans for overcoming any barriers they
faced in attendance and adhering to the prescribed treatment. Using the
PMI to evaluate the effectiveness of the PEI, Nock and Kazdin (2005)
found that increases in parent motivation predicted parents' ratings of
fewer barriers to their participation in treatment and, in turn, greater
treatment attendance. Furthermore, both parents and therapists reported
greater adherence to treatment plans as a result of the PEI.

The Family Check-Up

Dishion and Stormshak (2007) have developed the EcoFIT model,
which includes an assessment-driven feedback component delivered within
the context of MI and has been applied within the context of schools
(Dishion, Stormshak, & Siler, 2010). Dishion and Stormshak effectively
argue that the complex issues faced by families and their children cannot
be approached nor ameliorated with typical interventions that focus effort
on singular members of the family or single issues. Rather, an ecological
approach, which recognizes the importance of the individuals themselves
and their interactions with the environment and culture in which they live,
is necessary to facilitate change.

A hallmark component of the EcoFIT model, the Family Check-up,
was inspired by the Drinker's Check-up (Miller & Sovereign, 1989). The
content of the Family Check-up is focused on parenting behavior that promotes youth adjustment and competence. Shaw et al. (2006) adapted the
assessment battery and intervention to focus on developmental processes
and parent management strategies for parents of toddlers. The *structure* of
the intervention included three brief home visitations: (1) an initial contact

session, (2) an assessment session, and (3) a feedback session (Shaw et al., 2006). The *processes* embedded within the visitation structure included: adult and child questionnaires and a series of coded videotaped parent-child interactions were coded; a "get to know you" interview where parent concerns and critical family issues were discussed openly; and a feedback session, where the coach summarized the results of the assessment with MI strategies to explore the possibility of changing problematic parenting practices and in support of the parent's existing strengths. In addition, parents were offered up to six additional home visitations in support of their efforts. The *content* of these additional visitations included "parenting practices, other family management issues (e.g., coparenting), and contextual issues (e.g., child care resources, marital adjustment, housing, and vocational training)" (p. 5).

Researchers have conducted a series of notable studies of the Family Check-up program in early childhood; results demonstrated the positive longitudinal effects of the program on very young children who were identified as at-risk for early conduct problems. The intervention was implemented with 120 mother-child dyads who were recruited from eight Women, Infant, and Children (WIC) centers in a large metropolitan city. Provided by the United States Department of Agriculture's Food and Nutrition Service, the WIC program provides supplemental nutrition health care referrals and nutrition education for low-income pregnant women and infants and children up to age 5 who are found to be at nutritional risk. The results of this randomized, controlled trial indicate that maternal involvement was sustained for mothers assigned to the intervention group; in addition, a sustained reduction in disruptive behaviors resulted for children who participated in the intervention (Shaw et al., 2006). Children of low-income families who were randomly assigned to the Family Check-up condition demonstrated improvements in school readiness (i.e., inhibitory control and language development) through its effects on parents' provision of increased positive behavioral support (Lunkenheimer et al., 2008). Further study of the program demonstrated the program's effectiveness for families "with very high levels of distress and disadvantage compared with those who were more advantaged" (Gardner et al., 2009, p. 550). These effects were not as strong in single-parent families.

The Family Check-up is a long-standing intervention that leverages MI as a theory of behavior change, and was originally designed as a multi-tiered system of family support (Dishion, Nelson, & Kavanagh, 2003). Specific structure, processes, and content were utilized within "existing, nationally available service delivery settings" (p. 8) to facilitate change in the behavior of mothers who participated in the intervention group.

HomeBase

The development of the homeBase intervention began as an effort to bolster the existing home component of the First Step to Success (Walker et al., 1997; Walker et al., 2013) intervention for children with emerging school adjustment and behavioral issues (Frey et al., 2013a, 2015). In 2015, a new version of First Step to Success was published by Northwest Publishing (Walker et al., 2015); the new version, called First Step Next, includes home engagement activities but the home component was eliminated. As a result, homeBase, which was initially modeled off Dishion and Stormshak's (2007) Family Check-up, is a stand-alone intervention to improve parenting practices, or it can be used in combination with any school-based intervention.

Structurally, homeBase is completed in three to six 1-hour home visitation sessions with the parent(s). The *content* of homeBase focuses on parenting practices; specifically, the coach works with parents to help them consider modifying one or more of the five universal principles of positive behavior support: (1) establish clear behavioral and performance expectations; (2) directly teach the expectations; (3) reinforce their display in schoolwork; (4) minimize teacher attention for minor inappropriate student behaviors; and (5) establish clear consequences for unacceptable behavior. The *process* includes (1) engaging in values discovery, (2) assessing current practices, (3) sharing performance feedback, (4) offering extended consultation, education, and support, and (5) closure.

Following its development, the homeBase was delivered (in combination with the First Step intervention) to determine whether it could be implemented with fidelity, was perceived by key stakeholders as socially valid, and was associated with social competency and academic functioning (Frey et al., 2015). Forty-one children participated in two cohorts during the 2010–2011 and 2011–2012 school years. Children were screened using the Systematic Screening for Behavior Disorders' (SSBD) rank ordering and rating procedures (Walker & Severson, 1990; Walker, Severson, & Feil, 2014). Additionally, 18 teachers and 3 coaches participated in one of several focus groups to better understand their experiences with the intervention. Coaches' adherence to the intervention procedures was measured via the Home Module Fidelity Checklist, which assesses implementation adherence relating to the core processes of the home module. Results suggest the intervention was implemented with acceptable fidelity. Overall, based on coach reports, all program tasks were completed for the majority of families, and the majority of families committed to and implemented a change plan. Satisfaction data collected during the pilot study suggested participants were generally pleased with the homeBase intervention, and coaches also reported high levels of satisfaction. Finally, the proficiency with which coaches implemented MI was assessed by evaluating audio-recordings of coach-parent interactions, and were published separately (Frey et al., 2013b); these results clearly demonstrate coach proficiency in applying MI strategies within the context of the homeBase intervention. The homeBase intervention is currently the focus of a large-scale efficacy trial (IES Grant R324A150179).

The Classroom Check-Up

The Classroom Check-up leverages MI-based coaching procedures to assist teachers in making changes to their classroom management (Herman, Reinke, Frey, & Shepard, 2014). The *structure* of the Classroom Check-up intervention includes five steps: (1) assessing the classroom, (2) providing the teacher with feedback, (3) developing a menu of possible interventions, (4) choosing the intervention collaboratively with the teacher, and (5) having the teacher self-monitor implementation of the intervention, which were applied over the course of 60 days during the study. The duration of each step varied for each teacher in the study, and social validity results indicated the teachers believed the entire process was appropriate and acceptable.

The *processes* of the Classroom Check-up intervention begin with the coach using MI to establish a relationship with the teacher. This initial engagement helps the coach learn about the teacher (i.e., values, goals for the classroom) and serves as a vehicle to develop a working relationship (Reinke et al., 2008). Other processes of the Classroom Check-up intervention include: assessing the classroom, providing feedback to teachers on classroom behavior observations, encouraging the teacher to accept personal responsibility for decision making, developing a menu of options for the teacher, supporting the teacher by identifying strengths when teachers have engaged in changing behaviors in the classroom, and having the teacher self-monitor the implementation of the self-selected plan. The *content* of the Classroom Check-up intervention was determined individually by teachers, and included evidence-based teacher behaviors such as: (1) increasing specific praise, (2) decreasing reprimands, and (3) decreasing disruptive behaviors. Reinke et al. (2008) implemented the Classroom Check-up with teachers in a study utilizing single subject, multiple baseline methodology to measure changes in teacher classroom management performance resulting from particular coaching activities. Observations of same group instruction periods occurred during the baseline phase, the teacher's self-monitoring phase, and a coach performance feedback phase. Other than the coach performance feedback component, during which the coach provided feedback (e.g., strengths and weaknesses) based on the assessment results and observations, the interventions were teacher driven and monitored. Results from this study showed consistent increases in behavior specific praise and decreases in reprimands and disruptions from baseline to the intervention phase when the teachers received performance feedback from the consultant as opposed to when the teacher engaged in self-monitoring only (Reinke et al., 2008).

Reinke et al. (2012) adapted the Classroom Check-up to fit within the PATHS to PAX intervention program (Becker, Bradshaw, Domitrovich, & Ialongo, 2013) to compare its effectiveness with a standard coaching model that does not use MI. One coach, described as highly skilled by the authors, initiated the coaching model with each of six teachers using MI "to build a rapport, gain an understanding of the values and beliefs guiding the teacher's practices, and gather data on current and past teaching practices" (p. 221). Next, the coach gathered classroom data collected from classroom observations to create a menu of areas for improvement, which was presented to the teacher utilizing "specific motivational enhancement strategies" (p. 221) to personalize the feedback. Teachers then worked collaboratively with the coach to choose an area to address and create an action plan that the coach supported with modeling, role-play, rehearsal, and feedback. As the teachers showed improvement with a chosen menu item, the action plan was revised to include other areas of need, or the teacher could opt to end consultation. Teachers receiving the enhanced coaching showed significant gains on a measure of classroom atmosphere, whereas the control group did not. Although both groups showed gains in scores on an observation-based rating of their implementation quality, neither groups' scores were shown to be statistically significant.

The Classroom Check-up provides a strong representation of coaching that targets a teacher's motivations to implement EBPs using MI. Across both studies, teachers were satisfied with the coaching structure, processes, and content, and the coaching model resulted in measureable benefits in the use of evidenced based practices (Reinke et al., 2008) as well as classroom atmosphere (Reinke et al., 2012). Reinke and her colleagues' work demonstrates a coaching framework that targets teacher motivation through performance feedback used to identify discrepancy between their current practices and the EBPs available to them. In this work, teacher autonomy was highlighted in that teachers selected behavior change goals and collaborated with the coach to develop and monitor change plans. Furthermore, the Classroom Check-up approach provides teachers with a visual feedback system based on observed behaviors (e.g., specific praise and reprimands), an approach that was demonstrated effective in a previous study (Reinke. Lewis-Palmer, & Martin, 2007). Coach implementation integrity was measured robustly, although the quality of MI as provided by the coach was not.

First Step Classroom Check-Up

Based on the work of Reinke, Lewis-Palmer, and Martin (2007) and Reinke, Lewis-Palmer, and Merrell (2008), as described above, the First Step Classroom Check-up was developed to support and improve teachers' classroom management practices (Frey et al., 2013; Lee, Frey, Walker et al., 2014) as a component of the original First Step to Success intervention. The *process* is identical to that of the homeBase intervention. Additionally, the *content* is similar to homeBase in that it focuses on five universal principles of positive behavior support. The *structure* requires less time, with an initial session lasting 30 minutes, and four to six subsequent 20-minute meetings. Teacher satisfaction ratings were high for the coaching intervention. Audio-recordings of coach-teacher interactions clearly demonstrate coach proficiency in applying MI strategies within the context of the First Step Classroom Check-up intervention (see Frey et al., 2013; Lee, Frey, Herman, & Reinke, 2014).

Evidence from quasi-experimental studies of both homeBase and the First Step Classroom Check-up suggest the coaching structure, processes, and content were accepted well by teachers, parents, and coaches alike. The coaching process resulted in measureable benefits for parents, their children, and the teachers involved, and was an effective intervention for facilitating parent and teacher behavior change. Frey and his colleagues' work demonstrates a coaching framework that targets the motivations of parents and teachers using specific coaching structures, processes, and content. In this case, MI was combined with five universal principles of positive behavior support to identify discrepancy in the current practices of parents and teachers, thus cultivating importance. Modeling, practice, observation, and performance feedback were utilized to target skills and to build confidence. Coach implementation integrity was measured robustly, as was the quality of MI as provided by coaches (Frey et al., 2013).

The Daily Report Card

Owens and Coles (2014) used coaching to supplement the *Daily Report Card*, an intervention designed specifically for children with attention-deficit/hyperactivity disorder (ADHD) or at risk for diagnosis of ADHD. Thus, the *content* of the intervention was classroom behavior management strategies that are effective in reducing impairment and improving functioning in children with or at risk for diagnosis of ADHD.

The *structure* of their coaching model stems from a combination of research suggesting that change is dictated by an individual's knowledge, skills, and beliefs, and includes an introductory training, weekly observation, and biweekly performance feedback. Graduate students from a clinical psychology program served as the coaches in the study, and were trained over a 3-day period that culminated in mastery-based role play with the authors.

Coach *processes* included targeting teachers' skills, knowledge, and beliefs simultaneously, using individual strategies for each content area. To enhance skills, coaches completed weekly observations in which areas for growth were identified and targeted through modeling and role-play. Performance feedback also occurred biweekly in which coaches presented teachers with graphs of child behaviors, reviewed teacher adherence to the intervention, and acknowledged further areas for improvement. Coaches addressed teacher knowledge by providing an initial training, handouts including facts about ADHD, and a short vignette for discussion. Finally, coaches used MI to identify teacher beliefs and their top three teaching values as a means to anticipate and navigate potential barriers to implementing the intervention. During subsequent coaching sessions, the coaches relied on MI skills (questions & reflections) to elicit "change talk" and soften "sustain talk" to cultivate the importance of change behaviors prior to planning for implementation of the targeted change.

Evidence from case studies suggests the method was most effective for skills, but positive gains were also made in beliefs and knowledge. Owens and Coles's (2014) work demonstrates a coaching framework that targets the motivations of the teacher using specific processes and techniques. In this case, MI was combined with Socratic questioning to identify teacher values and beliefs and relate those beliefs to the perspective change, thus cultivating importance. Modeling, practice, observation, and performance feedback were utilized to target skills and to build confidence. Although teacher implementation integrity was measured robustly, the quality of MI as provided by coaches was not.

DISCUSSION

In this chapter, we identified MI as a promising framework for school-based coaching as a response to the call from several leading scholars to prioritize the role of motivation in coaching and consultation strategies that promote EBP implementation (Erchul, 2011, 2015; Guskey, 1994; and Lyon et al., 2011). We reviewed a variety of intervention programs that leverage MI-inspired coaching procedures to help teachers and parents better address the social competency and problem behavior of young children in preschool and the primary grades. We approached our review using Powell and Diamond's (2013) dimensions of structure, process, and content to promote comparisons across programs. These interventions utilized regularly scheduled meetings as the foundational structure for interacting with the teachers and parents with whom they worked. The meetings varied in length across programs, but focused almost exclusively on introductions, observations and assessment, feedback, and skill development.

While the specific processes identified within these structured meetings varied across programs, the choice to use introduction, assessment, and performance feedback meetings to consolidate motivation to change prior to goal setting and skill development are consistent in the MI-informed practices described herein. For example, several interventions identified "getting to know you" activities intended to develop working relationships. These introductory meetings allowed the coach to better understand the teacher or parent's values, ideals, and goals. The coaches then used this knowledge when providing performance feedback in order to establish discrepancies between the teacher or parent's current practices and their goals. Although not specifically addressed within the studies we reviewed, the process of developing discrepancy between current and goal behaviors is a primary means of cultivating importance (Miller & Rollnick, 2012). Furthermore, the feedback meetings provided opportunities for coaches to affirm the progress of the teachers and parents, building confidence.

There are two reasons why we advocate for the use of MI as a foundation for coaching, and both warrant additional research. First, adopting MI as a foundation for coaching allows for an identifiable skill set to be conceptualized, taught, and measured. Erchul (2015) identifies consultation procedural integrity (CPI) as the extent to which the coaching procedure is implemented as intended, and suggests that CPI will be critical in advancement of the coaching/consultation literature. Frey, Lee, Small, Walker, and Seeley (2017) developed the Motivational Interviewing Assessment and Treatment System (MITAS) to measure MI skill, competency, and proficiency, which is a critical aspect of CPI among school personnel. Using tools associated with the MITAS, MI skill and the quality with which school personnel utilize MI can be measured (see Lee et al., 2014; Small, Lee, Frey, Seeley, & Walker, 2014). While many coaching-based interventions identify the process that is used, and can therefore address compliance, the skill level, competency, and proficiency of coaches utilizing the interventions we reviewed were rarely reported. For example, Darling-Hammond (2009) suggest reflection is an important coaching activity, but current assessments can only indicate if reflection has taken place, not how well it was implemented. There are currently only two studies that demonstrate school personnel can learn to implement MI with proficiency (Frey et al., 2013; Frey et al., 2017; Lee, Frey, Walker, et al., 2014). Additional research is needed to validate the efficacy of the MITAS to develop MI proficiency among school-based personnel.

The second reason we advocate for MI is that it provides the opportunity to better understand the mechanisms of coaching that ultimately lead to behavior change. Over the past three decades, research involving MI has provided insight into the underlying mechanisms affecting behavior change, leading to a well-defined theory of change that is valid and empirically supported (Miller & Rollnick, 2012; Miller & Rose, 2009). Understanding the coaching mechanisms that lead to increased motivation and behavior change not only aligns strongly with the goals of coaching as defined by Denton and Hasbrouck (2009), but provides a framework for evaluating mechanisms of social influence, as recommended by Erchul (2011). Specifically, future research that documents the empirical association between: (1) a coach's MI proficiency and teacher or parent change talk and (2) teacher or parent change talk and behavior change will provide a powerful justification for the use of MI in the context of school-based practice and research.

CONCLUSION

Coaching is a promising approach to enhance the motivation of teachers to adopt and implement social behavioral and emotional EBPs, and MI-based coaching specifically may offer a particularly powerful framework given its theory of change. As diverse coaching strategies and models continue to be developed, it will be important to share information explicating coaching structure, process, and content. Furthermore, those developing coaching frameworks will need to clearly establish a theory of change that drives their coaching practice. While much still needs to be learned about the mechanisms of change that make coaching effective, establishing consistent means of communication and evaluation will be critical to ensuring that coaching is achieving its original intent: to inspire teachers and parents to adopt practices that will allow them to better guide the development of our future generations. Our review of programs involving MI-based coaching suggests there is a need for the further examination of coaching approaches that view teacher behavior change as a motivational deficit, rather than a skill deficit.

REFERENCES

Becker, K. D., Bradshaw, C. P., Domitrovich, C., & Ialongo, N. S. (2013). Coaching teachers to improve implementation of the Good Behavior Game. *Administration and Policy in Mental Health and Mental Health Services Research*, *40*(6), 482–493.

Becker, K. D., & Domitrovich, C. E. (2011). The conceptualization, integration, and support of evidence-based interventions in the schools. *School Psychology Review*, *40*(4), 582–589.

Darling-Hammond, L. (2009). Recognizing and enhancing teacher effectiveness. *The International Journal of Educational and Psychological Assessment*, *3*, 1–24.

Denton, C. A., & Hasbrouck, J. A. N. (2009). A description of instructional coaching and its relationship to consultation. *Journal of Educational and Psychological Consultation*, *19*(2), 150–175.

Dishion, T. J., Nelson, S. E., & Kavanagh, K. (2003). The Family Check-up with high-risk young adolescents: Preventing early-onset substance use by parent monitoring. *Behavior Therapy*, *34*(4), 553–571.

Dishion, T. J., Shaw, D., Connell, A., Gardner, F., Weaver, C., & Wilson, M. (2008). The Family Check-up with high-risk indigent families: Preventing problem behavior by increasing parents' positive behavior support in early childhood. *Child Development*, *79*(5), 1395–1414.

Dishion, T., & Stormshak, E. (Eds.). (2007). *Intervening in children's lives: An ecological, family-centered approach to mental health care*. Washington, DC: American Psychological Association.

Dishion, T., Stormshak, E., & Siler, C. (2010). An ecological approach to interventions with high-risk students in schools: Using the Family Check-up to motivate parents' positive behavior support. In M. R. Shinn & H. M. Walker (Eds.), *Interventions for achievement and behavior problems in a three-tier model including RTI* (pp. 101–124). Bethesda, MD: National Association of School Psychologists.

Driscoll, K. C., Wang, L., Mashburn, A. J., & Pianta, R. C. (2011). A description of instructional coaching and its relationship to consultation. *Early Education and Development*, *22*, 593–619.

Erchul, W. P. (2011). School consultation and response to Intervention: A tale of two literatures. *Journal of Educational and Psychological Consultation*, *21*(3), 191–208.

Erchul, W. P. (2015). Put me in, coach: Observations on selected studies implementing supportive interventions to teachers. *School Mental Health*, *7*, 74–79.

Forman, S. G., Olin, S. S., Hoagwood, K. E., Crowe, M., & Saka, N. (2009). Evidence-based interventions in schools: Developers' views of implementation barriers and facilitators. *School Mental Health*, *1*(1), 26–36.

Frey, A., Cloud, R., Lee, J., Small, J., Seeley, J., Fiel, E., Walker, H., & Golly, A. (2011). The promise of motivational interviewing in school mental health. *School Mental Health*, *3*(1), 1–12.

Frey, A. J., Lee, J., Small, J., Seeley, J., Walker, H., Feil, E. (2013a). Transporting Motivational Interviewing to school settings to improve the engagement and fidelity of tier 2 interventions. *Journal of Applied School Psychology*, *29*(2), 183–202. doi:10.1080/15377903.2013.778774

Frey, A. J., Lee, J., Small, J., Seeley, J., Walker, H., & Feil, E. (2013b). The Motivational Interviewing Navigation Guide: A process for enhancing teachers' motivation to adopt and implement school-based interventions. *Advances in School Mental Health Promotion*, *6*(3), 158–173. doi:10.1080/1754730X.2013.804334

Frey, A .J, Lee, J., & Small, J. W, Walker, H. M., & Seeley, J. R., (2017). motivational interviewing training and assessment system for school-based applications. *Emotional & Behavioral Disorders in Youth, 17*, 86–92.

Frey, A. J., Small, J., Lee, J., Walker, H., Seeley, J., Feil, E., & Golly, A. (2015). Expanding the range of the First Step to Success intervention: Tertiary-level support for children, teachers and families. *Early Childhood Research Quarterly, 30*(part A), 1–11. doi:10.1016/j.ecresq.2014.05.002

Frey, A. J., Walker, H., Seeley, J., Lee, J., Small, J., Golly, A., & Feil, E. (2013). *Tertiary First Step to Success Resource Manual.* University of Louisville, KY: Kent School of Social Work.

Gardner, F., Connell, A., Trentacosta, C. J., Shaw, D. S., Dishion, T. J., & Wilson, M. N. (2009). Moderators of outcome in a brief family-centered intervention for preventing early problem behavior. *Journal of Consulting and Clinical Psychology, 77*(3), 543–553.

Glynn, L. H., & Moyers, T. B. (2010). Chasing change talk: The clinician's role in evoking client language about change. *Journal of Substance Abuse Treatment, 39*, 65–70.

Guskey, T. R. (1994). *Professional development in education: In search of the optimal mix.* Paper presented at the Annual Meeting of the American Educational Research Association, New Orleans, LA.

Hemmeter, M. L., Snyder, P., Kinder, K., & Artman, K. (2011). Impact of performance feedback delivered via electronic mail on preschool teachers' use of descriptive praise. *Early Childhood Research Quarterly, 26*(1), 96–109.

Herman, K. C., Reinke, W. M., Frey, A. J., & Shepard, S. A. (2014). *Motivational interviewing in schools: Strategies for engaging parents, teachers, and students.* New York, NY: Springer.

Hsieh, W. Y., Hemmeter, M. L., McCollum, J. A., & Ostrosky, M. M. (2009). Using coaching to increase preschool teachers' use of emergent literacy strategies. *Early Childhood Research Quarterly, 24*, 229–247.

Lee, J., Frey, A. J., Herman, K., & Reinke, W. (2014). Motivational interviewing as a framework to guide school-based coaching. *Advances in School Mental Health Promotion, 7*(4), 225–239.

Lee, J., Frey, A. J., Walker, H. M., Golly, A., Seeley, J., Small, J., & Feil, E. (2014). Motivational interviewing in support of teacher behavior change. In E. McNamara (Ed.), *Motivational interviewing with children and young people II: Issues and further applications* (pp. 83–102). United Kingdom: Positive Behaviour Management.

Lunkenheimer, E. S., Dishion, T. J., Shaw, D. S., Connell, A. M., Gardner, F., Wilson, M. N., & Skuban, E. M. (2008). Collateral benefits of the Family Check-up on early childhood school readiness: Indirect effects of parents' positive behavior support. *Developmental Psychology, 44*(6), 1737–1752.

Lyon, A. R., Stirman, S. W., Kerns, S. E., & Bruns, E. J. (2011). Developing the mental health workforce: Review and application of training approaches from multiple disciplines. *Administration and Policy in Mental Health and Mental Health Services Research, 38*(4), 238–253.

Miller, W. R., & Rollnick, S. (2012). *Motivational interviewing: Helping people change.* New York, NY: Guilford press.

Miller, W., & Sovereign, R. G. (1989). The Check-up: A model for early intervention in addictive behaviors. In T. Loberg, W. R. Miller, P. E. Nathan, & G. A. Marlatt (Eds.), *Addictive behaviors: Prevention and early intervention* (pp. 219–231). Amsterdam, Netherlands: Swets & Zeitlinger.

Miller, W. R., & Rose, G. S. (2009). Toward a theory of motivational interviewing. *American Psychologist, 64*(6), 527–537.

Moyers, T. B., & Martin, T. (2006). Therapist influence on client language during motivational interviewing sessions. *Journal of Substance Abuse Treatment, 30*(3), 245–251.

Nock, M., & Ferriter, C. (2005). Parent management of attendance and adherence in child and adolescent therapy: A conceptual and empirical review. *Clinical Child and Family Psychology Review, 8*, 149–166.

Nock, M., & Kazdin, A. (2005). Randomized controlled trial of a brief intervention for increasing participation in parent management training. *Journal of Consulting and Clinical Psychology, 73*, 872–879.

Nock, M., & Photos, V. (2006). Parent motivation to participate in treatment: Assessment and prediction of subsequent participation. *Journal of Child and Family Studies, 15*, 345–358.

Owens, J. S., & Coles, E. K. (2014). *Development of strategies to increase teacher integrity in a daily report card intervention for children with or at risk for ADHD* (Institute of Education Sciences Grant R324A120272, in progress). Retrieved from http://ies.ed.gov/funding/grantsearch/details.asp?ID1361

Patterson, G. R., & Chamberlain, P. (1994). A functional analysis of resistance during parent training therapy. *Clinical Psychology: Science and Practice, 1*(1), 53–70.

Powell, D. R., & Diamond, K. E. (2013). Studying the implementation of coaching-based professional development. In T. Halle, A. Metz, & I. Martinez-Beck (Eds.), *Applying implementation science in early childhood programs and systems* (pp. 97–116). Baltimore, MD: Paul J. Brooks.

Powell, D. R., Diamond, K. E., Burchinal, M. R., & Koehler, M. J. (2010). Effects of an early literacy professional development intervention on Head Start teachers and children. *Journal of Educational Psychology, 102*, 299–312.

Ransford, C., Greenberg, M., Domitrovich, C., Small, M., & Jacobson, L. (2009). The role of teachers' psychological experiences and perceptions of curriculum supports on the implementation of a social and emotional learning curriculum. *School Psychology Review, 38*(4), 510–532.

Reinke, W. M., Herman, K. C., Darney, D., Pitchford, J., Becker, K., Domitrovich, C., & Ialongo, N. (2012). Using the Classroom Check-up model to support implementation of PATHS to PAX. *Advances in School Mental Health Promotion, 5*(3), 220–232.

Reinke, W., Lewis-Palmer, T., & Martin, E. (2007). The effect of visual performance feedback on teacher use of behavior-specific praise. *Behavior Modification, 31*(3), 247–263.

Reinke, W. M., Lewis-Palmer, T., & Merrell, K. (2008). The Classroom Check-up: A class-wide teacher consultation model for increasing praise and decreasing disruptive behavior. *School Psychology Review, 37*(3), 315–332.

Reinke, W. M., Stormont, M., Herman, K. C., Puri, R., & Goel, N. (2011). Supporting children's mental health in schools: Teacher perceptions of needs, roles, and barriers. *School Psychology Quarterly, 26*(1), 1–13.

Reyno, S. M., & McGrath, P. J. (2006). Predictors of parent training efficacy for child externalizing behavior problems: A meta-analytic review. *Journal of Child Psychology and Psychiatry, 47*(1), 99–111.

Rogers, C. R. (1959). A theory of therapy, personality, and interpersonal relationships as developed in the client-centered framework. In S. Koch (Ed.), *Psychology: The study of a science: Formulations of the person and the social contexts* (Vol. 3, pp. 184–256). New York, NY: McGraw-Hill.

Shaw, D. S., Dishion, T. J., Supplee, L., Gardner, F., & Arnds, K. (2006). Randomized trial of a family-centered approach to the prevention of early conduct problems: 2-year effects of the Family Check-up in early childhood. *Journal of Consulting and Clinical Psychology, 74*(1), 1–9.

Sellman, J. D., MacEwan, I. K., Deering, D. D., & Adamson, S. J. (2007). A comparison of motivational interviewing with non-directive counseling. In G. Tober & D. Raistrick (Eds.), *Motivational dialogue: Preparing addiction professionals for motivational interviewing practice* (pp. 137–150). New York, NY: Routledge.

Sellman, J. D., Sullivan, P. F., Dore, G. M., Adamson, S. J., & MacEwan, I. (2001). A randomized controlled trial of motivational enhancement therapy (MET) for mild to moderate alcohol dependence. *Journal of Studies on Alcohol, 62*(3), 389–396.

Siebert, C. J. (2005). Promoting preservice teachers' success in classroom management by leveraging a local union's resources: A professional development school initiative. *Education, 125*(3), 385–392.

Small, J., Lee, J., Frey, A. J., Seeley, J., & Walker, H.M. (2014). Measuring motivational interviewing quality for school-based applications. *Advances in School Mental Health Promotion, (7)*4, 240–254.

Stormont, M., Reinke, W. M., Newcomer, L., Marchese, D., & Lewis, C. (2015). Coaching teachers' use of social behavior interventions to improve children's outcomes: A review of the literature. *Journal of Positive Behavior Interventions, 17*(2), 69–82.

Vidair, H. B., Sauro, D., Blocher, J. B., Scudellari, L. A., & Hoagwood, K. E. (2014). Empirically supported school-based mental health programs targeting academic and mental health functioning. In H. M. Walker & F. M. Gresham (Eds.), *Handbook of evidence-based practices for emotional and behavioral disorders: Applications in schools* (pp. 15–53). New York, NY: Guilford.

Walker, H., & Severson, H. (1990). *Systematic screening for behavior disorders: User's guide and technical manual.* Longmont, CO: Sopris West.

Walker, H. M., & Severson, H. H., & Feil, E. (2014). *Systematic screening for behavior disorders (SSBD).* Longmont, CO: Sopris West.

Walker, H., Severson, H., Seeley, J., Feil, E., Small, J., Golly, A., ... Forness, S. (2013). The evidence base of the First Step to Success Early Intervention for preventing emerging antisocial behavior patterns. In H. Walker & F. Gresham (Eds.), *Handbook of evidence-based practices for students having emotional and behavioral disorders* (pp. 518–533). New York, NY: Guilford.

Walker, H. M., Stiller, B., Coughlin, C., Golly, A., Sprick, M., & Feil, E. G. (2015). *First Step Next*. Eugene, OR: Pacific Northwest Publishing.

Walker, H., Stiller, B., Golly, A., Kavanagh, K., Severson, H., & Feil, E. (1997). *First Step to Success: Helping children overcome antisocial behavior. Implementation guide.* Longmont, CO: Sopris West.

Wasik, B. A., & Hindman, A. H. (2011). Identifying critical components of an effective preschool language and literacy coaching intervention. In S. B. Neuman & D. K. Dickinson (Eds.), *Handbook of early literacy research* (Vol. 3, pp. 322–336). New York, NY: Guilford.

Wenz-Gross, M., & Upshur, C. (2012). Implementing a primary prevention social skills intervention in urban preschools: Factors associated with quality and fidelity. *Early Education and Development, 23*, 427–450.

CHAPTER 11

GANBARI

Cultivating Perseverance and Motivation in Early Childhood Education in Japan

Yoko Yamamoto and Eimi Satoh

How do Japanese early childhood education teachers try to build strong motivational values in young children that can carry on to later years of life? What are the important qualities believed to build a foundation for children's motivation to learn? Over the last half-century, Western scholars have paid great attention to Japanese students' learning processes, including motivation and engagement. Japanese students have consistently demonstrated high academic performance in international tests of mathematics, science, and language arts (Organization for Economic Cooperation and Development [OECD], 2016; Stevenson & Stigler, 1992). To identify key elements that explain such academic achievement, many scholars from the United States and Europe have conducted intensive research on Japanese schools and families (Ben-Ari, 1997; Cave, 2007; Holloway, 2000; Lewis, 1995; Peak, 1991; Rohlen & LeTendre, 1996; Tobin, Wu, & Davidson, 1989; White, 1987).

In addition to structural differences in compulsory schooling between the United States and Japan, scholars have found that Japanese students' commitment to hard work and perseverance sustains their long-term motivation to learn (Stevenson & Stigler, 1992; White, 1987). These scholars

Contemporary Perspectives on Research on
Motivation in Early Childhood Education, pp. 229–248
Copyright © 2019 by Information Age Publishing
All rights of reproduction in any form reserved.

observed that Japanese students are willing to invest in their learning even when their academics are difficult or not enjoyable (DeVos, 1996; Lewis, 1995; Stevenson & Stigler, 1992; Tucker & Razzi, 2011; White, 1987). Several cross-cultural experimental studies have supported these observations: Japanese students demonstrate longer attention spans and more task persistence, even after failure than North American students (Blinco, 1992; Heine et al., 2001). Even though recent studies have revealed socioeconomic differences in academic motivation and aspirations within Japan (Kariya, 2009; Matsuoka, Nakamuro, & Inui, 2015; Yamamoto, 2015), researchers have identified the role of schools, including early childhood institutions, in cultivating what they call Japan's "human capital": people's motivation, determination, and commitment to hard work (Blinco, 1992; DeVos, 1996; Rohlen & LeTendre, 1996; Shimizu, 1992; Stevenson & Stigler, 1992; Tucker & Razzi, 2011). But how can qualities like diligence, perseverance, and endurance be cultivated at school, especially during early childhood? Is it even possible to teach such qualities to young children? Increasing attention has been paid to perseverance and persistence in students' learning processes as critical components of motivation (Duckworth, 2016; Schunk & Zimmerman, 2008).

In this chapter, we introduce and describe the Japanese concept of *ganbari*, which means trying hard, persisting, and persevering, by examining interdisciplinary studies. Scholars have acknowledged the powerful influence of cultural milieu and values in children's development of motivational beliefs (Eccles & Wigfield, 2002; Li, 2012). Even so, few researchers have studied such cultural milieus themselves and processes of teaching or cultivating cultural values that build a foundation for learning motivation (Li, 2012). While *ganbari* may not seem to be a direct construct of motivation, it is considered a key value and virtue that guides Japanese children's learning motivation (Amanuma, 1987; Ben-Ari, 1997; Singleton, 1989). By introducing this distinctive Japanese concept, we highlight a cultural virtue that children are expected to internalize from a young age and hope to provide a unique viewpoint that could enrich discourse related to learning motivation. Based on reviews of research on Japanese childcare, preschools, and elementary schools, we also present how teachers cultivate this virtue in young children within the classroom.

In the following sections, we first describe the concept of *ganbari* and its relations to learning motivation. After an overview of Japan's early childhood education system, we examine sociocultural contexts to describe why and how *ganbari* is promoted and valued in Japanese education. Then, we elaborate on how early childhood education teachers implicitly and explicitly cultivate *ganbari* in young children. We conclude with a discussion focusing on what we can learn from *ganbari*, its role in motivation, and the challenges associated with its implications.

WHAT IS *GANBARI?*

Definitions and Meanings

Ganbari, often translated as endurance, endeavor, and persistence, means the exertion of hard work and effort (Amanuma, 1987; Samimy, Liu, & Matsuta, 1994; Shimizu, 1992; Singleton, 1989). *Ganbari* is often cited as a unique cultural virtue explaining Japanese people's behaviors (Amanuma, 1987). *Ganbaru* (or spelled as *gambaru*), the verb form of *ganbari*, means trying and exerting hard work and effort, often by hanging on and persevering even in the face of adversity or failure. Inextricably linked to *ganbari* are its sub-branches, *isshōkenmei* and *gaman*. *Isshōkenmei* is used to describe giving one's all to accomplish a goal or a task (Moeran, 1984). Similar in meaning to *ganbari*, *isshōkenmei* implies the existence of many degrees of *ganbari*, in which *isshōkenmei* is the highest and utmost tier. On the other hand, *gaman* is the combined practice of restraint, patience, and tolerance, especially during unpleasant situations (Kuwayama, 1996; Peak, 1991; White, 1987). *Gaman* as a facet of *ganbari* implies that the ability to reconcile hardship and distress in less-than-ideal circumstances is also an important part of effortful progress.

Other words in Japanese have meanings similar to *ganbari*, such as *doryoku* (endeavor), *akiramenai* (not giving up), and *nebarizuyoi* (persevering). However, *ganbari* is unique as it is the only word that includes all of these multifaceted meanings and is most frequently used in daily life. The imperative and command forms of *ganbari*, such as *"ganbatte"* and *"ganbare"* (Hang on! Don't give up! Try harder! Good luck!) are commonly used in everyday life at home, school, and work in Japan (Amanuma, 1987). Scholars have witnessed diverse contexts and situations beyond educational ones in which *ganbari* is used and promoted. For example, Moeran (1984) found how promoting *ganbari* could help a team overcome athletic difficulties in professional baseball. Other scholars have also detailed how *ganbari* (effort, persistence, and endurance) is emphasized to counter challenges, to conquer difficult tasks, and to improve difficult conditions like the aftermath of natural disasters (Amanuma, 1987: DeVos, 1996; Tsuneyoshi, 2008). In this sense, *ganbari* manifests itself in a wide range of contexts. Embedded within *ganbari* is the belief that continuous motivation and hard work lead to progress and better results. As Amanuma (1987) argues,

> When placed in an extremely difficult situation, Japanese think that they have to exert *ganbari* (put effort), pledge to do *ganbari*, exchange encouragement such as *"ganbarō!"* (Let's persevere together), and send encouragement like *'ganbare!'* (Hang on! Work hard!), regardless of age or gender. (p. 3)

Ganbari and Motivation

Why does *ganbari* play an important role in children's motivation and learning processes? Motivation is usually translated as "*yaruki*," defined as the "active feeling and will to do something" (Shimura, 2008, p. 2849). Another word used for motivation is "*iyoku*," or "active feeling and will to do specific things" or "selective things" (Shinmura, 2008, p. 203). As these definitions indicate, motivation is considered to depend on mind and heart rather than drive or desire. Because an individual's will to do something largely depends on their effortful decision to act upon their will and feeling, motivation is strongly tied to *ganbari*.

While scholars have examined cognitive and affective aspects and processes related to learning motivation, some demonstrate that fostering effort and perseverance leads to positive emotions and behaviors that help to sustain a child's motivation (Duckworth, 2016; Dweck, 2006; Schunk & Zimmerman, 2008). Children's putting forth effort to learn a difficult task can lead to higher levels of mastery. Motivation to persist can also promote independence and self-reliance, ultimately helping children learn on their own (Duckworth, 2016; Heine et al., 2001; Schunk & Zimmerman, 2008). Emphasizing effort also helps to reduce negative affect associated with learning such as feelings of helplessness or overt frustration and may sustain long-term motivation (Blackwell, Trzensniewski, & Dweck, 2007; 2017; Dweck, 2017; Schunk & Zimmerman, 2008). These studies suggest that *ganbari* can lead to both behavioral forms of motivation, such as task persistence and mastery, and affective forms of motivation, such as self-satisfaction, joy associated with learning, and self-efficacy (e.g., "You can do it with effort").

Ganbari shares some overlaps with critical concepts of motivation and learning in psychological studies, such as implicit theories of intelligence and grit (Blackwell et al., 2007; Dweck, 2006, 2017; Duckworth, 2016). The implicit theory of intelligence suggests that children with an incremental theory, or commonly called a growth mindset, tend to perceive ability and intelligence to be malleable through effort and one's mastery of learning, whereas children with an entity theory or a fixed mindset tend to view ability and intelligence as innate and unchangeable (Blackwell et al., 2007; Dweck, 2006, 2017). A growth mindset was found to enhance achievement motivation (Blackwell et al., 2007). In the face of setbacks or failure, children with a growth mindset tend to persist because they perceive adversity as a learning opportunity to become more intelligent. On the other hand, children with a fixed mindset tend to demonstrate helpless reactions (Dweck, 2006, 2017). *Ganbari* seems to be related to a growth mindset as cultivating *ganbari* is tied to cultivating effort orientation, perseverance, and persistence. However, a major difference between *ganbari* and a growth mindset lies in their respective emphases on intelligence and learning processes. Under *ganbari*, effort and character, not intelligence, are believed to determine learning outcomes (Holloway, 1988; Tobin et al., 1989). This reflects Japanese perceptions of ability as a combination of social and mental competence rather than just cognitive competence (Holloway, 1988). Thus, *ganbari* seldom emphasizes intelligence in learning processes and outcomes.

Another construct similar to *ganbari* is *grit*, defined as the determination to persevere and persist for a long-term goal despite failure or adversity (Duckworth, 2016; Duckworth, Peterson, Matthews, & Kelly, 2007). Grit is not associated with IQ but has been identified as an important predictor of academic achievement such as grade-point average (GPA) and highest level of education (Duckworth, 2016; Duckworth et al., 2007). *Grit* and *ganbari* share a key quality: the determination to persist and persevere until task completion despite failure or adversity. However, sharp distinctions exist between *grit* and *ganbari* in their sources and constructs. While *grit* tends to be defined as a personality or trait (Duckworth, 2016; Duckworth et al., 2007), *ganbari* is considered a moral characteristic and attitude cultivated mainly through experiences and training. Second, a sense of obligation and commitment, not passion or interests, may drive the act of *ganbari*. People are usually expected to exert *ganbari* for any task or work they have, are responsible for, or committed to even when it is not enjoyable or interesting (Amanuma, 1989; Singleton, 1989; Tsuneyoshi, 2008). Third, motivational sources of *ganbari* are often strongly connected with collectivistic goals, such as goals of groups and societal well-being in addition to an individual's goals (Ben-Ari, 1997; Shimizu, 1992; Tucker & Razzi, 2011), while the motivational sources of *grit* are tied to individual benefits. Lastly, while success or achievement is the ultimate goal fueled by *grit*, sheer effort itself could become a goal of *ganbari* (Amanuma, 1989; Singleton, 1989). Under *ganbari*, students may consider the effort and time devoted to studying more important than the achievement-based outcomes themselves.

STRUCTURE OF JAPAN'S EARLY CHILDHOOD EDUCATION SYSTEM

Before describing *ganbari* in educational contexts, we explain the Japanese education system with a focus on early childhood education. In Japan, preprimary school is not mandatory, but most children spend a few years attending some type of preschool/childcare institution before entering elementary school. In 2008, more than 95% of 4- and 5-year olds and about 64% of 3-year olds attended a preschool or childcare center (Ministry of Health, Labour and Welfare, 2008 [hereafter called Ministry of Health]). Like the distinction between preschool and childcare centers in the United

States, three types of preprimary schools exist in Japan, each with different objectives in terms of education and care: *yōchien*, *hoikuen*, and *kodomoen*. These distinct early childhood education institutions were established to meet the diverse needs of parents in Japan.

Managed by the Ministry of Education, Culture, Sports, Science, and Technology (MEXT), the main goal of *yōchien* is to provide social and educational stimulation rather than to provide full day care for children of working parents (Holloway & Yamamoto, 2003; Moriue, Oomameuda, & Mitani, 2016; Tobin, Hsueh, & Karasawa, 2009). *Yōchien* enrolls children from 3 to 5 years of age until they start first grade and embodies a slight cognitive focus by introducing very elementary academic concepts (Holloway & Yamamoto, 2003; Imoto, 2007; Moriue et al., 2016). For a long time, *yōchien* did not offer full day care as it aimed to serve children with stay-at-home mothers. With the lowering birth rate and increasing numbers of working mothers, however, *yōchien* began extending its school hours and offering enrichment programs to compete with *hoikuen* (Imoto, 2007; Tobin et al., 2009). The maximum number of children per teacher at *yōchien* is 35. However, most preschool institutions have smaller teacher to student ratios as a result of Japan's decreasing birth rate. Most *yōchien* (63%) are privately run; of the children attending *yōchien*, approximately 83% attended a private one in 2015 (Moriue et al., 2016).

The *hoikuen*, on the other hand, more closely resembles a childcare center as it provides full day care for children whose parents work full-time (Holloway & Yamamoto, 2003; Imoto, 2007; Tobin et al., 2009). Parental full-time employment or a condition requiring full-time care (e.g., parents' illness) is a requirement to enroll children in an accredited *hoikuen*, managed by the Ministry of Health. For an accredited *hoikuen*, the maximum number of children per care provider is 6 for 1- and 2-year olds, 20 for 3-year olds, and 30 for 4- and 5-year olds. About 61% of accredited *hoikuens* in Japan were private institutions in 2014 (Moriue et al., 2016).

In 2006, the MEXT and the Ministry of Health introduced a new type of preschool, *kodomoen*, translated as children's center/garden, as a hybrid of the *yōchien* and *hoikuen*. Now under the management of the Cabinet Office, *kodomoen* does not require full-time parental employment to enroll children, meaning parents who work part-time or those who are not employed at all can also enroll their children from 0 years of age. Supplying the functions of both the *yōchien* and the *hoikuen*, the *kodomoen* offers more flexibility and choice in the type of care offered within the institution and also aims to offer additional support to parents and families (Imoto, 2007; Moriue et al., 2016). As of 2015, about 80% of *kodomoen* were private institutions. The number of accredited *kodomoen* has increased drastically from 1,360 in 2014 to 2,836 in 2015 (Moriue et al., 2016).

Consistent with a rise in the number of families with working parents, the enrollment for *yōchien* has steadily decreased from an all-time high of 64% in 1981 to 54% in 2015 (Moriue et al., 2016). On the contrary, the demand for *hoikuen* has steadily increased due to its ability to care for children starting at a younger age (Imoto, 2007; Tobin et al., 2009). These trends have created a disparity between the increased demand in enrollment and the limited numbers of openings available in *hoikuens*, resulting in a new phenomenon called *taiki jidō*, a literal translation of 'waiting child.' As of 2015, the number of children waiting to attend a *hoikuen* was 23,167 (Moriue et al., 2016). The recent establishment of the *kodomoen*, the newest of the pre-primary institutions, is a direct response to this supply and demand gap.

Elementary education is compulsory and begins in the first grade at age 6. It lasts for 6 years, followed by 3 years of compulsory middle school. Although the 3 years of high school education are not compulsory in Japan, 98% of students attend and more than 90% follow to completion. About 71% of high school graduates pursue higher education, such as junior college, 4-year university, or vocational education (MEXT, 2015).

JAPANESE EDUCATION AND SOCIALIZATION OF *GANBARI*

Ganbari is a key virtue promoted in Japanese schools emphasizing the ideology of meritocracy and equal educational opportunities. Because of this ideology, public elementary schools usually have no tracking or ability grouping. The standardized entrance examination has been the predominant criterion determining students' enrollment at the university and high school level, although this practice is changing. Standardized testing is believed to be more objective and egalitarian than teacher recommendations or participation in extracurricular activities that could be influenced by subjective judgement or family background (Kariya, 2009; Okano & Tsuchiya, 1999; Tsuneyoshi, 2008). Heavy reliance on standardized testing emphasizes the importance of effort, as students are required to master subject material by studying hard (Kariya, 2009; Okano & Tsuchiya, 1999; Tsuneyoshi, 2008). Because graduating from a high-ranked university is inextricably tied to future career prospects and income, educational success is highly valued in Japan (Kariya, 2009; Okano & Tsuchiya, 1999).

With a belief that hard work and devotion are needed to succeed, it is common for students to spend long hours studying by getting tutoring services or attending additional private academic schools (Kariya, 2009; Okano & Tsuchiya, 1999). Although it is difficult to deny the interplay of talent or ability, school institutions emphasize the heightened importance of effort and diligence in achieving goals (Singleton, 1989). Scholars argue that this is the key factor that the Japanese education system seeks to communicate from the onset: one can overcome disadvantages associated with family or socioeconomic background, and ability can be fluidly nourished with the correct spirit of *ganbari* (Kariya, 2009; Samimy et al., 1994; Tsuneyoshi, 2008). Although school teachers and the media have raised concerns about academic pressure, it is believed that the intensity of exam preparation strengthens students' spirits of *ganbari* by providing the experience of overcoming hardship through perseverance and commitment (Singleton, 1989).

Japanese teachers tend to assume that all students are innately capable of putting forth effort, and that everyone can be motivated to succeed and has opportunities to succeed (Blinco, 1993; Stevenson & Stigler, 1992; Tsuneyoshi, 2008). They share the premise that effort, not innate ability, leads to good academic performance. Assessment for intelligence (e.g., IQ tests) is rarely administered in Japanese schools. Teachers usually do not consider differing innate abilities of students or concepts such as "gifted children" (Lewis, 1995; Stevenson & Stigler, 1992; Tobin et al., 1989; Tsuneyoshi, 2008). Japanese teachers list perseverance, concentration, and the ability to function as a member of a group, as critical preacademic skills (Hendry, 1986; Lewis, 1995). Japanese students and parents also attribute academic success or failure to effort more than U.S. counterparts who tend to credit aptitude (Holloway, 1988). Japanese students tend to associate their failures with their lack of hard work, not lack of innate abilities (Holloway, 1988; Stevenson & Stigler, 1992; Tsuneyoshi, 2008).

Socialization of attitudes connoting *ganbari* begins early as a way to cultivate motivational habits. Experiences of endurance and effort are seen as critical for young children's character development and personal and social growth. Learning to stick to a task, no matter how difficult or unpleasant, is believed to strengthen the inner self (Ben-Ari, 1997; Singleton, 1989). Thus, cultivating *ganbari* is a pivotal socialization goal in early childhood education. The first instances of *ganbari* are fostered within the home. For example, parents may encourage their children to *ganbaru* as early as infancy in their attempts to crawl or to walk (Samimy et al., 1994). By listening to their parents' encouragement with *"ganbare"* or *"ganbatte"* (Hang on! Don't give up! Good luck!), the *ganbari* attitude becomes an integral part of children's lives from an early stage. Japanese mothers tend to focus on developing emotional bonds and reciprocal relationships with their children (DeVos, 1996; Holloway, 1988). Thus, children generally understand their parents' efforts and love in raising them and feel a sense of reciprocal obligation to return the favor by showing their *ganbari* to their parents from a young age (DeVos, 1996). Parental support for developing *ganbari* is likely to nurture affective ties between children and their parents, ties that evolve into children's feelings of responsibility and obligation to their parents (DeVos, 1996; Holloway, 1988; Samimy et al., 1994). It is important to note, however, that this obligation is usually not forced; rather, it suggests a willingness in the children to sustain healthy familial relations. By the time they begin formal schooling, children become relatively well-accustomed to *ganbari* (Duke, 1986).

Taken together, early socialization processes of *ganbari* begin at home, and preschool and elementary school teachers prioritize effort over inherent ability. They consider that children's ability to exert *ganbari* indicates valued characteristics such as self-control, emotional maturity, and social courtesy (Samimy et al., 1994; Stevenson & Stigler, 1992).

FOSTERING AND CULTIVATING *GANBARI* IN EARLY CHILDHOOD EDUCATION

How do early childhood education teachers cultivate *ganbari* in young children? How do preschool children internalize *ganbari* as a source of motivation? The words *ganbari* and *ganbaru* do not appear in the official guidelines for preschools issued by the MEXT. The guidelines do not explicitly state cultivating effort or perseverance as a developmental goal. However, teachers constantly convey the value of *ganbari*, motivate children to put forth effort, and encourage them to persevere. In doing so, Japanese preschool (and elementary school) teachers rarely lecture on the importance of *ganbari*. Contrary to the stereotypical view of East Asian teachers, Japanese teachers are generally reluctant to act as authority figures (Holloway & Yamamoto, 2003; Izumi-Taylor, 2013). They rarely give worksheets or academic material for preschool children to practice the value of hard work. Even though there are preschools that focus on academic work, the central goals shared in most Japanese preschools are to promote children's social development, group consciousness, social values, and self-reliance (Ben-Ari, 1997; Holloway, 2000; Izumi-Taylor, 2009; Lewis, 1995; Tobin et al., 2009; White, 1987). As cultural members share an unspoken agreement about values and transmit various cultural standards to young children, socialization for *ganbari* often happens informally (Ben-Ari, 1997; Shigaki, 1983).

Implicit Instructions

At the preschool level, elements of *ganbari* often appear in informal and implicit ways through a "hidden curriculum"" (Singleton, 1989). Japanese teachers foster *ganbari* through experiences rather than explicit instructions, and such experiences are sometimes carefully constructed

(Izumi-Taylor, 2013; Shigaki, 1983; Singleton, 1989). Preschool teachers and caregivers at childcare centers use an intentional set of practices—implicit signaling and verbal designation—to develop motivation and *ganbari* in young children.

Focus on effort and the value of struggling in the learning process. When children are involved in activities and engaged in tasks, teachers tend to focus on their attitudes, especially effort and persistence, rather than on performance or outcome. They praise children's accomplishment, but focus more on praising children who try hard. For example, Izumi-Taylor (2009) observed that when a preschool child could not finish her lunch, the teacher praised the child for trying to finish regardless of the fact that she was unable to do so. Teachers especially encourage children to put forth effort when engaged in a project or task. For instance, when children are engaged in art activities such as coloring or pasting, teachers encourage them to complete the task by emphasizing the ability to persevere. Young children may have difficulty completing tasks due to their limited fine motor skills and short attention span. They also face distractions from peers, but teachers verbally encourage them to exercise patience and self-restraint. When children struggle with tasks or assignments, teachers tend to watch and wait to intervene by standing or sitting nearby and only provide assistance after the child has made an effort (Ben-Ari, 1997: Izumi-Taylor, 2013; Peak, 1991). Throughout these activities, however, teachers' comments and support usually focus more on effort. If teachers think that effort was not made to complete the task, they may withhold recognition and support. They may also criticize work that does not reflect the child's best effort (Ben-Ari, 1997; Hendry, 1986; Lewis, 1995).

American teachers may avoid frustrating situations or struggles in an effort to build self-confidence (Stevenson & Stigler, 1992). On the other hand, Japanese teachers usually believe that children need to struggle and make mistakes in order to learn from their errors and to overcome overreliance on adults (Stigler & Hiebert, 1999). Peak (1991) observed that a childcare provider usually waits to help young children so that they can master self-reliant skills, such as changing clothing and going to the bathroom, by themselves. At the elementary school level, teachers occasionally create challenging experiences that may cause students to struggle by designing academic tasks that are slightly beyond their capabilities (Stigler & Hiebert, 1999; Tucker & Razzi, 2011). Teachers do not view struggling as a sign of low ability, but rather as a natural opportunity to solve problems and further learning. Through these experiences, teachers point out to their students that they can accomplish a task through perseverance and hard work (Stigler & Hiebert, 1999; Tsuneyoshi, 2008). They believe that *ganbari* (effort) made after struggling enhances the self through commitment to work (Stigler & Hiebert, 1999; Tsuneyoshi, 2008;

White, 1987). However, teachers do not continue to push young children; rather, they provide support when necessary. Teachers and caregivers tend to be sensitive to young children's capabilities and will help or intervene before children become too frustrated (Izumi-Taylor, 2013; Shigaki, 1983). As Ben-Ari (1997) states, "The trick (as all preschool teachers know) is to place the tasks at a level which will not frustrate the children because it is too difficult or bore them because it is too easy" (p. 88).

These teacher practices are likely to help children learn how to persevere, embrace struggle, learn from setbacks, and keep moving forward. Fundamentally, accomplishing a goal through hard work can enhance a child's self-reliance, pride, self-satisfaction, and confidence (Amanuma, 1987; Singleton, 1989).

Cultivating ganbari in group settings. Japanese early childhood education teachers rarely provide material rewards such as prizes or stickers or use punishment to discipline young children. Instead, they focus on fostering children's motivation and willingness to try hard by emphasizing each individual's role in a bigger group. From the beginning of the school year, Japanese preschool and elementary school teachers try to create a home-like environment in the classroom by enhancing children's bonding experiences in their classroom community (Cave, 2007; Holloway & Yamamoto, 2003; Lewis, 1995). Teachers aim to foster children's feelings of connectedness to their groups and classmates (Ben-Ari, 1997; Cave, 2007; Lewis, 1995; White, 1987). Activities are organized to encourage cooperative learning and emphasize learning kindness and collaboration. Groups and classes become like families, and students become motivated to put forth effort and do their best for other group members (Izumi-Taylor, 2013; Lewis, 1995). Frequently, teachers divide children into small groups and assign a task or responsibility to each group, such as taking care of class plants or serving school lunch to classmates. These group-based activities and tasks help children understand that others count on their individual hard work in achieving a goal together. Children are encouraged to pursue their respective tasks and goals with effort through cooperative group activities (Izumi-Taylor, 2013; Lewis, 1995; Singleton, 1989).

At the elementary school level, teachers often divide children into small groups for academic work by mixing students of various academic abilities (Cave, 2007; Stevenson & Stigler, 1992; White, 1987). Forming small groups that consist of advanced students and students experiencing academic difficulties is considered to be an effective way to motivate all students. Motivated students—advanced or not—sometimes encourage unmotivated students to pay attention and try hard; they teach them by working together as a group. In other cases, a contributor gains self-recognition and social reward because the group depends on individual contributions for achievement, and young students become motivated to work hard and persist on the task (Blinco, 1993; Tucker & Razzi, 2011). Teachers tacitly use these group-based, cooperative learning activities to facilitate children's reflecting on their actions in relation to the well-being of their group (Izumi-Taylor, 2013; Lewis, 1995). They learn that committing to do one's best is a critical part of character development. They also learn that individual effort is connected to overall group well-being (Shimizu, 1992; Tucker & Razzi, 2011).

Teachers also praise students' effort in class by highlighting their hard work or success after perseverance. For example, Lewis (1995) witnessed a first-grade student who could not give a short speech in front of the class. After trying for several days, the student finally gave a speech. The teacher asked her students to clap for this student's hard work, thereby emphasizing the child's perseverance and emotional engagement over acquired skills or knowledge. By encouraging the other children's affirmation, the teacher further enhanced the student's personal sense of satisfaction and awareness of others' appreciation.

Explicit Instructions: Creating Opportunities to Cultivate *Ganbari*

Setting goals and reflecting one's attitudes through **hansei.** Transmission of *ganbari* values is implicit in many ways, but sometimes teachers and schools intentionally create opportunities to overtly teach the value of *ganbari*. For example, some schools or classrooms display slogans and goals on banners such as "TRYING HARD" or "DOING MY BEST" (Izumi-Taylor, 2009; Lewis, 1995). Some schools designate days to promote *ganbari*: children select their own goals for the day, such as "doing one's best" (Cave, 2007). In many kindergartens and elementary schools, teachers also provide opportunities or lessons for young children to discuss *ganbari*. Children often select goals for self-improvement that require effort. Examples vary widely from academic to social and behavioral areas that require effort: being responsible, being nice to others, writing the alphabet more neatly, or running around the track without stopping (Lewis, 1995). These lessons are often given in the beginning of the year, trimester, or new season, but also in the middle of trimesters. On other occasions, these goals are revisited to reflect on progress.

When preschool and elementary school teachers give feedback, they find areas where children can exert more effort. Even when children show good performance, teachers tend to identify what they could do better (Izumi-Taylor, 2009; Stevenson & Stigler, 1992; White, 1987). This practice is critical but constructive and does not seek to point out flaws. Providing constructive criticism for young children is not considered harsh in

Japan where *hansei*, or reviewing, evaluating, and critiquing past behavior, is widely practiced in everyday life. *Hansei*, reflection and self-evaluation, is considered an opportunity to promote introspection and commonly practiced at Japanese schools. *Hansei* is self-evaluation that focuses on room for improvement, especially areas that require more effort (Izumi-Taylor, 2009).

In some schools, teachers encourage more formal self-reflection. For example, teachers may ask children to individually rate their goals or to report their self-evaluations. In other schools, children rate their goals as a whole class. Teachers may direct a discussion by asking questions such as, "What things (or incidents) did you like (or dislike)?" or "What could you try harder to improve?" Many elementary schools also set up time for *hansei* at the end of the day to help students reflect on their daily attitudes and behaviors (Izumi-Taylor, 2009; Lewis, 1995; White, 1987). This time for reflection provides opportunities for children to focus on areas they did poorly or well and find ways to improve next time. The opportunities for self-evaluation become powerful tools for children to recognize social, emotional, or school-related work in which they need to invest more effort.

Western observers may be worried about children's self-esteem due to these self-evaluation processes that sometimes involve criticism. These processes may challenge young children, but they are not self-negating. Since *hansei* focuses on improving one's attitudes rather than evaluating outcomes, it can create optimism. Self-monitoring effort is likely to reduce the feeling of helplessness and build self-efficacy. Scholars found that in an environment with a supportive teacher and classmates, *hansei* provides pleasant moments for children (Izumi-Taylor, 2009; Lewis, 1995). By promoting children's feelings of group belonging, many scholars argue that Japanese preschool teachers succeed in maintaining a cheerful and lively atmosphere, making the classroom a happy place (Ben-Ari, 1997; Izumi-Taylor, 2009; Lewis, 1995; Tobin et al, 1989).

Activities, events, and training. In general, Japanese preschools and elementary schools focus on whole-child development (Cave, 2007; Holloway & Yamamoto, 2003; Lewis, 1995; White, 1987). Japanese elementary school students spend more time on nonacademic subjects such as art, music, and physical education than American students do (Cave, 2007; Lewis, 1995; Stevenson & Stigler, 1992). There are also various school-wide events and activities that involve both students and teachers such as sports day, field trips, seasonal festivals, and events such as apple-picking, leaf-gathering, or digging up sweet potatoes. School events are included as an official part of the national curriculum (Cave, 2007). These events are intended to foster students' sense of belonging and positive feelings toward school, and often serve as opportunities to cultivate *ganbari*.

One example is the annual sports day held by most preschools and elementary schools in Japan. Sports day usually lasts 3 to 4 hours and features races, group competitions such as tug-of-war and ball-toss games, obstacle courses, and other activities. All children are required to participate, and parents are usually invited. Many preschools hold practice sessions for this special day. During sports day, teachers repeatedly emphasize the importance of *ganbari*, or doing your best and trying hard (Peak, 1991). Group competitions encourage children to work hard for the group and foster a sense of pride (Tobin et al., 1989). Throughout the practices and events, children and teachers continue to shout the word, "*ganbare!*" (Keep on trying? Don't give up!) to encourage classmates. Shigaki (1983) reported this observation in a day care when children practiced for sports day by running across a large sports field. When a child fell halfway through, the caregivers at the finish line yelled "*ganbare!* (don't give up!)" The child picked himself up even though he was crying, finished the course, and received warm embraces and praise for his perseverance. Even after losing, collective effort is valued more than the outcome (Tobin et al., 1989).

Some preschools and schools organize events and activities that involve mild hardship to enhance children's *ganbari* and dedication to task completion. Among many, a common activity is marathon running, one that promotes habits and positive attitudes toward physical fitness and exercise but also emphasizes effort (Ben-Ari, 1997; Cave, 2007; Holloway, 2000). All children are expected to participate. For preschoolers, marathons are shorter. Usually, no expected goal or competition is involved in these sessions, but children may receive cards to record their progress. Emphasis is placed on individual effort. Children may run together with other students and exchange words of support and encouragement. Cave (2007) argues that these activities are designed to teach children that they have the power to accomplish things through effort and perseverance.

Other activities such as running the obstacle courses and going on a difficult hike serve as training for *ganbari* (Ben-Ari, 1997; Holloway, 2000). At a preschool visited in 2016, the first author observed a unicycle training session. In this preschool, teachers begin providing unicycle instructions when students are 3-year olds and aim to have them ride a unicycle by graduation around age 6. They purposefully chose this challenging physical activity for preschoolers. While some children are quick to learn, others have to spend years to master the skill. For such children, teachers give individual lessons by allocating extra time. One may wonder why it is so important to teach young children how to ride a unicycle. While the teacher mentioned that this lesson could help children improve their gross motor skills and physical coordination, she emphasized the major goal for teaching this: setting goals, exerting effort, and not giving up.

As mentioned before, however, opportunities to cultivate *ganbari* are incorporated into everyday experiences and instructions in many preschools. In general, preschool and childcare teachers value spontaneous learning opportunities through activities and play rather than formal lessons (Izumi-Taylor, 2013; Lewis, 1995; Tobin et al., 1989). Preschool and elementary school teachers usually share all activities with their students. They are present on the playground and play with children during breaks. They also eat lunch with their students in their classrooms. These opportunities allow teachers to know each child's characteristics, behavioral patterns, *ganbari* (effort), and progress over the course of the year.

DISCUSSION AND CONCLUSION

What can we learn from Japanese early childhood educators' emphasis on *ganbari*? Persistence is a critical component of motivation (Schunk & Zimmerman, 2008), but studies demonstrate that a significant number of North American children and students fail to persist in the face of challenge (Heine et al., 2001; Smiley & Dweck, 1994). As described in this chapter, Japanese teachers foster the development of *ganbari* (effort and perseverance) in young children as a moral endeavor and characteristic. From early stages, teachers and parents try to foster *ganbari* to help children become responsible and motivated learners who are willing to exert effort. Through implicit and explicit instruction, teachers encourage children to put forth more effort, be persistent, and not give up. In doing so, Japanese teachers tend to focus on acknowledging children's effort and hard work rather than on their ability or outcomes.

Fundamentally, *ganbari* reflects the belief that outcomes and even abilities depend on effort. As the implicit theory of intelligence suggests (Blackwell et al., 2007; Dweck, 2006, 2017), views of ability as malleable are likely to create optimism and increase motivation to learn. An intervention study conducted for seventh graders in the U.S. demonstrates that a growth mindset can be cultivated and taught to enhance adolescents' motivation in the classroom (Blackwell et al., 2007). Even though perceptions of and attitudes toward intelligence may be different between Japan and the United States, our review suggests that it may not be too early to cultivate the perception of malleable ability from the preschool stage. Japanese teachers share the belief that effort determines success and that all children possess abilities to exert effort; such messages are promoted and conveyed in everyday discussions and activities. These practices are likely to also help young children believe that struggling and failing are natural and critical parts of learning, as they show that effort and perseverance are necessary to overcome challenges.

However, it is also important to note that *ganbari* does not come with simple optimism. The practice of *hansei*, self-reflection, helps children recognize areas of weakness that require more effort. Children are constantly encouraged to reflect on their own behaviors to find areas for more effort and improvement. Furthermore, Japanese teachers sometimes create experiences of struggle and wait to provide support to show the importance of perseverance and self-reliance. They believe that struggling and making mistakes provide opportunities to learn from setbacks, ultimately enhancing long-lasting motivation. Studies based on implicit theories of intelligence suggest that simply praising children and telling them that they can accomplish anything may not promote children's attribution to effort (Dweck, 2017). Practices used in Japan such as setting aside time for student self-reflection and self-evaluation may be useful for teachers and practitioners in other countries as they aim to foster a growth mindset and effort-orientation in children.

It is also important to note that Japanese early childhood teachers cultivate *ganbari* in generally fun, warm, and cooperative environments. While teachers try to foster *ganbari* in academic processes for older students, early childhood educators foster *ganbari* through everyday activities and tasks with interpersonal cooperation. They focus on developing children's trust in their teachers and classmates through a sense of community in the classroom. Children's affection toward classmates helps them become motivated to persist through difficult assignments and persevere as a way to contribute to group well-being. Development of the whole-child, social skills, and group consciousness are connected with the development of *ganbari* in Japanese early childhood education.

While *ganbari* continues to be perceived as a core cultural value for motivation and human capital in Japan, globalization and Japan's prolonged economic recession have challenged the cultural assumptions of *ganbari*. When the first author interviewed Japanese mothers of elementary-school-aged children in 2015 and 2016, they demonstrated mixed messages related to the concept of *ganbari* (Yamamoto, 2016). Many mothers articulated the importance and benefits of *ganbari*, such as inviting positive feelings and sense of achievement to children, enabling them to "change inborn abilities," and fostering "abilities to continue to do something." But some mothers noted that *ganbari* is unnecessary in areas that children do not enjoy, and *ganbari* should not be pushed by others. One mother talked about the importance of providing "time and places to relax" at home, as children are expected to exert *ganbari* at school (Yamamoto, 2016).

It is also important to note the negative aspects associated with this concept. Sometimes, *ganbari* can falsely lead one to believe that everything can be achieved through effort and perseverance. In doing so, *ganbari* can endlessly pressure one to exert effort until exhaustion (Nakano, 2014;

Tsuneyoshi, 2008). Moreover, effort itself becomes the goal, and the process may become inefficient and unproductive. In some cases, people feel discouraged to seek help or to try different strategies, thinking that the only way out of a bad situation is through constant effort and persever-ance (Borovoy, 2008). As Borovoy (2008) states, "Because of the emphasis on effort and comportment, teachers also often lack awareness of how to classify or differentiate slovenliness or disobedience from a more systemic developmental problem or illness" (p. 562). Teachers may assume that a child's academic problems are indicative of their lack of effort or poor support from parents without paying attention to individual differences and possible learning disabilities (Borovoy, 2008; Tsuneyoshi, 2008). Japan has become increasingly aware of such drawbacks, especially the pressure and sacrifice associated with *ganbari*. Social phenomena such as sudden death and suicide associated with overwork have led the Japanese govern-ment to regulate employees' work hours and promote work-life balance. Some best-selling books encourage people to pursue lifestyles beyond *ganbari*, which include not pushing oneself to the brink or blindly focusing on effort (Nakano, 2014).

Ideally, if work were fun for children, students would continue to feel motivated to learn. In the process of long-term learning, however, students are likely to face challenges. Mastery of academic content may become more difficult as they grow, and learning may not always be fun or interest-ing. A cross-cultural study found that students become less interested in learning and less inclined to do difficult work during adolescence regard-less of cultural orientation (Wang & Pomerantz, 2009). When subject content becomes more challenging and not necessarily enjoyable, *ganbari*, that places value on diligence and endurance, may become a protective factor in maintaining students' motivation to learn. Perceiving struggle as a natural process and having accumulated experiences of overcoming struggle may help students be willing to exert more effort without being overly frustrated and giving up. As such, how to foster *ganbari* that con-tributes to children's motivation, success, and well-being is considered to be an important theme in Japan's early childhood education scene. Our review suggests that examinations of cultural milieus and cultural values such as *ganbari* that cultivate achievement motivation could provide useful insights for educational researchers and practitioners. We hope to see more research and theories that investigate cultural context in relation to chil-dren's learning motivation in future studies.

ACKNOWLEDGMENT

A part of this review research was supported by a grant from the Mayekawa Foundation.

REFERENCES

Amanuma, K. (1987). *Ganbari no kōzō: Nihonjin no kōdō genri* [The structure of ganbari: Principles of Japanese behavior]. Tokyo: Yoshikawa Kōbunkan.

Ben-Ari, E. (1997). *Body projects in Japanese childcare: Culture, organization and emotions in a preschool.* Richmond, Surrey: Curzon Press.

Blackwell, L. S., Trzesniewski, K. H., & Dweck, C. S. (2007). Implicit theories of intelligence predict achievement across an adolescent transition: A longitudinal study and an intervention. *Child Development, 78,* 246–263.

Blinco, P. M. A. (1992). A cross-cultural study of task persistence of young children in Japan and the United States. *Journal of Cross-Cultural Psychology, 23*(3), 407–415.

Blinco, P. M. A. (1993). Persistence and education: A formula for Japan's economic success. *Comparative Education, 29*(2), 171–183.

Borovoy, A. (2008). Japan's hidden youths: Mainstreaming the emotionally distressed in Japan. *Culture, Medicine, and Psychiatry, 32*(4), 552–576.

Cave, P. (2007). *Primary school in Japan: Self, individuality and learning in elementary education.* London, England: Routledge.

DeVos, G. A. (1996). Psychocultural continuities in Japanese social motivation. In D. W. Shwalb & B. J. Shwalb (Eds.), *Japanese childrearing: Two generations of scholarship* (pp. 44–84). New York & London: Guilford Press.

Duckworth, A. L. (2016). *Grit: The power of passion and perseverance.* New York, NY: Scribner.

Duckworth, A. L., Peterson, C., Matthews, M. D., & Kelly, D. R. (2007). Grit: Perseverance and passion for long-term goals. *Journal of Personality and Social Psychology, 92*(6), 1087–1101.

Duke, B. C. O. (1986). *The Japanese school: Lessons for industrial America.* New York, NY & London, England: Praeger.

Dweck, C. S. (2006). *Mindset: The new psychology of success.* New York, NY: Random House.

Dweck, C. S. (2017). The journal to children's mindsets—and beyond. *Child Development Perspectives, 11*(2), 139–144.

Eccles, J. S., & Wigfield, A. (2002). Motivational beliefs, values, and goals. *Annual Review of Psychology, 53,* 109–132.

Heine, S. J., Kitayama, S., Lehman, D. R., Takata, T., Ide, E., Leung, C., & Matsumoto, H. (2001). Divergent consequences of success and failure in Japan and North America: An investigation of self-improving motivations and malleable selves. *Journal of Personality and Social Psychology, 81*(4), 599–615.

Hendry, J. (1986). *Becoming Japanese: The world of the pre-school child.* Honolulu, Hawaii: University of Hawaii Press.

Holloway, S. (1988). Concepts of ability and effort in Japan and the United States. *Review of Educational Research, 58*(3), 327–345.

Holloway, S. D. (2000). *Contested childhood: Diversity and change in Japanese preschools.* New York, NY & London, England: Routledge.

Holloway, S. D., & Yamamoto, Y. (2003). Sensei! Early childhood education teachers in Japan. In O. Saracho & B. Spodek (Eds.), *Contemporary perspectives in early childhood education: Studying teachers in early childhood setting* (pp. 181–207). Charlotte, NC: Information Age Publishing.

Imoto, Y. (2007). Japanese preschool in transition. *Research in Comparative and International Education, 2*(2), 88–101.

Izumi-Taylor, S. (2009). Hansei: Japanese preschoolers learn introspection with teachers' help. *Young Children, 64*(4), 86–90.

Izumi-Taylor, S. (2013). Scaffolding in group-oriented Japanese preschools. *Young Children, 68*(1), 70–75.

Kariya, T. (2009). *Kyōiku to byōdō* [Education and equality]. Tokyo, Japan: Chūōkōron Shinsha.

Kuwayama, T. (1996). "Gasshuku": Off-campus training in the Japanese school. *Anthropology & Education Quarterly, 27*(1), 111–134.

Lewis, C. C. (1995). *Educating hearts and minds: Reflections on Japanese preschool and elementary education.* Cambridge, England: Cambridge University Press.

Li, J. (2012). *Cultural foundations of learning: East and West.* New York, NY: Cambridge University Press.

Matsuoka, R., Nakamuro, M., & Inui, T. (2015). Emerging inequality in effort: A longitudinal investigation of parental involvement and early elementary school-aged children's learning time in Japan. *Social Science Research, 54*, 159–176.

Ministry of Education, Culture, Sports, Science and Technology. (2015). *Heisei 27 nendo gakkō kihon chōsa no kōhyō ni tsuite* [Report on the 2015 basic school survey results]. Retrieved from http://www.mext.go.jp/component/b_menu/other/__icsFiles/afieldfile/2016/01/18/1365622_1_1.pdf

Ministry of Health, Labour and Welfare. (2011). *Heisei 21 nendo zenkoku katei jidō chōsa kekka no gaiyō* [Overview of the 2008 national families and children survey results]. Retrieved from http://www.mhlw.go.jp/stf/houdou/2r9852000001yivt.html

Moeran, B. (1984). Individual, group and seishin: Japan's internal cultural debate. *Man, 19*(2), 252–266.

Moriue, S., Oomameuda, H., & Mitani, D. (Eds.). (2016). *Saishin hoiku shiryōshū* [Updated childcare data and information]. Kyoto: Mineruva Shobō.

Nakano, N. (2014). *Doryoku fuyōron* [The theory of no effort]. Tokyo, Japan: Foresuto Shuppan.

Organisation for Economic Co-operation and Development. (2016). *Launch of 2015 results of the OECD Programme for International Student Assessment (PISA).* Retrieved from http://www.oecd.org/pisa/launch-of-pisa-2015-results.htm

Okano, K., & Tsuchiya, M. (1999). *Education in contemporary Japan: Inequality and diversity.* Cambridge, England: Cambridge University Press.

Peak, L. (1991). *Learning to go to school in Japan: The transition from home to preschool life.* Berkeley, CA & London, England: University of California Press.

Rohlen, T. P., & LeTendre, G. K. (1996). *Teaching and learning in Japan.* Cambridge, England: Cambridge University Press.

Samimy, K., Liu, J., & Matsuta, K. (1994). Gambare, amae, and giri: A cultural explanation for Japanese children's success in mathematics. *Journal of Mathematical Behavior, 13*(3), 261–271.

Schunk, D. H., & Zimmerman, B. J. (Eds.). (2008). *Motivation and self-regulated learning: Theory, research, and applications.* New York, NY: Routledge.

Shigaki, I. (1983). Child care practices in Japan and the United States: How do they reflect cultural values in young children? *Young Children, 38*(4), 13–24.

Shimizu, K. (1992). Shido: Education and selection in a Japanese middle school. *Comparative Education, 28*(2), 109–129.

Shinmura, I. (2008). (Ed.). *Kōjien* [Japanese dictionary] (6th ed.). Tokyo, Japan: Iwanami Shoten.

Singleton, J. (1989). Gambaru: A Japanese cultural theory of learning. In J. J. Shields, Jr. (Ed.), *Japanese schooling* (pp. 8–15). University Park, PA & London, England: Pennsylvania State University Press.

Smiley, P. A., & Dweck, C. S. (1994). Individual differences in achievement goals among young children. *Child Development, 65*(6), 1723–1743.

Stevenson, H. W., & Stigler, J. W. (1992). *The learning gap: Why our schools are failing and what we can learn from Japanese and Chinese education.* New York, NY & London, England: Summit Books.

Stigler, J. W., & Hiebert, J. (1999). *The teaching gap: Best ideas from the world's teachers for improving education in the classroom.* New York, NY: Free Press.

Tobin, J. J., Hsueh, Y., & Karasawa, M. (2009). *Preschool in three cultures revisited: China, Japan, and the United States.* Chicago & London: University of Chicago Press.

Tobin, J. J., Wu, D. Y., & Davidson, D. H. (1989). *Preschool in three cultures: Japan, China, and the United States.* New Haven, CT & London, England: Yale University Press.

Tsuneyoshi, R. (2008). *Kodomotachi no mittsu no kiki: Kokusaihikaku kara miru nihon no mosaku* [The three risks facing children: Comparing Japan with international standards]. Tokyo, Japan: Keisō Shobō.

Tucker, M. S., & Razzi, B. B. (2011). Japan: Perennial league leader. In M. S. Tucker (Ed.), *Surpassing Shanghai: An agenda for American education built on the world's leading systems* (pp. 79–112). Cambridge, MA: Harvard Education Press.

Wang, Q., & Pomerantz, E. M. (2009). The motivational landscape of early adolescence in the United States and China: A longitudinal investigation. *Child Development, 80*(4), 1272–1287.

White, M. (1987). *The Japanese educational challenge: A commitment to children.* New York, NY: Free Press.

Yamamoto, Y. (2015). Social class and Japanese mothers' support for young children's education: A qualitative study. *Journal of Early Childhood Research, 13*(2), 165–180.

Yamamoto, Y. (2016). *In-depth interviews with Japanese mothers.* Unpublished raw data.

PART V

CONCLUSION

CHAPTER 12

MOTIVATION RESEARCH, CONTRIBUTIONS, AND RECOMMENDATIONS

Olivia N. Saracho

Young children have an inherent need to interact with their environment, which provides them with a source of knowledge that motivates them to learn. Such motivation to learning is grounded exclusively within the children without any outside rewards for its continuation (Deci, 1975). When young children first experience academic situations, several of them have lost their interest in learning (Stipek, 1988). Carlton and Winsler (1998) raise several questions: "What happens to this motivation? What can we do to foster its development?" (p. 159). It is essential to find ways to support the young children's motivation to promote their academic learning.

MOTIVATION PROGRESS

Motivation can considerably contribute to the field in the 21st century, but it needs to consider its countless transformations and increase its practices to diverse populations. Educational psychologists will have access to colleagues in other countries and consider using their expertise (e.g., through collaborations, replicating their studies, integrating their research as part

Contemporary Perspectives on Research on
Motivation in Early Childhood Education, pp. 251–262
Copyright © 2019 by Information Age Publishing
All rights of reproduction in any form reserved.
251

of their theoretical frameworks). Motivation assumes an important function in early childhood theories, research, and practices. Researchers perceive motivation to be an essential element of the individuals' behavior and the development of theories that inform practice. Undoubtedly, motivation is submerged in numerous disciplines such as psychology, anthropology, and early childhood education.

The progress in early childhood education and information technologies have created modifications that are reforming the young children's world. They change the young children's behavior and the way teachers instruct them. Motivating them has become an essential and multifaceted undertaking for educators. The solution to achieving this undertaking well is to learn about the elements that motivate young children. In addition, contemporary education has beneficial devices (e.g., computers, smartboards, faxes, iPhones, videoconferencing aids, etc.) that were inaccessible throughout most of the 20th century. Instructional approaches and classroom configurations have been transformed. Despite these transformations, how to motivate individuals continues to be an issue (Graham & Weiner, 2012), especially with young children. As a result, this area has attracted the attention of both research and scholarly journals throughout the last decades. Although most articles report theories and the progress in motivation, this chapter will focus on the contributions, recommendations for research and practice, future of motivation theories, and ways to broaden, modify, and develop new motivation models that contribute to future society. A prerequisite for this knowledge is establishing the basics for motivation.

THE BASICS OF MOTIVATION

Motivation is concerned with the internal elements that require action and external elements that can stimulate action. Three facets of action that influence motivation include direction (choice), intensity (effort), and duration (persistence). Numerous factors guide the individuals' motivations. There are three key fundamentals to motivation: activation, persistence, and intensity (Cherry, 2017).

1. **Activation** refers to the introduction of behavior.
2. **Persistence** refers to the persistent attempt to achieve a goal regardless of its barriers.
3. **Intensity** refers to the application and determination in achieving a goal.

In addition, the following components are important in motivation (Kleinginna & Kleinginna, 1981):

- internal state or condition that triggers behavior and provides it with direction;
- desire or want that invigorates and guides goal-oriented behavior;
- needs and desires that induce the strength and course of behavior.

Motivation indicates the reasons for the individuals' behaviors. Motivation has had an impact on the individuals' skills and abilities and how they use them (Locke & Latham, 2004). Motivation in early childhood education has been a concern for at least 45 years (Pakdel, 2013). Motivational researchers study the individuals' actions, *choice* of behavior; time to begin a task, or the *latency* of the behavior; challenges encountered in achieving the task, or *intensity* of behavior; continuance with the task, or the *persistence* of behavior; and thoughts and emotion while working on the task, or the *cognitions* and *emotional reactions* toward the behavior (Weiner, 1995).

Individuals need to have knowledge about motivation. They can establish goals based on their expectations of themselves and others for the appropriate reward systems. This knowledge can also assist them in avoiding various myths. Motivation requires learning that activates, directs, and sustains goal-directed behavior. It specifies the reasons for the individuals' behaviors. In relation to academic achievement, motivational issues refer to the causes that prompts certain students to finish tasks regardless of huge barriers, whereas various students would quit at the smallest difficulty, or the reasons several students establish high expectations for themselves that failure is inevitable (Weiner, 1995).

HISTORICAL PERSPECTIVES

The word motivation has a Latin origin. According to Pintrich (2003), "the term motivation is derived from the Latin verb movere, which means to move. In other words, motivational theories attempt to answer questions about what gets individuals moving (energization) and toward what activities or tasks" (p. 669). The theory of motivation can be found during the period of the ancient Greeks (e.g., Socrates, Plato, Aristotle). Plato proposed a categorized hierarchy such as dietary, emotional, and sensible components. For more than two decades, Aristotle supported a spiritual hierarchy, although he used different transformations which differ from his earliest belief. He thought that dietary and emotional elements are pertinent to the body and a portion related to motivation. They can make several sensors similar to development, physical well-being (food) and certain physical experiences such as hurt and contentment (emotional). These two segments were the foundation of an unreasonable motivation strength. The early Greeks acknowledged three elements: the body's desires, pleasures, and pains (senses and efforts of will and spirit) in a hierarchical organization for the primary theoretical rationalization of the motivational undertakings. After the Renaissance, René Descartes differentiated between inactive and active features of motivation. Descartes thought that the body is a passive aspect of motivation, whereas determination is a functioning aspect of motivation. Body has a physical and mechanical disposition with nourishment wishes that respond to those desires through senses and physiological responses to the external atmosphere. Determination is the power of motivation. Initially, Descartes attributed motivation entirely to the willpower of man and the initial distinguished theory of motivation for philosophers (Pakdel, 2013).

Emergence of Theories

The quantity of investigations on motivation varies throughout the different periods. Through the 1930s and 1940s, drive theories (i.e. reinforcement, need theories) dominated motivation. These theories increased during the 1950s and 1960s with researchers such as Vroom (1964) and Locke (1968). In the 1950s motivation shifted to the individuals' motivation and achievement attempts that prompted another general type of grand motivation theory identified as expectancy-value theory (Atkinson, 1957), where behavior is the result of the interaction between the individuals' expectancies about the results of their actions and the value they assign to those results. Atkinson's (1957) expectancy-value theory is based on three elements: the reason for achievement, the likelihood of being successful, and the stimulus value for success.

Additional theories have concentrated on explicit psychological methods, as does Vroom's theory. Skinner's (1938) behavioristic philosophy ignored the significance of consciousness. Such method emphasizes the spontaneous function of rewards and feedback on motivation, which affects its psychological practices such as goals, self-efficacy (Bandura, 1986; Locke, 1977). Goal-setting theory (Locke & Latham, 2002) and control theory (Lord & Hanges, 1987) concentrate on the effects of conscious goals as motivators of task performance. Attribution theory (Weiner, 1986) is based on how individuals make the attributions concerning their own or peers' performance, which have an impact on their later selections and actions. Bandura's (1986) social-cognitive theory focuses on self-efficacy, which has a strong motivational impact on task performance (Bandura, 1997). Personality theory has had strong support. For example, McClelland and his contemporaries (e.g., McClelland, Atkinson, Clark, & Lowell, 1953; McClelland & Winter, 1969) emphasized the outcome of intuitive motivation, including the need for achievement. Lately, these studies have focused on the conscious and self-reported characteristics such as conscientiousness (Barrick & Mount, 2000).

Conflicting Motivators: Intrinsic Versus Extrinsic Motivation

Psychology researchers continue to be curious about what motivates the individuals' behaviors. In striving to determine what best motivates individuals, they have identified the two opposing motivators: extrinsic motivation (e.g., rewards/punishment) versus intrinsic motivation. Motivation is how children initiate and continue a goal-directed activity. Goal-directed behavior can be intrinsically motivated, extrinsically motivated, or a combination of the two motivators. Intrinsic motivation refers to the children's wish to engage in an activity simply for pleasure that results from that activity (Pintrich, Schunk, & Meece, 2008). On the other hand, an extrinsically motivated activity refers to the children's participation to achieve a desirable end result (e.g., praise, reward). Intrinsic motivation is related to the children's learning and achievement (Pintrich et al., 2008). It is assumed that this improvement of learning occurs because intrinsically motivated children are more engrossed in their learning, and they practice strategies to support profound understanding and forthcoming use of that learning. Intrinsically motivated children experience greater pleasure from their learning, obtain more knowledge and understanding, feel better about themselves, and may continue in goal-directed activities (Barrett & Morgan, 1995, Pintrich et al., 2008). If intrinsically motivated learning is greater than extrinsically motivated learning, it seems that it is important to know about the purpose and development of this type of motivation (Carlton & Winsler, 1998). Researchers have both extrinsic and intrinsic motivation, clarified any uncertainties, and identified theoretical advances in motivational research.

These theories have weaknesses, although they offer certain beneficial understandings about the individuals' motivation. It is obvious that the motivation field needs to develop, even though it continues to grow in numerous ways. Nonetheless, the information on motivation continues to develop.

RECOMMENDATIONS

In considering the next step, Locke and Latham (2004) made the following recommendations, which are briefly described in the next section.

- Use the results of existing meta-analyses to integrate valid aspects of extant theories.
- Create a boundaryless science of work motivation.
- Identify how general variables such as personality get applied to and are mediated by task and situationally specific variables, how they are moderated by situations, and how they affect situational choice and structuring.
- Study subconscious as well as conscious motivation and the relationship between them.
- Use introspection explicitly as a method of studying and understanding motivation
- Acknowledge the role of volition on human action when formulating theories.

Integrate Applicable Characteristics of Existing Theories

After starting to review the plethora of current motivation theories, readers might become confused at the enormous diversity in the concepts and methods. However, such motivation theories with their limitations (Miner, 2002) compliment each other. Hence, it is essential to integrate these theories as much as possible to develop a general model. Schmidt (1992) recommended that researchers conduct a meta-analyses on several theoretical studies to integrate the theories and develop a model theory, which he labeled as "mega-analysis." Motivation theory can also be combined into macrotheories. For example, motivation at the macro level can support the individuals' interaction and functioned in relation to social control (Locke & Latham, 2004).

Extend Knowledge to Include Neglected Motivation Areas

Motivation theory needs to be stretched into several areas beyond psychology and include other task performance situations. It needs to include knowledge that has been overlooked. Motivation should include more than young children but include the motivation of teachers, parents, team effectiveness, and others. For example, researchers can examine team effectiveness and concentrate on explicit behaviors that team members use to motivate and demotivate one another. For instance, team members might encourage one another through building efficacy, convincing, or proposing valuable recommendations. In this situation, researchers can examine problems like personality conflicts, values, and/or aims that have been excluded in motivation theories. Motivation should include decision making. Knight, Durham, and Locke (2001) show that goals influence the amount of risk individuals assume in making decisions.

Identify the Application of General Variables (Such as Personality) to Specific Variables in Different Situations and Structures

Motivation theories need to relate general and particular variables such as the impact of personality on motivation. The individuals' characteristics are grounded in well-articulated motivation theories. The personality attributes are extremely wide-ranging in application, intercepting in several motivation variables (e.g., achievement striving, competence, order, dutifulness), or characteristics that influence motivation in specific circumstances (Judge & Ilies, 2002). Thus, personality is integrated in motivational theory. It is important to understand that no action in general is mutually exclusive. Each action has a specific task and situation. Also, specific instruments usually predict actions better than general assessments, although general instruments predict more broadly than do precise ones (Judge et al., 2002).

Examine the Motivation of Both the Subconscious and Conscious and Their Relationship

When individuals interpret their thoughts, they believe that they have caused that act. They assume that their conscious experience is the basis for their main concern and uniqueness of their thought about their action. The thought must appear before the action, be constant with the action, and not be attended by other causes. Wegner and Wheatley's (1999) study showed that individuals mistakenly concluded that they were deliberately responsible for an action that in reality they were required to perform when they were merely directed to consider the action just before it took place.

Individuals can behave without being conscious of the reasons and beliefs that affect their performance. This belief needs to go beyond the use of an unconscious consisting of primitive instincts lacking any contact with the conscious mind. It needs to recognize that the subconscious may not have unconscious powers that control all behaviors (Wegner & Wheatley, 1999). This belief is obviously subjective. Such allegation merely needs admission that the subconscious is a warehouse of knowledge (Murphy, 2001) and that availability to this accumulated information varies within and between individuals.

Examining the subconscious is problematic specifically because individuals, including subjects, are unable to persistently access the stored information. Thus, indirect measures are required. Some researchers (Lilienfeld, Wood, & Garb, 2000) use projective measures (e.g., Rorschach Inkblot Test, Thematic Apperception Test [TAT], human figure drawings), but these measures have a low internal reliability and the results become distrustful. These measures fail to provide scientists with accurate information about the subjects' responses and have difficulty knowing which concept they actually mean. Some researchers (e.g., Miner, Smith, & Bracker, 1994) proposed other types of projective techniques such as the incomplete sentence blank (ISB, Loevinger, 1957; Rohde, 1946) where subjects are presented with several sentence stems and asked to complete them.

The subconscious can also be examined through "priming," where individuals are provided with information that is obviously irrelevant to the task but can unconsciously influence their responses which have been used in several motivation studies (e.g., Bargh, Gollwitzer, Lee-Chai, Barndollar, & Troetschel, 2001; Earley & Perry, 1987). For trustworthy results, a variety of projective techniques can be used and compared. Then effect sizes and any interactions between the conscious versus subconscious can be assessed (Locke & Latham, 2004).

Employ Introspection to Explicitly Examine and Understand Motivation

Since motivational circumstances are in the consciousness, introspection needs to be examined. It influences the generation and understanding of psychological concepts (e.g., desire, self-efficacy, purpose, satisfaction, belief). Locke and Latham (2004) identified the following essential advantages to determine the individuals' motivation.

- Understanding traits and motives.
- Increasing accurate assessments.
- Understanding the effects of attitudes.
- Learning how individuals develop and use principles (e.g. general truths) instead explicit theories
- Understanding self-motivation such as what do individuals do to motivate others.
- Understanding the relationship between motivation and knowledge.

Use the Individuals' Decisions in Establishing Theories

When researchers are developing theories, they need to accept and use the individuals' way of making decisions and integrate them into their theories. Individuals use several methods to make decisions. For example, Beach's (1990) image theory states that individuals use a definite method (e.g., value images, trajectory images, strategic images) to make decisions. Appropriate methods need to be identified and implemented to develop and extend motivation theories.

Summary

The aforementioned recommendations can assist researchers to advance the understanding, interpretation, and development of motivation theories. Locke and Latham (2004) believe that motivation needs to be examined using new perspectives. Their six recommendations are merely the beginning to new directions in the study of motivation.

CONCLUSION

This chapter reviews some of the history of motivation, its basic elements, and several recommendations. New studies have influenced the most important transformations in the field, which has resulted in "chaos with the decline of the grand theories of motivation along with the novelty characterizing the new approaches" (Graham & Weiner, 2012, p. 393). Although motivation research has been conducted for several decades, there has been little progress in the field, a lack of innovative concepts, and an absence of interventions based on motivation theory. It is important to support the recommendation by Locke and Latham (2004) to advance motivation research beyond what has been reported. Graham and Weiner (2012) suggest the following tasks:

- Examine multiple realms and that theoretically apply to distinctive, interconnected paradigms.
- Make distinctions among achievement goals
- Identify contributory beliefs and social outcomes of achievement performance.

New research methods and theoretical concepts have been developed to study these and related issues. There are also many motivation packages that are supported by experimental literatures and potential scientific frameworks. Accordingly, there is a basis to consider that this is a time of exploration and the environment can suggest how to promote a theoretical development, enhancement, and sustained vigor in the study of motivation (Graham & Weiner, 2012). It is important to accept that the progress so far in motivation is an incomplete task. Researchers need to assess and implement their area of interest to determine the next steps.

REFERENCES

Atkinson, J. W. (1957). Motivational determinants of risk-taking behavior. *Psychological Review*, *64*(6), 359–372. doi:10.1037/ h0043445

Bandura, A. (1986). *Social foundations of thought and action: A social-cognitive theory.* Englewood Cliffs, NJ: Prentice-Hall.

Bandura, A. (1997). *Self-efficacy: The exercise of control.* New York, NY: Freeman.

Bargh, J., Gollwitzer, P., Lee-Chai, A., Barndollar, K., & Troetschel, R. (2001). The automated will: Nonconscious activation and pursuit of behavioral goals. *Journal of Personality and Social Psychology*, *81*(6), 1014–1027. doi:10.1037// 0022-3514.81.6.1014

Barrett, K. C., & Morgan, G. A. (1995). Continuities and discontinuities in mastery motivation during infancy and toddlerhood: A conceptualization and review. In R. H. MacTurk & G. A. Morgan (Eds.), *Mastery motivation: Origins, conceptualizations, and applications* (pp. 57–93). Norwood, NJ: Ablex.

Barrick, M., & Mount, M. (2000). Select on conscientiousness and emotional stability. In E. Locke (Ed.), *Handbook of principles of organizational behavior* (pp. 15–28). Malden, MA: Blackwell.

Beach, L. (1990). *Image theory: Decision making in personal and organizational contexts.* Hoboken, NJ: John Wiley & Sons.

Carlton, M. P., & Winsler, A. (1998). Fostering intrinsic motivation in early childhood classrooms. *Early Childhood Education Journal*, *25*, 159–166.

Cherry, K. (2017). Motivation: psychological factors that guide behavior. Retrieved from https://www.verywell.com/what-is-motivation-2795378

Deci, E. (1975). *Intrinsic motivation.* New York, NY: Plenum Press.

Earley, C., & Perry, B. (1987). Work plan availability and performance: An assessment of task strategy priming on subsequent task completion. *Organizational Behavior and Human Decision Processes*, *39*(3), 279–302. doi:10.1016/0749-5978(87)90025-2

Graham, S., & Weiner, B. (2012). Motivation: Past, present, and future. In K. R. Harris, S. Graham, T. Urdan, C. B. McCormick, G. M. Sinatra, & J. Sweller (Eds.), *APA educational psychology handbook: Theories, constructs, and critical issues* (Vol. 1., pp. 367–397). doi:10.1037/13273-013

Judge, T., Bono, J., Tippie, H., Erez, A., Locke, E., & Thoreson, C. (2002). The scientific merit of valid measures of general concepts: Personality research and core self-evaluation. In J. Brett & F. Drasgow (Eds.), *The psychology of work: Theoretically based empirical research* (pp. 55–77). Mahwah, NJ: Lawrence Erlbaum Associates.

Judge, T. A., & Ilies, R. (2002). Relationship of personality to performance motivation: A meta-analytic review. *Journal of Applied Psychology*, *87*(4), 797–807.

Kleinginna, P., Jr., & Kleinginna A. (1981). A categorized list of motivation definitions, with suggestions for a consensual definition. *Motivation and Emotion*, *5*(3), 263–291. doi:10.1007/BF00993889

Knight, D., Durham, C., & Locke, E. (2001). The relationship of team goals, incentives, and efficacy to strategic risk, tactical implementation, and performance. *Academy of Management Journal*, *44*, 326–338.

Lilienfeld, S., Wood, J., & Garb, H. (2000). The scientific status of projective techniques. *Psychological Science in the Public Interest*, *1*, 27–66. doi:10.1111/1529-1006.002

Locke, E. (1977). The myths of behavior mod in organization. *Academy of Management Review*, *3*, 594–601.

Locke, E. A. (1968). Towards a theory of task motivation and incentives. *Organizational Behavior and Human Performance*, *3*(2), 157–189. doi:10.1016/0030-5073(68)90004-4

Locke, E., & Latham, G. (2002). Building a practically useful theory of goal setting and task motivation: A 35-year odyssey. *American Psychologist*, *57*(9), 705–717. doi:10.1037//0003-066X.57.9.705

Locke, E., & Latham, G. (2004). What should we do about motivation theory? Six recommendations for the twenty-first century. *The Academy of Management Review*, *29*(3), 388–403. doi:10.2307/20159050

Lord, R., & Hanges, P. (1987). A control system model of organizational motivation: Theoretical development and applied implications. *Behavioral Science*, *32*, 161–178.

Loevinger, J. (1957). Objective tests as instruments of psychological theory. *Psychological Reports*, *3*(3), 635–694. doi:10.2466/pr0.1957.3.3.635

McClelland, D., & Winter, D. (1969). *Motivating economic achievement*. New York, NY: Free Press.

McClelland, D., Atkinson, R., Clark, R., & Lowell, E. (1953). *The achievement motive*. New York, NY: Appleton-Century Crofts.

Miner, J. (2002). *Organizational behavior theory*. New York: Oxford University Press.

Miner, J., Smith, N., & Bracker, J. (1994). Role of entrepreneurial task motivation in the growth of technologically innovative firms: Interpretations from follow-up data. *Journal of Applied Psychology*, *79*(4), 627–630. doi:10.1037/0021-9010.79.4.627

Murphy, S. T. (2001). Feeling without thinking: Affective primary and the nonconscious processing of emotion. In J. A. Bargh & D. K. Apsley (Eds.), *Unraveling the complexities of social life: A festschrift in honor of Robert B. Zajonc* (pp. 39–53). Washington, DC: American Psychological Association.

Pakdel, B. (2013). The historical context of motivation and analysis theories individual motivation. *International Journal of Humanities and Social Science*, *3*(18). Retrieved from http://www.ijhssnet.com/journals/Vol_3_No_18_October_2013/23.pdf

Piaget, J. (1952). *The origins of intelligence in children*. New York, NY: International Universities Press.

Pintrich, P.R. (2003) A motivational science perspective on the role of student motivation in learning and teaching context. *Journal of Educational Psychology*, *95*(4), 667–686. doi:10.1037/0022-0663.95.4.667

Pintrich, P. R., Schunk, D. H., & Meece, J. (2008). *Motivation in education: Theory, research, and applications* (3rd ed). New York, NY: Pearson.

Rohde, A. R. (1946). Explorations in personality by the sentence completion method. *Journal of Applied Psychology*, *30*(2), 169–181. doi:10.1037/h0063621

Schmidt, F. (1992). What do data really mean? Research findings, meta-analysis, and cumulative knowledge in psychology. *American Psychologist*, *47*(10), 1171–1181. doi:10.1037//0003-066X.47.10.1173

Skinner, B.F. (1938). *Behavior of organisms.* New York, NY: Appleton-Century-Crofts.

Stipek, D. J. (1988). *Motivation to learn: From theory to practice.* Englewood Cliffs, NJ: Prentice-Hall.

Vroom, V. H. (1964). *Work and motivation.* New York, NY: Wiley.

Wegner, D., & Wheatley, T. (1999). Apparent mental causation: Sources of the experience of will. *American Psychologist*, *54*(7), 480–492.

Weiner, B. (1986). *An attributional theory of motivation and emotion.* New York, NY: Springer-Verlag.

Weiner, B. (1995). Lessons from the past. *Psychological Inquiry*, *6*(4), 319–321. doi:10.1207/s15327965pli0604_11

ABOUT THE AUTHORS

Kristen A. Archbell is a PhD candidate in the Department of Psychology at Carleton University (Ottawa, Canada) and completed a Bachelor of Education (Primary/Junior) at the Schulich School of Education—Nipissing University (North Bay, Canada). Broadly speaking, her research is related to social withdrawal and social anxiety in children and emerging adults, and implications for socioemotional and academic development.

Bryce L. C. Becker is a doctoral student in Language, Literacy, and Culture at the University of California Berkeley Graduate School of Education. She earned her BA in Linguistics and German at the University of California, Berkeley, and her EdM in Language and Literacy from Harvard University Graduate School of Education. Her research background includes both qualitative and quantitative methods, broadly exploring the early literacy experiences and development of young learners both in and out of the classroom. Her academic motivation is fueled by her interest in racialized linguistic ideologies and their effects on the classroom and assessment experiences of youth from nondominant backgrounds within the U.S cultural political economy.

Alison K. Billman is Director of Early Elementary Curriculum and a principal investigator at the Lawrence Hall of Science at the University of California, Berkeley where she currently leads an Institute of Educational Sciences research project: First Grade, Second Language: Uniting Science Knowledge and Literacy Development for English Learners. She received her PhD in Educational Psychology from Michigan State University. Her research interests focus on the contexts and materials that support reading to learn in primary grade classrooms, including the design of integrated curricula that support language development and literacy. Related research focuses on the design and use of nonlinguistic features in science informational texts for beginning readers and particularly how these features support beginning readers' comprehension of science texts. She began her career teaching first grade, and her experiences with young children continue to fuel her motivation to learn.

Amanda Bullock is a postdoctoral fellow in the School of Psychology and Cognitive Science at East China Normal University (Shanghai, China), Adjunct Research Professor in the Department of Psychology at Carleton University (Ottawa, Canada), and scientist at the Department of National Defence (Ottawa, Canada). Her research is related to personal and interpersonal stressors and protective factors related to children and families' well-being in different context.

Robert J. Coplan is a Professor in the Department of Psychology at Carleton University (Ottawa, Canada) and Director of the Pickering Centre for Research in Human Development. His research is related to children's socioemotional development, with a particular focus of the development of shyness and social anxiety in childhood. He has served as Editor of the journal *Social Development,* and his recent books include the *Handbook of Solitude: Psychological Perspectives on Social Isolation, Social Withdrawal, and Being Alone* (2014, Wiley-Blackwell) and *Quiet at School: An Educator's Guide to Shy Children* (2016, Teachers College Press).

Sandy L. R. Dietrich is an adjunct professor at George Mason University in the Department of Psychology with more than 7 years of experience conducting research related to disadvantaged populations. She received her doctorate degree in developmental psychology from the University of Miami. She is currently collaborating with a local pediatric hospital in developing and implementing a STEM program for underserved children, grades K–2, in the Washington D.C. metropolitan area. She has participated in evaluation projects that assessed programs designed to reduce social and environmental risk factors. She has also contributed to research and publications that identified risk and protective factors for youth at risk of poor developmental outcomes (e.g., minority youth of low economic background, youth with medical/physical disability or limitation).

Rebecca Dowling is a doctoral student in the Applied Developmental Psychology program at the University of Maryland, Baltimore County. Her research examines the associations between early childhood classroom practices and learning in diverse populations.

Andy J. Frey is a Professor at the University of Louisville, Kent School of Social Work and coordinator of the School Social Work Specialization. He is a senior scholar within the context of a social-emotional intervention development for school-based applications. Dr. Frey has a successful record of disseminating research findings, having had 70 peer-reviewed articles and chapters accepted for publication since becoming an Assistant Professor in 2000; many of his most recent publications are related to motivational interviewing. He received the Distinguished University Teaching Award and the Distinguished Scholarship, Research, and Creative Activity in Social Sciences Award from the University in 2009 and 2015, respectively. In 2015, he was recognized by his alma mater, the University of Denver, as a School of Social Work Master Scholar.

Jessica R. Gladstone is a doctoral student in the Department of Human Development and Quantitative Methodology at the University of Maryland. She studies students' achievement motivation and engagement, with a focus on how they can be influenced by various social and internal factors.

Laura Kelley, is an Assistant Professor at Slippery Rock University of Pennsylvania, where she teaches in the early childhood teacher preparation program. Prior to earning her PhD in developmental and learning sciences, she was a preschool and elementary classroom teacher. Dr. Kelley's work center's on teachers' use of language to support children's social-emotional development and their willingness to engage with challenge.

Stefanie Kraft is a PhD student at the University of Innsbruck, Austria. In her doctoral thesis she focuses on mind-mindedness in infant child-care.

Jon Lee is an Associate Professor of early childhood education at Northern Arizona University, where he teaches undergraduate and graduate students in the early childhood licensure program. Prior to his work in higher education, he enjoyed a 17-year career as an Early Childhood Special Education teacher and administrator. Dr. Lee's research includes the development of interventions to support and enhance the social and emotional development of children in early childhood and the primary grades. As a member of the Motivational Interviewing Network of Trainers (MINT), Dr. Lee focuses on the use of motivational interviewing in school-based applications and has applied these skills in the development and innovation of multiple lines of inquiry, including applications in early childhood.

Robert Pasnak lived in New Mexico until he was 9 years old. Then he moved to the Maryland suburbs of Washington, DC and ultimately attended the University of Maryland. Upon graduating he attended The Pennsylvania State University for 4 years, obtaining his MA, and PhD in psychology. His first professional employment was as an assistant professor at the Catholic University of America in Washington, DC from 1968 to 1972. From there he moved to George Mason University in suburban Virginia where he was first an assistant professor, then an associate professor, and ultimately a full professor. He has published four books and written numerous journal articles on diverse topics, including motivation in preschoolers. He is currently working on his fourth large grant from the Department of Education to facilitate the academic achievement of disadvantaged young children.

Geetha B. Ramani is an Associate Professor in the Department of Human Development and Quantitative Methodology at the University of Maryland. Her research focuses on understanding how children's social interactions influence their cognitive development, mainly in the areas of mathematics and problem solving.

Eimi Satoh is a master's student in Education at the University of Oxford and a recent graduate of Brown University, where she was involved in Dr. Yoko Yamamoto's research project examining Japanese children's socialization processes. Her research interests lie in the areas of academic freedom, university admissions practices and policies, and the history of American higher education.

Nicole R. Scalise is a doctoral student in the Department of Human Development and Quantitative Methodology at the University of Maryland. Her research focuses on sources of variability in children's early mathematical knowledge, including informal learning activities and interactions with parents and teachers.

Wilfried Smidt is a professor of educational science with a focus on early childhood education at the University of Innsbruck, Austria. His research interests focus on educational quality in early childhood education, preschool teacher personality, professionalization in early childhood education, early literacy, and leadership in preschools.

Susan Sonnenschein is a professor and Graduate Program Director in the Applied Developmental Psychology program at the University of Maryland, Baltimore County. Her research focuses on ways to promote the academic success of children from different demographic backgrounds (e.g., low income, minority, ELL). Much of her research has focused on children's reading, language, and math development.

Zachary Warner, MEd, is a doctoral candidate and adjunct professor at the University of Cincinnati where he is studying instructional design and technology. He holds a master's degree from Miami University in educational psychology and is currently a senior consultant and learning strategist at TiER1 Performance Solutions. His research focuses on the development of theoretically grounded training environments, educational game design, and the intersection of qualitative methodologies and experiential learning.

Yoko Yamamoto, PhD, is an adjunct faculty in the Department of Education at Brown University. Her research focuses on family and educational processes and young children's development related to culture, socioeconomic status, and immigrant contexts. She is currently involved in several research projects that investigate socialization processes and children's development of beliefs related to learning in Japan and the United States.

CPSIA information can be obtained
at www.ICGtesting.com
Printed in the USA
BVHW040253030819
555013BV00010B/44/P